DYLAN, LENNON, MARX AND GOD

Bob Dylan and John Lennon are two of the most iconic names in popular music. Dylan is arguably the twentieth century's most important singer-songwriter. Lennon was founder and leader of the Beatles who remain, by some margin, the most covered songwriters in history. While Dylan erased the boundaries between pop and poetry, Lennon and his band transformed the genre's creative potential. The parallels between the two men are striking but underexplored. This book addresses that lack. Jon Stewart discusses Dylan's and Lennon's relationship; their politics; their understanding of history; and their deeply held spiritual beliefs. In revealing how each artist challenged the restrictive social norms of their day, the author shows how his subjects asked profound moral questions about what it means to be human and how we should live. His book is a potent meditation and exploration of two emblematic figures whose brilliance changed Western music for a generation.

JON STEWART is guitarist for platinum-selling Britpop band Sleeper and, since 2019, for influential indie pioneers The Wedding Present. He is Course Leader for the MA in Popular Music Practice at BIMM Institute in Brighton and has published academic research on The Archies, Devo and Brian Eno, Robert Johnson, Joe Meek, grassroots venues, music memoirs, protest songs, *The Wire*, and *YouTube*.

DYLAN, LENNON, MARX AND GOD

JON STEWART

CAMBRIDGE
UNIVERSITY PRESS

CAMBRIDGE
UNIVERSITY PRESS

University Printing House, Cambridge CB2 8BS, United Kingdom

One Liberty Plaza, 20th Floor, New York, NY 10006, USA

477 Williamstown Road, Port Melbourne, VIC 3207, Australia

314–321, 3rd Floor, Plot 3, Splendor Forum, Jasola District Centre,
New Delhi – 110025, India

103 Penang Road, #05–06/07, Visioncrest Commercial, Singapore 238467

Cambridge University Press is part of the University of Cambridge.

It furthers the University's mission by disseminating knowledge in the pursuit of
education, learning, and research at the highest international levels of excellence.

www.cambridge.org
Information on this title: www.cambridge.org/9781108489812
DOI: 10.1017/9781108779470

First published 2022
Reprinted 2022

Printed in the United Kingdom by TJ Books Limited, Padstow Cornwall.

A catalogue record for this publication is available from the British Library.

Library of Congress Cataloging-in-Publication Data
NAMES: Stewart, Jon, 1961– author.
TITLE: Dylan, Lennon, Marx and God / Jon Stewart.
DESCRIPTION: Cambridge, England ; New York, NY : Cambridge University Press, [2022] |
Includes bibliographical references and index.
IDENTIFIERS: LCCN 2021020717 (print) | LCCN 2021020718 (ebook) | ISBN 9781108489812
(hardback) | ISBN 9781108779470 (ebook)
SUBJECTS: LCSH: Dylan, Bob, 1941 – Criticism and interpretation. | Lennon, John, 1940–1980 –
Criticism and interpretation. | Popular music – Political aspects. | Music and philosophy.
CLASSIFICATION: LCC ML420.D98 S75 2022 (print) | LCC ML420.D98 (ebook) | DDC
782.42164092/2–dc23
LC record available at https://lccn.loc.gov/2021020717
LC ebook record available at https://lccn.loc.gov/2021020718

ISBN 978-1-108-48981-2 Hardback

In memory of my dad, George R. Stewart

Contents

Figures

Tables

Preface

One hundred thousand Americans are dead from a virus. A feat of space flight demonstrates American ingenuity. In cities across the country, protests sparked by racial injustice are showing an ugly side of America to the world. In November voters must choose between a Republican running on a law-and-order platform, and an uninspiring vice-president running for the Democrats. The year is 1968. It is also 2020.

The Economist, 6 June 2020

This book explores three themes in popular music and society – protest movements, cultural history and the psychology of belief. These perennial topics become increasingly urgent during periods of crisis, and in that context a book discussing the struggles of the 1960s and 1970s could not be more prescient. The times, it seems, are a-changin' at a rapid pace; yet the concerns Dylan and Lennon articulated half a century ago remain pressing imperatives today. A climate emergency is undermining the sustainability of global capitalism. The COVID-19 pandemic has drawn attention to the very fragility of human existence, triggering unprecedented economic instability and accentuating political polarisation. Two decades after the enormous worldwide demonstrations against the 2003 invasion of Iraq, mass mobilisation has once again become an agent of change as Black Lives Matter, Extinction Rebellion, the Hong Kong protests, the Women's March and the *gilets jaunes* take to the streets. Meanwhile, social media has enabled influential figures to communicate directly and instantly with their audiences, allowing musicians, sportspeople and other celebrities to make increasingly bold political interventions. It is tempting to 'Imagine' how John Lennon might use such platforms today as the tensions brought forth in his biggest post-Beatles song – between faithful and secular, left and right, global and local, rich and poor – remain entirely unresolved.

Acknowledgements

With love to my fiancée Mari Maeda and to my family: Ann and Derek King; and Phil, Lisa, Finn and Molly Stewart.

I would like to extend my enormous appreciation and total respect to my friends and band mates David Lewis Gedge, Jessica McMillan, Melanie Howard and Chris Hardwick from The Wedding Present; Louise Wener, Andy Maclure and Kieron Pepper from Sleeper. You are all incredibly gifted and I feel privileged just to know you.

Thank you to Professor Laurie Stras (University of Southampton) for her constructive and patient guidance on the original version of this manuscript.

I am also truly grateful to the following people: Dr Kate Brett and Hal Churchman (Cambridge University Press); Professor Sarah Hill (Oxford University), Dr Matthew Shlomowitz, Professor Stephen Bygrave and Professor David Nicholls (University of Southampton); editors Kerry Boettcher and Anne Elliott-Day; readers James Kendall (BIMM Institute, Brighton), Dr Steve Gamble (University College Cork) and Omar Joel Zaki; John Pring at Designbysoap for his eye-catching cover design; Peter Dean (Kite Printing) for permission to use his artwork; senior colleagues Martin Wright and Tony Shepherd (BIMM Institute, Brighton); Rob Ilies for tech support; Tristan Wilson (Downtown Music Publishing) and Dean Marsh (creativelaw.eu) for copyright advice.

My thanks to Bob Dylan, David Beal (Special Rider Music) and Marc Cimino (Universal Music) for permission to reprint lyrics from the following works:

CHAPTER I

Introduction

Bob Dylan and John Lennon are two of the most influential figures in popular music history. Dylan is arguably the twentieth century's most important singer-songwriter. His works have been covered more often than any other solo composer, and sales of his records put him comfortably in the thirty most popular performers in United States' history. Lennon was founder and erstwhile leader of the Beatles who remain, by some margin, the most covered songwriters ever and all-time top-selling popular music entertainers worldwide (Clark, 2020; Hamlin, 2015). While Dylan erased the boundary between poetry and popular music, Lennon and his group entirely transformed the genre's creative potential. Each artist challenged the restrictive social norms of their day and asked profound moral questions about what it means to be human and how we should live.

This book compares Dylan's and Lennon's output and legacy in four areas: their own relationship, their politics, their appreciation of history and their deeply held spiritual beliefs. It draws on the work of two notable Marxist scholars, sociologist R. Serge Denisoff and cultural theorist Fredric Jameson, plus recent research on the evolutionary psychology of faith by J. Anderson Thomson and Clare Aukofer. It offers a new explanation of the differences in Dylan's and Lennon's approach to protest music, explores the postcolonial legacy underlying much of Lennon's distinctive imagery and the historical basis for Dylan's romantic attraction to nature, and closes with a groundbreaking analysis of their spiritual convictions. In so doing, it reveals their shared enthusiasm for best-selling conspiracy theorists, their emphatic disavowals of human evolution and a 'lost' co-written song that never actually existed ... but can now be heard on Spotify.

A great deal of literature already exists on Dylan and Lennon as individuals. The earliest publications were biographical accounts, although the last two decades have seen some excellent monographs incorporating a variety of academic approaches.[1] A comparative study by Ian Inglis (1996b) drew useful parallels between Dylan and the Beatles, but until now no one has considered the specific correlations between Dylan and Lennon. Chapter 2, 'Dylan, Lennon and Dual Biography', introduces Eloise Knapp Hay's (1984) concept of dual biography and explains why Dylan and Lennon are such appropriate subjects. It examines their known meetings, intertextual references, reciprocal influences and other forms of interaction. As the dual biography unfolds it elicits findings that a study of each performer alone could not disclose. The cultural mythology around their fleeting encounters, such as when Dylan apparently introduced the Beatles to marijuana or when Dylan and Lennon filmed a *cinéma vérité* scene together, demonstrates the symbiotic nature of their ongoing relationship.

Chapter 3, 'Dylan, Lennon and Anti-War Protest Music' uses a modified version of R. Serge Denisoff's (1968) Marxist analysis of class consciousness in protest music to explain the differences in Dylan's and Lennon's anti-war output during the Vietnam era. It synthesises this with Ron Eyerman and Andrew Jamison's (1998) theorisation of the 'movement artist', offering new explanations for the divergence in Dylan's and Lennon's outlook. Dylan's initial period as a peace campaigner was surprisingly brief, lasting for just over a year, at which point he turned towards more ambiguous anti-war lyrics. Meanwhile, at the height of the Beatles' international popularity, Lennon began to advocate for universal love but was gradually drawn into militant revolutionary politics. Their work traced a mirror image, just as Dylan retreated from the role of movement artist, Lennon enthusiastically embraced it.

Chapter 4, 'John Lennon and History' and Chapter 5, 'Bob Dylan and History' examine Dylan's and Lennon's conspicuous and copious allusions to events, characters and literature from the past using a framework inspired by the Marxist historiography of Fredric Jameson (1981). They reveal the similarities and dissimilarities between Dylan's and Lennon's worldview, and show how each artist's appreciation of history informed their work. Dylan's romantic attachment to nature has parallels with nineteenth-century New England transcendentalism and was rooted in his Midwestern upbringing on the Minnesotan Iron Range. Lennon's colonial nostalgia coincided with the Beatles' propulsion to international

---

[1] Examples include Boucher and Browning, 2004; Elliott, 1995; Frontani, 2009; Hersch, 1998; Hislope, 2018; Hollingshaus, 2013; Inglis, 2000a; Mäkelä, 2004; Marshall, 2013; Meisel, 2010; Schneider, 2008; Sullivan, 1995; Womack, 2009; Womack and Davis, 2006; Zak, 2005.

stardom during the dissolution of the British Empire, and was further complicated by his predilection for transgressive humour – which included ironic Nazi salutes before vast open-air crowds and acts of grotesque mimicry while performing onstage. Each chapter explores the basis of Dylan's and Lennon's historical awareness and their response to cultural tensions that arose at the end of the post-war economic boom.

Chapter 6, 'Dylan, Lennon and Spirituality' uses J. Anderson Thomson and Clare Aukofer's (2011) meta-analysis of the evolutionary basis for faith to compare Dylan's and Lennon's supernatural beliefs. These manifest as profound spiritual convictions that resisted the conventional strictures of mainstream religion. Their similarities and differences demonstrate, once again, how dual biography elicits outcomes that a stand-alone individual assessment cannot produce. Dylan and Lennon, widely regarded as innovative mavericks, were both active participants in thought-reform movements on at least one occasion. Each also, at different times, identified with the figure of Jesus Christ so completely that this transformation in their private disposition became conspicuous in their public lives. As the first study of its type, this chapter demonstrates the potential for further interdisciplinary research between popular music scholars and evolutionary psychologists.

To paraphrase David McCullough (2017) history explains *who* we are, *where* we are and *why* we are the *way* we are – and this theme threads through every section of this book. What follows is structured sequentially around three pivotal moments in social discourse over the last half century, each almost twenty years apart. Denisoff's research documented changes in protest music that he observed during the 1960s. Jameson theorised the relationship between global capitalism and postmodern culture as it materialised during the early 1980s. The evolutionary analysis of faith was J. Anderson Thomson and Clare Aukofer's contribution to 'New Atheism' in the first decade of the 2000s – almost thirty years after Dylan's conversion to Christianity and what Paul McCartney later called Lennon's 'martyrdom' (Hawksley, 2015). As the work moves forward through time its focus pulls gradually outward: from the acute political difficulties caused by an unjust imperialist war, across the broad historical underpinnings of twentieth-century capitalism, then wider still to encompass the entire pre-history of humanity. Our story begins, however, with the relationship between two individuals whose output shaped Western popular music for a generation.

CHAPTER 2

Dylan, Lennon and Dual Biography

Introduction: Dual Biography

Bob Dylan and John Lennon certainly share *something* in common, they are the two most thoroughly examined figures in popular music's canon. Arguably, little remains to be written about them as performers, recording artists and songwriters. As one author asked in his opening sentence: 'Why on earth would anyone need another book about the Beatles?' (Stark, 2005: 1). Dylan, too, has acknowledged this glut of literature:

> Everybody knows ... there's a gazillion books on me either out or coming out in the near future. So I'm encouraging anybody who's ever met me, heard me or even seen me, to get in on the action and scribble their own book. You never know, somebody might have a great book in them. (Dylan, 2011)

One unexplored concept is dual biography: the itemisation and analysis of similarities and differences in the life and work of two related artists. What follows synthesises Eloise Knapp Hay's (1984) method with Ian Inglis' (1996b) work on Dylan and the Beatles. It expands and updates existing research, and provides a framework for discussing other correlations between Dylan and Lennon. Hay (1984) demonstrated the scholarly possibilities for dual biography in her essay on Rudyard Kipling and E. M. Forster. This drew on Friedrich Schlegel's notion of two writers who inform each other's work to such an extent that, once this association is recognised, any singular account of their lives becomes inadequate. She concluded that Kipling and Forster present an ideal comparison because only by studying them together can we fully understand each as an individual:

> The two writers ... may be seen as complementary rather than antagonistic figures. Each of their biographies is incomplete without the other; both our criticism and our biographies of each would profit greatly if we could set

them in a single focus … By analogy we should arrive at the word 'Symbiography', following Schlegel's hint about two German writers when he said, 'Wieland and Barger [together] would make one good poet'. Similarly, one might say, Kipling and Forster together would make one good novelist. (Hay, 1984: 124–5)

Hay compared Kipling's poem 'The Ballad of East and West' (1889) and the denouement of Forster's *A Passage to India* (1924) as 'scenes that speak to each other in their writing' where 'a man of the West rides forth into an allegorical Indian landscape with a fellow horseman, a man from the East' (Hay, 1984: 130). While Kipling's characters meet as enemies but part as friends, Forster's protagonists were not able to reconcile their differences – which leads Hay to ask how Schlegel's 'symbiography' might explain 'why Kipling's men can shake hands but Forster's cannot?' Hay, 1984: 130).

Although relatively underused in academia, dual biographies date back to Plutarch's Greco–Roman *Parallel Lives* and are common in commercial publishing. Popular examples include Kenneth Marc Harris' *Carlyle and Emerson* (1978) and Allan Bullock's *Hitler and Stalin* (1993). Some notable figures such as Charles Darwin and Abraham Lincoln even have multiple dual biographies (Contosa, 2008; Lander, 2010). The format gradually gained traction in popular music with Stephen Citron's (1996, 2001, 2005) dual biographies on Broadway composers and David Browne's (2001) monograph on Jeff and Tim Buckley. More relevantly David Boucher (2004a) compared Bob Dylan and Leonard Cohen as rock poets, Wade Hollingshaus (2013) analysed the performance styles of Bob Dylan, Jimi Hendrix and David Bowie, while Andrew Muir (2019) explored the parallels between Dylan and Shakespeare. Peer-reviewed journals sometimes offer musicological comparisons too. Examples include Greg Clydesdale (2006) on the Beatles and Brian Wilson, John McMillian (2013) on the Beatles and the Rolling Stones, Ian Inglis (1996a) on Elvis Presley and the Beatles and Albin Zak (2005) on Bob Dylan and Jimi Hendrix.

An obvious criticism of the dual biography format is its resemblance to Thomas Carlyle's (1841) 'great man' theory of history. What follows, however, is not a tale of heroic accomplishment or leadership. It is intended more as a framework to contextualise two flawed individuals who became influential songwriters. The works cited above do all happen to discuss male subjects – as, of course, does the rest of this book – but it is also worth noting the growing range of dual biographies about women. Recent examples include Clare Mulley's (2017) account of Hanna Reitsch and Melitta von Stauffenberg, two female test pilots of the Third Reich, and Lindy Woodhead's (2017) work on Elizabeth Arden and Helena Rubinstein. Interestingly, a prominent academic dual biography from Yale University Press compares male and female political figures from Napoleonic France – Benjamin Constant and Germaine de Staël (Winegarten, 2008).

Dylan and the Beatles: Mutual Approbation, Balanced Reciprocity

The remainder of this section expands on Ian Inglis' (1996b) work on Dylan and the Beatles, then focuses on Dylan and Lennon's cultural correlations and personal encounters to explain why they are best suited for a dual biography. Inglis unpacked the musical and professional commonalities between Dylan and the Beatles using two concepts. *Synergy*, from business studies scholar Yoneji Masuda (1990), showed how individuals achieve shared goals more effectively by acting together; *balanced reciprocity*, from anthropologist Marshall Sahlins (1972), analysed common ideals, professional interactions and mutual approbation in relationships.

Inglis began by cataloguing similarities and intersections in Dylan and the Beatles' formative years. All were born in the early 1940s and raised over the ensuing two decades in relatively unfashionable and unsophisticated industrial regions. They shared similar rock and roll influences – they were all were fans of Buddy Holly and Little Richard, for example – but they were equally inspired by different musical traditions, too. For Dylan these included country artist Hank Williams and folk singer-songwriter Woody Guthrie; for the Beatles, trad jazz and skiffle performer Lonnie Donegan, music hall artist George Formby and BBC radio's *The Goon Show*. Dylan and the Beatles each built loyal local followings in New York and Liverpool, respectively, before attaining national international success in 1963–4. Their parallel careers allowed for numerous interesting coincidences and historical ironies, including the occasion of their first British radio exposure. Dylan's earliest airplay in the UK was his recording of 'Freight Train Blues', played on the BBC Light Programme's *Twelve O'Clock Spin* on 30 October 1962. The Beatles' debut BBC appearance was their single 'Love Me Do', broadcast on the same show the following day (Lewisohn, 2013).

Mutual approbation and *balanced reciprocity* became an important factor as Dylan and the Beatles' public renown mushroomed (Inglis, 1996b). Interviews such as this 1965 exchange between Dylan and a British journalist are typical:

'Would you say the Beatles are your biggest unofficial press agents in this country?'

'Gee I don't know. I hope so'.

'They have done an awful lot of good, Bob, over here in the last nine months. Talking an awful lot about you to the trade press and so on'. (Dylan in Jarosinski, 2006: 128)

The Beatles' most consequential public advocacy for Dylan was their 1965 'Beatles Say – Dylan Shows the Way' *Melody Maker* interview with Ray Coleman, which helped trigger what Robert Shelton (1986: 288) called '*Dylan*-mania' across the UK. Two years later his portrait from the cover of *Highway 61 Revisited* (1965) was included on the *Sgt. Pepper's Lonely Hearts Club Band* (1967) artwork. Dylan featured prominently in the image, staring down directly at the viewer from the top right corner of the sleeve. Other than 'WELCOME THE ROLLING STONES' embroidered on the Shirley Temple doll's sweater and the cut-out of Dion DiMucci from Dion and the Belmonts chosen by Peter Blake, he was the only contemporary musician featured. The omission of other key influences – from Elvis Presley and Little Richard to Lonnie Donegan, George Formby and Bert Weedon – perhaps indicated Dylan's importance to the band at this time.

While the Beatles helped promote Dylan in the UK, he, too, remained an advocate for them in American and British media. 'Oh, I think they're the best', he told *Melody Maker* in 1965 (Jarosinski, 2006: 119). A decade later, in 1976, Dylan commented: 'America should put up statues to the Beatles. They helped give this country's pride back to it. They used all the music we'd been listening to, everything from Little Richard to the Everly Brothers. A lot of barriers broke down, but we didn't see it at the time because it happened so fast' (Jarosinski, 2006: 523).

Dylan had various connections with each member of the Beatles but shared an enduring friendship with guitarist George Harrison. Like Lennon, Harrison made key contributions to the band's catalogue that betrayed his own profound fandom. His autobiography *I Me Mine* (2004) also revealed Dylan's *Blonde on Blonde* (1966) as the only western pop record he carried on the Beatles' visit to Rishikesh, India in 1968. Later that year Dylan and Harrison co-wrote 'I'd Have You Anytime' when the guitarist visited Dylan over Thanksgiving. In May 1970 they recorded together in Columbia Studio B, New York. Harrison also facilitated two of Dylan's rare live appearances around this time: the 1969 Isle of Wight Festival and the 1971 Concert for Bangladesh in Madison Square Garden. Dylan and Harrison subsequently teamed up with Roy Orbison, Jeff

Lynne and Tom Petty for the Traveling Wilburys, and Harrison played lead guitar on the title track of Dylan's *Under the Red Sky* (1990).

Ringo Starr is the only other ex-Beatle to have recorded or performed with Dylan; each has appeared on singles released by the other and they have appeared onstage together several times. Dylan and McCartney's relationship remains the most equivocal of the three. His famous 1966 remarks disparaging the Beatles' 'smoothness' were directed specifically at McCartney compositions 'Michelle' and 'Yesterday' (Shelton, 1986). McCartney has worked with numerous well-known artists over the years but never collaborated with Dylan. A brief period of press speculation in 2009 inspired conjecture about how Dylan's dry vocal style might compliment McCartney's melodicism, much as Lennon's had done decades earlier, but this collaboration now seems unlikely to materialise.

For a list of the documented interactions between Bob Dylan and John Lennon see Table 2.1. A comprehensive timeline of Dylan's and Lennon's lives, works and interactions is mapped alongside the important cultural and political events of their day in Appendix 1: Detailed Chronology. An account of Dylan's relationship with Harrison, Starr and McCartney including their interactions, recordings and performances is also provided in Appendix 2: Bob Dylan and the Beatles.

Table 2.1 *Known interactions between Bob Dylan and John Lennon*

	1964
17 May	London: Lennon sends a supportive telegram to Dylan at his first UK concert at the Royal Festival Hall.
28–9 August	New York City: Dylan meets the Beatles at Hotel Delmonico, and again the next day. Dylan takes Lennon for breakfast in Greenwich Village.
20 September	New York City: the Beatles play Paramount Theater, attended by Dylan and his manager Albert Grossman, who then accompany the band to the Riviera Motel near John F. Kennedy Airport prior to their flight home.
	1965
9 May	London: the Beatles see Dylan play the Royal Albert Hall, then visit him at the Savoy Hotel. Lennon publicly defends Dylan's decision to stay at the Savoy.
15–16 August	New York City: the Beatles play Shea Stadium. They are visited by Dylan at the Warwick Hotel after the show and again the following day.

Table 2.1 (*cont.*)

1966	
26–9 May	London: Lennon and Harrison attend Dylan's Royal Albert Hall concert. Lennon visits Dylan at The May Fair Hotel. Dylan visits Lennon's house, Kenwood, in Surrey. They are filmed in Dylan's limousine the next morning.
1969	
30 August	Isle of Wight: Lennon and Ono travel to the Isle of Wight and meet Dylan in rehearsal at Forelands Farm.
31 August	Isle of Wight: Dylan performs at the Isle of Wight Festival watched by Lennon and Ono, George Harrison and Ringo Starr.
1 September	Dylan visits Lennon's new house at Tittenhurst Park, Berkshire, but declines to play on 'Cold Turkey'.
1971	
9 October	Syracuse, NY: Dylan attends the opening of Ono's *This Is Not Here* at Everson Museum of Art and contributes a guest work of art (a copy of his Nashville Skyline album).
November	New York City: Dylan, Lennon, Ono tour Greenwich Village.
1972	
January	New York City: Dylan visits Lennon in the studio as he is producing David Peel and The Lower East Side's album *The Pope Smokes Dope* and hears 'The Ballad of Bob Dylan'.
1974	
31 January	New York City: Lennon and Ono see Bob Dylan and The Band perform at Madison Square Garden.
1980	
December	New York City: Dylan visits Ono after Lennon's assassination.

Dylan and Lennon, 1964–1966

Hay argued that dual biography is most useful when a simultaneous examination of two artists contributes to a better understanding of their individual work. In this sense, as founder and erstwhile leader of the Beatles it is Lennon who provides the most obvious counterpart to Dylan. Their noticeable aesthetic and cultural correlations were immediately apparent. Noted musicologist Wilfred Mellers (1974: 163) regarded Lennon's 'achievement as an Englishman' as 'collateral with Bob Dylan's as a white American'. Elsewhere, Lennon was described as 'Dylan's English reflection' (Aronowitz, 1994: 49), Dylan's 'principal rival' or someone 'born half-American' (Goldman, 1988: 43) – just as Dylan was perceived as 'a semi-Brit' (Silverton, 2011). Michael Gray (2008: 41) noted the pair's obvious stylistic resemblances: 'as the most acerbic Beatle, John was the one regarded as most similar to Dylan'.

Dylan had infrequent personal contact with Lennon but their few documented meetings generated considerable interest. Some, such as their introduction in New York's Hotel Delmonico in 1964 or Dylan and Lennon's limousine journey through London in 1966, have attained legendary status. Most scholars of mythology, from Claude Lévi-Strauss (1978) to Karen Armstrong (2004), view history and legend as two honest attempts to interpret past events and distinguish the latter by its lack of written records. Dylan and Lennon's rare interactions have become mythologised by precisely this process: as culturally significant but unreliably reported encounters where the hazy remembrances of those present became magnified and misremembered in the re-telling, then consolidated in published biographical accounts.

Their correspondence began in May 1964, three months *before* they met in person, when Lennon reached out to congratulate Dylan on the occasion of his first major London concert. According to Dylan's biographer Howard Sounes (2011a: 191): 'Lennon found time to send a telegram saying they wished they could be at the Festival Hall. Unfortunately, they had a filming commitment.' In fact, Lennon was *not* filming. He was on vacation with Harrison in Tahiti at the time (Goodden, 2014g). Nevertheless, when Dylan read the message backstage during his show's intermission, it attracted great interest from those present: 'Oh Man! That's pretty neat', exclaimed his friend John Bucklen – who also recalled that Dylan himself was more sanguine: 'pleased, but not impressed' (Sounes, 2011a: 191).

On 28 August 1964 Dylan and the Beatles finally met face-to-face at the Hotel Delmonico, New York City. 'john lennon goovy also ringo' Dylan wrote in a letter to his friend Tony Glover soon after their encounter (Brinkley, 2020). It is now, of course, best known in rock folklore as the occasion Dylan introduced the band to cannabis. Dylan and Lennon's entourage, which included journalist Michael Aronowitz, personal assistant Peter Brown and press officer Derek Taylor, portrayed this as a defining moment for both artists: 'a friendship instigated and pursued through mutually admired recordings *made flesh through marijuana and the sacred exploration of deepest inner space*' (Taylor, 1987: 92, my italics). In truth, this was *not* the first time Lennon had experimented with the drug. Cavern Club DJ Bob Wooler remembered the Beatles bringing marijuana back from

London in 1962 (Goodden, 2017). George Harrison also recalled smoking it while in the nearby resort town of Southport:

> We first got marijuana from an older drummer with another group in Liverpool. We didn't really try it until after we'd been to Hamburg. I remember we smoked it in the band room in a gig in Southport and we all learnt do to the Twist that night, which was popular at the time . . . . Everybody was saying, 'This stuff isn't doing anything'. It was like that old joke where a party is going on and two hippies are up floating on the ceiling, and one is saying to the other, 'This stuff doesn't work, man'. (Harrison, in Roylance, 2000: 158)

Lennon probably first tried cannabis as early as 1960 in Liverpool. That same year, two months prior to the band's initial Hamburg trip, beat poet Royston Ellis also showed him how to extract Benzedrine from a Vicks inhaler: 'Everybody thought, "Wow! What's this?" and talked their mouths off for a night' (Goodden, 2017: 13). During their second trip to Germany he developed a robust appetite for Preludin and other forms of amphetamine that continued well into the mid-1960s (Inglis, 2012). A habitual substance misuser, Lennon was familiar with a variety of drug-culture tropes. In the 'coke snorting scene' at the beginning of *A Hard Day's Night* (1964), filmed four months before his first meeting with Dylan at Hotel Delmonico, he repeatedly sniffed at a bottle of Pepsi-Cola then flashed a knowing smile at fellow cast member Wilfrid Brambell. Although unnoticed at the time by the British Board of Film Censors, this was quite clearly a covert drug reference (Horgan, 2012). What is more, he had already written about cannabis ('Indian Hump') in the prose-poem 'Neville Club' from *In His Own Write* (1964), published six months before his meeting with Bob Dylan in New York, in August 1964:

> All of a southern I notice boils and girks sitting in hubbered lumps smoking Hernia taking Odeon and going very high. Somewhere 4ft high but he had Indian Hump which he grew in his sleep. Puffing and globbering they drugged theyselves rampling or dancing with wild abdomen, stubbing in wild postumes amongst themselves. (Lennon, 1964: 60)

In that context, the significance of the Beatles' smoking marijuana during their first meeting with Dylan seems, perhaps, rather overstated. In truth, Dylan's impact on Lennon's drug taking was far less consequential than his influence on Lennon's *songwriting*. That same year the Beatles began what John Covach (2006) called their journey from 'craftsmen' to 'artists', gradually integrating more imaginative ideas into standardised pop arrangements. Aided by producer George Martin, the band collated an impressive range of new source material. Lyrically, however, Lennon was inspired by one voice: 'I remember the early meetings with Dylan – he was always saying, "Listen to the words, man", and I said, "I can't be bothered. I listen to the sound of it, the overall sound"' (Harry, 2000: 217). The profundity of Dylan's insight motivated the Beatles' to bring increasingly adventurous subjects into their own work. Lennon turned inwards, using rumination as a writing tool to explore more intense themes. As a result, the first three songs from what he later called 'my Dylan period' all contained introspective expressions of self-doubt: 'I Should Have Known Better' and 'I'll Cry Instead' on *A Hard Day's Night*, then 'I'm a Loser' on *Beatles For Sale* (1964). The depiction of chronic depression in the latter became the Beatles' earliest attempt to address personal concerns beyond the immediate pain and pleasure of youthful courtship: 'I started thinking about my own emotions – "I'm a Loser" or "Hide Your Love Away" – those kind of things – I would just try to express what I felt about myself which I'd done in my books ... Dylan helped me realise that ... just by hearing his work' (Lennon in Wenner, 2000: 83–4).

Happy to share the inspiration behind his new direction, Lennon publicly declared: 'I could have made "I'm a Loser" even more *Dylanish* if I'd tried.' In the same interview he revealed that 'A Hard Day's Night' was originally conceived in the same style, 'but later we Beatle-ified it before we recorded it' (Coleman, 1965: 3). Lennon's harmonica introduction for 'I Should Have Known Better' further demonstrated this capability for 'Dylanish' music. Longstanding companion Pete Shotton provided a behind-the-scenes perspective: 'John was particularly impressed and amused by Dylan's way with words; he often quoted, with enormous relish, lines like "even the president of the United States sometimes must have to stand naked"' (Shotton and Schaffner, 1983: 110).

Shotton's memoir offered a thoughtful account of this transformative period:

> My personal association with John's songwriting began at a time when he was first starting to repudiate the greeting-card sentiments of the Beatles' early hits. In this respect he was strongly influenced by the lyrics of Bob Dylan. Until he heard Dylan, it never occurred to John that the words of popular songs could or should amount to anything more than meaningless hackwork, and he contented himself with channelling his literary talents into his little books. Dylan's success came as a real revelation to John, who suddenly realised that there was nothing to stop him from expressing his poetic and even political ideas within the framework of the Beatles' music. (Shotton and Schaffner, 1983: 110)

These innovations included new writing techniques, too. Prior to 1964, Beatles songs usually originated with a short vocal refrain that they developed and refined into a more complete instrumental composition. Once this was arranged, the remaining lyrics were then finalised over the existing music. After meeting Dylan in New York, Lennon experimented with writing 'words first', weaving his melodies around semi or even fully formed lyrical structures. Here, Lennon drew from Dylan just as Dylan had drawn from Woody Guthrie.[1] The outcome, in compositions such as 'Norwegian Wood (This Bird Has Flown)' (1965), was a series of Beatles songs whose artful poeticism threatened to outshine their musical sophistication (MacDonald, 1994).

While Dylan influenced Lennon's songwriting, Lennon influenced Dylan as an author. Dylan's early published poetry included 'Go Away You Bomb' (1962) and '11 Outlined Epitaphs', the substantial sleeve notes for *The Times They Are A-Changin'* (1964). In January 1964, three months before the publication of Lennon's *In His Own Write*, Dylan also disclosed that he was working on a novel and a play. Lennon's success encouraged Dylan's manager Albert Grossman to negotiate a publishing deal with Macmillan and coax Dylan into completing the work (Dalton, 2012; Heylin, 1996):

> As for Lennon, well I was encouraged by his book. Or the publishers were encouraged, because they asked me to write a book and that's how *Tarantula* came about. John has taken poetics pretty far in popular music. A lot of his work is overlooked, but if you examine it, you'll find key expressions that have never been said before to push across his point of view. Things that are symbolic of some inner reality and probably will never be said again. (Dylan in Jarosinski, 2006: 542)

Where Lennon presented nonsense poetry accompanied by illustrations, Tarantula (1971) poured stream of consciousness prose into large avant-garde blocks. Nevertheless, there were many similarities between their experimental texts. Each used puns or purposeful misspellings, often in their characters' names, and ignored grammatical or syntactical conventions. The likenesses between their fractured and scatological writing style caused both authors to be compared to avant-garde modernist James Joyce (Dalton, 2012; Doggett, 2009).

---

[1] In an unpublished 1971 interview with long-term friend Tony Glover, Dylan offered a rare insight into this songwriting technique: 'The songs of *John Wesley Harding* were all written down as poems, and the tunes were found later' (Brinkley, 2020).

In the early days of their relationship Dylan reciprocated Lennon's admiration, mainly when talking to the British media. Interviewed for *Melody Maker* in May 1965, he said: 'I dig John. As a writer, a singer, and a Beatle. There are very few people I dig every time I meet them, but him I dig' (Jarosinski, 2006: 157). At this time, Dylan was still groping towards what he later called his own 'thin, wild, mercury sound'. Four months later, having recorded *Highway 61 Revisited*, he became noticeably more ambivalent about the Beatles' impact on his music in press conferences outside the UK. This example is from Austin, Texas, in September 1965:

> [Interviewer] Have the Beatles had any influence on your work?
> [Dylan] Well, they haven't influenced the songs or sound. I don't know what other kind of influence they might have. They haven't influenced the songs or the sound. (Dylan in Jarosinski, 2006: 186)

There are several interesting but ambiguous references to the Beatles in Dylan's output. Clinton Heylin (2010a), Keith Negus (2007) and others have argued, with some credibility, that the 'no no no's' in 'It Ain't Me Babe' were an ironic quotation of the 'yeah yeah yeah's' in 'She Loves You'. Less convincingly, Heylin also asserts that 'If You Gotta Go, Go Now', first recorded in January 1965, was purposefully written in the style of the Beatles after Dylan's meeting with the band at New York's Hotel Delmonico the previous August: 'Dylan was smart enough to feel the wind of change the Beatles blew in on, and some part of him wanted to be part of the same mighty storm' (Heylin, 2010a: 213). This is, however, probably incorrect. 'If You Gotta Go, Go Now' is indeed one of Dylan's earlier 'electric' recordings, and it certainly has a Merseybeat rhythm, but this track was originally put to tape as a solo acoustic folk song with the other musicians layered on *after the fact* by producer Tom Wilson. Later that same year Wilson would repeat the same experiment more successfully by over-dubbing a band on the acoustic recording of Simon and Garfunkel's breakthrough hit 'Sound of Silence' (1965). Dylan *did* record two conspicuously Beatles-influenced songs with his group the Hawks during the first studio sessions for *Blonde on Blonde* in October 1965: 'Can You Please Crawl Out Your Window' and 'I Wanna Be Your Lover'. The latter appropriated a line from the chorus of Lennon/McCartney's 'I Wanna Be Your Man' (1963) for its title, and an early take of 'Leopard Skin Pillbox Hat' from these sessions even segued into a parody version of 'Drive My Car' (1965) (Heylin, 2010a). This project was, however, abandoned when Dylan relocated to Nashville, Tennessee to record the definitive version of *Blonde on Blonde*.

Dylan and Lennon's mutual influence was equally apparent in their choice of clothes and accessories during this period. Dylan wore brown suede Cuban heels at the Newport Folk Festival in July 1965, but a month later at the Forest Hills Music Festival in Queens he changed to black 'Beatle boots' – the distinctive style Lennon and McCartney commissioned in 1961 from Carnaby Street cobbler Anello and Davide – and wore these throughout his 1966 World Tour. Lennon, of course, had imitated Dylan by sporting a black peaked Breton cap in Paris and on the Beatles' first visit to North America in early 1964. This resembled the hat worn by Dylan on the cover of his debut album *Bob Dylan* (1962) and in other publicity photographs during that time. Lennon later explained: 'If I see or meet a great artist, I love 'em. I go fanatical about them . . . If they wear green socks I'm liable to wear green socks for a period too' (Wenner, 2000: 148). Indeed, around this time Lennon confided to The Animals' Alan Price that other members of his own band had begun 'taking the mickey out of him' due to his enthusiasm for Dylan (MacDonald, 2008: 163). His Dylan-influenced 'Norwegian Wood (This Bird Has Flown)' (1965) met with a veiled reply on *Blonde on Blonde* (1966) where '4th Time Around', effectively Dylan-doing-Lennon-doing-Dylan, cautioned against using Dylan as a 'crutch'. 'I was very paranoid about that', Lennon confessed shortly afterwards, 'I remember he played it to me when he was in London' (Colt, 1968).

This was at their fifth known meeting, on 26–7 May 1966, when Dylan performed two concerts at London's Royal Albert Hall as the closing dates of his world tour (Goodden, 2014h; MacDonald, 1994). The encounter coincided with the culmination of the 1964–6 trans-Atlantic 'British Invasion', uniting Britain and North America's two most influential popular songwriters just as *Time* magazine celebrated 'Swinging London' with a colourful cover by Geoffrey Dickinson. Lennon was at a creative peak, having recorded and mixed 'Tomorrow Never Knows', 'Dr Robert', 'And Your Bird Can Sing' and 'I'm Only Sleeping' the previous month. The outcome, *Revolver* (1966), proved a pivotal Beatles' release. Positioning relatively conventional song structures alongside more adventurous arrangements, melodies, timbres and lyrics emancipated popular music from conventional templates and validated the genre as an authentic art form (Everett, 1999; Valdez, 2017). *Revolver* also paved the way for what became known as the band's masterpiece, *Sgt. Pepper's Lonely Hearts Club Band*. Retrospectively, it has now begun to rival that album as their most culturally impactful collection of songs (Rodriguez, 2012; Whiteley, 2008).

Dylan, meanwhile, was 'putting his head in the lion's mouth' (Scorsese, 2005) on his 1966 World Tour, delivering some of the most atmospheric, controversial and edgy live performances yet witnessed by British popular music concertgoers. The near-mythological events that transpired have since generated a cultural momentum of their own. In what turned out to be his last tour for eight years, Dylan performed an acoustic set before a captivated audience who then booed and slow hand-clapped in almost equal measure when his backing band the Hawks appeared for the second half of the show. In a now iconic confrontation at Manchester's Free Trade Hall, Dylan paused briefly when an angry fan screamed 'Judas!' at him from the nearby balcony. As the singer struggled to respond the interruption was greeted by a roar of enthusiastic applause. Every performance on the tour was taped by Columbia Records for a planned live album, although this never materialised. Meanwhile Dylan was shadowed, onstage and off, by stills photographer Barry Feinstein and accompanied by a four-person team of cinematographers and sound recordists filming what became *Eat the Document* (1972), as depicted in Figure 2.1.

Commissioned by American broadcaster ABC TV and shot by D. A. Pennebaker and Howard Alk under the erstwhile direction of Dylan himself, it was eventually deemed too impenetrable to be shown on television. Two grainy ten-minute reels, shot at dawn in London, captured Dylan and Lennon in conversation while travelling through the outskirts of the city in a chauffeured limousine: 'I've never seen it, but I'd love to see it. I was always so paranoid', Lennon later recalled. 'I'm just blabbing off and commenting all the time, like you do when you're very high and stoned. I had been up all night' (Wenner, 2000: 149).[2]

Although witnessed by thousands of fans, archiving errors caused significant ongoing confusion over the order of events on this leg of Dylan's World Tour. Columbia's master tapes from the Manchester Free Trade Hall 'Judas!' show were accidentally mislabelled 'Royal Albert Hall' by an audio engineer. As a result, for decades afterwards it was assumed this incident occurred in the famous London venue (Heylin, 2016). Thirty years later, Columbia released the live album, calling it *The Bootleg Series Vol. 4: Bob Dylan – Live 1966 – The 'Royal Albert Hall' Concert* (Sony Music, 1998), even though they knew it was recorded at the Free Trade

---

[2] *Mojo* magazine's 1993 launch issue provided images, a transcript and an analysis of this conversation, which was relatively undocumented at the time (Williams, 1993). The footage is now available in its entirety on *YouTube* (Wylde, 2020).

Figure 2.1 Bob Dylan at The May Fair Hotel, London, 3 May 1966, with cinematographer Howard Alk in the background. (© Pictorial Press Ltd / Alamy Stock Photo)

Hall, Manchester. On the fiftieth anniversary of the tour the actual master tapes from Dylan's London set, which obviously contained none of the shouted interruptions, were released as *The Real Royal Albert Hall 1966 Concert! Live in London 1966* (Sony Music, 2016). That same year every surviving master tape was compiled into a box set of thirty-six CDs and released by Columbia as *Bob Dylan: The 1966 Live Recordings* (Sony Music, 2016).

Other incidents were confused or inflated by second-hand accounts – such as the recollections of Dylan's former drummer, Levon Helm: 'Upset by the walkouts and booing ... the Beatles came backstage after the show to commiserate with the boys. *John Lennon had been hanging out with Bob at the hotel*' (Helm and Davis, 2000: 135–6, my italics). It is most unlikely that Helm was present during this stage of Dylan's trip. He had left backing band the Hawks six months earlier and, according to journalist Dave Lifton (2016), was in New Orleans at this time where he eventually found work on an oil rig, so it is reasonable to assume Helm could not have witnessed these encounters. Maybe he was relying on reminiscences from his former band-mates Rick Danko and Richard Manual. If so, they also, it seems, passed on another untrue anecdote about a violent incident at Dylan's De Montfort Hall show in Leicester in which enraged audience members stormed the stage and attacked Bob, pinning him to the floor (Lifton, 2016). Mickey Jones, the Hawks' replacement drummer, who *was* present at this concert, did *not* include the incident in his memoir. Nor did it feature in Clinton Heylin's exhaustive analysis of the tour. There was particularly energetic booing in Glasgow, even reports of a physical confrontation at Dylan's hotel, but no onstage assault (Feinstein, 2009; Heylin, 2016; Jones, 2007; McKay, 2019).

Dylan himself was a notoriously unreliable narrator having invented elements of his own backstory during previous encounters with the media, a habit that also helped build the mythology around his mid-1960s British tours. At times in early career interviews Dylan claimed to have been raised in an orphanage or to have run away from home and worked as a carnival huckster (Shumway, 2014: 72–3). This make-believe was exposed by *Newsweek* in November 1963, yet Dylan refused to abandon the strategy. Later, when asked directly whether he had ever sung with the Beatles, he responded equivocally – teasing his questioner with allusions to a previous collaboration: 'No, no. Well, I think we may have messed around in London, but no, I don't think anything serious' (Jarosinski, 2006: 243). As a 'true liar' Dylan demonstrated what Rob Coley (2015) labelled Deleuzian 'powers of the false' in the creative 'fabulation' of his past. The prospect of working with Lennon became so enticing that two decades on, in his interview for the *Biograph* (1984) sleeve notes, even Dylan seemed to believe they must have written together at some point:

> It's an interesting footnote to music history that on an English tour, Dylan and Lennon penned a song together. 'I don't remember what it was, though', said Dylan. 'We played some stuff into a tape recorder but I don't know what happened to it. I can remember playing it and the recorder was on. I don't remember anything about the song.' (Crow, 1985)

Eventually, forty years later, respected Dylan scholar Michael Gray unearthed a long-lost Dylan/Lennon/McCartney collaboration in his definitive *The Bob Dylan Encyclopedia* (Gray, 2006). Called 'Pneumonia Ceilings', the song was composed on 25–6 May 1966, at some point during their meeting between the two Royal Albert Hall concerts on the British leg of Dylan's infamous tour. Apparently written 'words first' using Dylan's preferred technique, the lyrics were typed on a single leaf of notepaper then discarded in his hotel room wastebasket:

> Words and phrases right
> Cigarette ash keeps me up all nite
> How come your mama types so fast?
> Is daddy's flag flyin' at half mast?
> Pneumonia ceilings, pneumonia floors
> Daddy ain't gonna take it no more
> Elephant guns blazing in my ears
> I'm sick and tired of your applesauce tears!
> Thermometers don't tell time no more
> Since aunt mimi pushed them off the 20th floor
> So say goodby to skyscrapers
> You'll read about it in the evening paper
> I picked my nose & i'm glad i did

(Gray, 2008: 442)

Sadly, this story is also untrue. 'Pneumonia Ceilings' never existed. The story originated in Mark Shipper's (1978) parody novel, *Paperback Writer*. Once again, the creative potential in Dylan and Lennon's relationship proved so compelling that fiction was repeated as myth and then recorded as fact. Today 'Pneumonia Ceilings' appears in both the original and the revised and updated editions of Gray's (2006, 2008) otherwise masterful *The Bob Dylan Encyclopedia*. It is a powerful example of wishful thinking bias, in which an observer's attention is drawn towards their preferred outcomes. As a *fictional* entry in a publication whose rationale is to provide a definitive reference work, this also constitutes an ironic postmodern artefact. Perhaps inevitably, two songs called 'Pneumonia Ceilings' have now been recorded on commercially available albums: *Holiday at Wobbledef Grunch* (1997) by The Tables, whose version actually incorporates a word-for-word rendition of Shipper's invented lyric; and *No Flowers for a Friend* (2013) by Willie and the Hand Factory, who simply borrowed the song's title. Both are available on Amazon and Spotify. Probably the most convincing element of Shipper's creation, however, is that it was grounded so firmly in Lennon's conspicuous veneration of Dylan: '"I'm a big fan of yours. A big fan". Lennon was in heaven . . . This was as *cool* as Lennon had ever experienced it' (Shipper, 1978: 45). This only confirmed the powerful synergy between these two individuals, both in Shipper's mind and in the perception of his readers who found it so credible.

Dylan and Lennon, 1968 Onwards

Dylan and Lennon's next known encounter was when Lennon and Yoko Ono travelled to see Dylan perform at the 1969 Isle of Wight Festival. Afterwards George Harrison escorted the singer to Lennon's recently acquired mansion, Tittenhurst Park in Berkshire. Here, Lennon failed to persuade Dylan to contribute to what became the Plastic Ono Band's second single: 'He came to our house with George after the Isle of Wight and when I had written "Cold Turkey" . . . I was just trying to get him to record. We had just put him on piano for "Cold Turkey" to make a rough tape but his wife was pregnant or something and they left' (Lennon in Wenner, 2000: 148).

Unofficial extracts from the Beatles' January 1969 recordings in Twickenham Film Studios and their basement facility in Apple Corps Ltd at 3 Savile Row, London hold more evidence of Lennon and Harrison's ongoing Dylan fandom during this period. Around sixteen of his songs were improvised or attempted by the group at these sessions.[3] This compares to sixteen Little Richard songs, fourteen by Chuck Berry, eleven by Elvis Presley, eight by Buddy Holly, seven by Ray Charles and half a dozen each by Lonnie Donegan and Carl Perkins (Goodden, 2014e; Lewisohn, 2004). The majority were initiated by the most consistent and enthusiastic Dylan fan within the band at that time, George Harrison, who had clearly heard versions of 'Get Your Rocks Off' and 'Please Mrs Henry' (1967) some months before they were illicitly released on popular music's first notable bootleg album, *Great White Wonder* (1969). Dylan had possibly given him a copy of the tapes distributed privately by his publishing company Dwarf Music (Sounes, 2011a). Only three songs in the session were initiated by Lennon: 'Blowin' in the Wind' (1963), 'Rainy Day Women #12 & 35' (1966) and a fifteen-minute improvisation in which he repeatedly sang the title of Dylan's biggest hit single, 'Like a Rolling Stone'. Fifty seconds of this performance subsequently appeared on *Let It Be* (1969) as the track 'Dig It'.

Lennon also acknowledged Dylan by name three times in his songs from 1968 to 1970. In 'Yer Blues' (1968), Dylan's lyrics were cited as a measure of Lennon's own inner turmoil. In 'Give Peace a Chance' (1969) he was included in a semi-random series of culturally influential people mostly

---

[3] They include 'All Along the Watchtower' (1967), 'I Shall Be Released' (1967), 'I Threw It All Away' (1969), 'I Want You' (1966), 'It Ain't Me Babe' (1964), 'Mama, You Been on My Mind' (1964), 'The Mighty Quinn' (1967), 'My Back Pages' (1964), 'Please Mrs Henry' (1967), 'Positively 4th Street' (1965) and 'Stuck Inside of Mobile With the Memphis Blues Again' (1966).

compiled from the attendees at that year's week-long Montreal Bed-in for Peace: Alan Ginsberg, Timothy and Rosemary Leary, American comedian Thomas Smothers, Lennon's press officer Derek Taylor, plus Norman Mailer and British comedian Tommy Cooper. Finally, in 'God' (1970), Dylan was included in a list of concepts and individuals that Lennon now publicly disavowed: magic, the I-Ching, the Bible, the Tarot, Adolf Hitler, Jesus, the Kennedys, Buddha, mantras, the Bhagavad Gita, yoga, kings, Elvis Presley, 'Zimmerman' and the Beatles themselves. The order of this list, where 'Zimmerman' appeared in penultimate position immediately before Lennon loudly disowned his own band, revealed the true extent of Dylan's influence (Inglis, 1996b). The use of his family name also indicated the intensity of Lennon's growing disenchantment at that time: 'Dylan is bullshit', he complained to *Rolling Stone*, 'Zimmerman is his name' (Wenner, 2000: 11). 'That's his problem, not mine', Dylan retorted, during an unpublished interview for *Esquire* magazine: 'Lennon is into that shit, taking his pants off, you know? That's where he's at. His record is about the same kind of things as that – who gives a fuck, you know?' (Brinkley, 2020).

Over the next decade Dylan and Lennon's relationship become increasingly complex and equivocal as their mutual approbation threatened to unravel. After Lennon disavowed Dylan in his song 'God', he also criticised the albums *John Wesley Harding* (1967) and *New Morning* (1970): 'I haven't been a Dylan follower since he stopped rocking' (Lennon in Wenner, 2000: 19). For the first time, Lennon consciously underplayed the influence of Dylan on his work, rescinding his usual openness and transparency on such matters. The folk song 'Working Class Hero' (1970) was, he now maintained, inspired by traditional English sources. Lennon vaguely identified these as: 'those miners up in Newcastle ... it doesn't sound like Dylan to me. Does it sound like Dylan to you? ... I never listened that hard to him, you know?' (Wenner, 2000: 6). Elsewhere in the same conversation he accused Dylan of harming Yoko Ono's reputation by initiating malicious gossip: 'Dylan and a few people said she'd got a lousy name in New York and that she gave off bad vibes' (Wenner, 2000: 45). In response, Dylan critiqued Lennon and Ono's political posturing during their interview on *The Dick Cavett Show*: 'I couldn't believe it ... I just felt like throwing something at the set when it was over, you know? I just went to bed and was pissed off' (Brinkley, 2020).

In late 1971, Lennon and Ono relocated to New York City, settling in an apartment at 105 Bank Street, Greenwich Village. Here they aligned with local counterculture figures Jerry Rubin, David Peel and A. J. Weberman and, for a brief period, endorsed Weberman's bizarre Dylan Liberation Front (DLF) – which attempted to harass the singer back into activism by generating critical press coverage, staging protests outside his Greenwich Village apartment and rifling through his domestic refuse. Lennon even sported a 'FREE BOB DYLAN DLF' button badge at one photo shoot. Dylan, who lived in nearby MacDougal Street at the time, took the couple on a walking tour of the neighbourhood, and introduced them to the area (Henke, 2003). Soon afterwards, Lennon withdrew his backing for Weberman and publicly denounced him in *The Village Voice*: 'Weberman is to Dylan as Manson is to the Beatles – and uses what he interprets from Dylan's music to try and kill Dylan' (Lennon in Doggett, 2007: 462). At the same time, he financed Dylan's recording sessions with Alan Ginsberg at The Record Plant studio in New York, intending to release it as the album *Holy Soul & Jelly Roll* on Apple Records, although this project never came to fruition. The following year, Dylan reciprocated by writing to the Immigration and Naturalisation Service in support of Lennon's fight against deportation:

> John and Yoko add a great voice and drive to this country's so called ART INSTITUTION. They inspire and transcend and stimulate, and by doing so can help put an end to this mild dull taste of petty commercialism which is being passed off as artist art by the overpowering mass media . . . Let John and Yoko stay! (Dylan in Wiener, 1991: 237–8)

Dylan and Lennon's last documented reunion occurred in January 1972, also at The Record Plant, where Lennon and Ono were producing David Peel and The Lower East Side's album *The Pope Smokes Dope*. Lennon invited Dylan to hear Peel's song 'The Ballad of Bob Dylan', which celebrated the singer's history as a campaigning political songwriter and encouraged him to return to this role once more, urging him not to fear the consequences of writing protest songs. Lennon's intention was to persuade Dylan to join an anti-Nixon peace concert outside the Republican Party National Convention in San Diego that August. Instead, Dylan walked out of the session objecting to the thinly veiled criticism in Peel's lyrics (Doggett, 2007; Goldman, 1988; Peel, 2011, pers. comm.).

Encouraged by intelligence gained from an over-enthusiastic informant, the Federal Bureau of Investigation mistakenly believed Dylan and Lennon were now involved with Rubin's anti-Nixon campaign. Internal reports suggested that Lennon planned to appear at a Peoples' Coalition for Peace and Justice benefit concert to be held at the March 1972 New Hampshire Republican Primary – although, again, this was untrue (Wiener, 1999).

That year Lennon also attended a preview screening of Harrison's film *The Concert for Bangladesh* at The DeMille Theater, New York City, but apparently left the building during Dylan's segment of the show (Badman, 2001). Details of further encounters may yet be revealed in any future volumes of Dylan's memoir, or if Yoko Ono ever comments on such matters. It would be interesting, for example, to know what happened backstage when Lennon and Ono attended Bob Dylan and The Band's concert at Madison Square Garden in January 1974 (Epstein, 2011).

Lennon continued to cite Dylan in his published and unpublished lyrics throughout the 1970s. 'The Luck of the Irish' from *Some Time in New York City* (1972) referenced 'With God on Our Side' in the final verse. In 1973 he inserted another Dylan song title, 'Blowing in the Wind', into an early version of the lyrics for 'Mind Games' (Anon., 2008). During his 'Lost Weekend' away from Ono in Los Angeles, Lennon produced Harry Nilsson's *Pussy Cats* (1974) which featured a cover of Dylan's 'Subterranean Homesick Blues', and also used Dylan's song title 'Like a Rolling Stone' in his own lyrics for a second time, on this occasion in 'Scared' on *Walls and Bridges* (1974).

In July 1975, Yoko Ono entered the third trimester of her pregnancy and the couple discovered she was expecting a boy. Lennon wrote to his press agent Derek Taylor suggesting the name Dylan: 'How does DYLAN ONO LENNON grab ya? It's a pity the BIG ZIMM copped the name ... but ... by the time he (for it is (a) HE) goes up ... Bobbie will be an OLD COPYWRITE!!! [sic]' (Davies, et al., 2012: 330). After Dylan labelled the Beatles' masterpiece *Sgt. Pepper's Lonely Hearts Club Band* as 'indulgent' in December 1978 (Jarosinski, 2006: 665), Lennon produced three critical parodies of Dylan now posthumously available on the *John Lennon Anthology* (1998). These include 'Stuck inside of Lexicon with the Roget's Thesaurus Blues Again' (an improvised commentary on geopolitics that criticised Dylan's wordiness) and 'Knockin' on Dylan's Door' (a rewrite of 'Knocking on Heaven's Door', which also refers to 'Dylan's Mister Jones'). Dylan's public display of religiosity at the February 1980 Grammy Award ceremony where he performed 'Gotta Serve Somebody' (1979) inspired another parody: 'Serve Yourself' (1980) (Goodden, 2014 k). The twelve different home recordings of this song currently available on unauthorised releases include a punk rock version and a piano blues arrangement, among others, suggesting Lennon was willing to spend considerable time developing this composition. Dylan later visited Ono in her apartment at The Dakota, New York City, shortly after Lennon was assassinated in December 1980 (Epstein, 2011).

Over the decades that followed, Dylan occasionally performed Beatles songs at concerts or in rehearsal, and continued to acknowledge their influence in his press interviews. In June 1981 he played Harrison's 'Here Comes the Sun' at London's Earl's Court. In August 1985 he reflected on Lennon's legacy in an interview for the sleeve notes of *Biograph*: 'People who praise you when you're dead, when you were alive they wouldn't give you the time of day. I like to wonder about some of these people who elevated John Lennon to such a mega-god as if when he was alive they were always on his side' (Dylan in Jarosinski, 2006: 851). In December of the same year he recorded a memorable version of Lennon's 'Come Together', featuring backing vocals from The Queens of Rhythm, during tour rehearsals with Tom Petty and the Heartbreakers at Stage 41 in Universal Studios, Hollywood. In November 2002 he delighted the audience at New York City's Madison Square Garden with Harrison's 'Something', possibly in recognition of the ex-Beatle's recent death. In August 1990 Dylan even performed Lennon's 'Nowhere Man' at the Northern Alberta Jubilee Auditorium in Edmonton, Canada.

Then, in May 2009, as the UK leg of his European tour reached Liverpool, interest in Dylan and Lennon's cultural correspondence unexpectedly intensified when the singer travelled incognito alongside fourteen other tourists on an excursion to Lennon's childhood home at Mendips in Woolton. Here, he viewed photographs and memorabilia at the newly restored house. Dylan 'appeared to enjoy himself', a National Trust press officer recalled: 'He took one of our general minibus tours. People on the minibus did not recognise him apparently ... He could have booked a private tour but he was happy to go on the bus with everyone else' (Anon., 2009). Dylan reportedly left the group before they reached their second stop, McCartney's childhood home at 20 Forthlin Road, Allerton, which is interesting, as this was also during a period when the two were publicly discussing whether they might work together.

Three years later Dylan closed his *Tempest* (2012) album with the unexpected tribute 'Roll on John'. This track references the Quarrymen, the Beatles in Hamburg, Lennon's infamous 1963 Royal Variety Performance quip – 'Would the people in the cheaper seats clap your hands, and the rest of you if you'll just *rattle* your *jewellery*' (Smeaton and Wonfor, 1995) – plus lyrics from 'A Day in the Life' and 'Come Together'. *Uncut Magazine* awarded *Tempest* a 10/10 review and declared 'Roll on John' to be 'as direct and heartfelt as anything since "Sara". The affection expressed for Lennon in the song is tangible, makes it glow like a force-field ... by the end is totally disarming ... a spine-tingling elegy' (Jones,

2012). *Atlantic Magazine* observed that Dylan's imagery in 'Roll on John' was 'rooted in American folk traditions' and argued that it 'only really makes sense seen as a sad lament in the tradition of tragic ballads about larger-than-life folk figures such as Stagger Lee or John Henry. "Roll on John" is ... Dylan acknowledging that Lennon has become legend – another mythic character to populate his songs' (Beauchamp and Shephard, 2012).

The Beatles were also one of many artists referenced in Dylan's song about President John F. Kennedy's assassination, 'Murder Most Foul' from *Rough and Rowdy Ways* (2020). Dylan correlated the unique appeal of the band's English charm with the depressed state of United States popular culture during a period of national mourning after Kennedy's death, a version of history that Ian Inglis (2000b) had previously critiqued as the two-step 'Kennedy – gloom – Beatles' model.

Conclusion: Dylan's and Lennon's Cultural Correlations

Dual biography remains an underused analytical framing device. Given their influence and their relationship to wider social changes during the 1960s and 1970s, Bob Dylan and the Beatles are deserving subjects for this mode of examination. While every band member established a relationship with Dylan, John Lennon is the most appropriate choice for a comparative analysis. George Harrison may have been a closer companion and more productive collaborator, but as two artists who shared unparalleled influence in the 1960s and 1970s, Dylan and Lennon's encounters carried greater cultural potential. The infrequency of these events, their significance and the absence of reliable documentation has allowed half-remembered and poorly sourced accounts to slip into the historical record. Dylan's influence on Lennon is apparent in the form and subject matter of his songs, his adoption of acoustic guitar folk stylings, and the politicisation of his lyrics. This continued throughout Lennon's life, as is evidenced by his ongoing intertextual references to Dylan's work. Conversely, the Beatles inspired Dylan's explorations of his 'electric' sound in early 1965, and Lennon influenced his decision to publish a monograph. The claim that 'you'd be hard-pressed to find a trace of Lennon's influence in any Bob Dylan record' (Beauchamp and Shephard, 2012) was belied by Dylan's recent releases, 'Roll on John' and 'Murder Most Foul', both of which confirmed the reciprocity in a relationship between two artists who shared a unique and unprecedented cultural correspondence during the second half of the twentieth century.

CHAPTER 3

Dylan, Lennon and Anti-War Protest Music

Introduction

The conflict in Vietnam was a significant source of social and political unrest in the United States during the late 1960s and early 1970s. Opposition to the war came from a broad coalition that included religious groups, the New Left, the counterculture, the civil rights movement and others. It inspired large and frequent demonstrations, many notable protest songs and other significant cultural artefacts and events.

Dylan and Lennon composed some of the era's best known and most impactful anti-war compositions; this chapter compares their output by drawing on the work of Marxist sociologist R. Serge Denisoff who documented the significant changes that occurred in protest music at this time. Denisoff (1966, 1968, 1969a, 1969b, 1970, 1972, 1973, 1983; Denisoff and Levine, 1971; Denlsoff and Fandray, 1977) conducted numerous studies that codified political popular songs during the Vietnam War and civil rights era. He classified such music according to two functions, 'magnetic' and 'rhetorical', then hypothesised a third mode, 'introspective', but did not fully develop this concept. In this chapter, for the first time, Dylan's and Lennon's compositions are categorised according to all three formats: magnetic, rhetorical *and* introspective. Two additional song types, 'magnetic–rhetorical' and 'rhetorical–introspective', are also introduced to describe compositions that sit between Denisoff's original classifications. Denisoff's revised typology is then synthesised with Ron Eyerman and Andrew Jamison's (1998) theorisation of the 'movement artist' to compare Dylan's and Lennon's responses to the opportunities and problems created by their interventions.

While Dylan and Lennon sang and spoke out about various social injustices, this chapter concentrates exclusively on their anti-war material, also referred to as their peace songs. These compositions offered or implied criticism of government policies or military actions, or contained a strong message of peace and love. There are several advantages in concentrating on this one theme. First, because most military conflicts stem from geopolitical disputes, anti-war music offers the opportunity to evaluate the work of artists writing about the same issue from different countries – which is not always possible in lyrics that discuss, say, a domestic civil rights campaign. Second, while Denisoff's work on protest music covered a wider range of concerns, the restrictions of this study allow it to focus Dylan's and Lennon's output in a single sub-set of discourse and, in so doing, to compare changes in their beliefs and goals over time. What follows reveals a near mirror image in the form of their output. While Dylan moved from explicit to ambiguous anti-war protest songs during the early 1960s, Lennon pushed forward and became increasingly politicised during the second half of that decade.

R. Serge Denisoff: Magnetic, Rhetorical and Introspective Songs

Denisoff's main period of research coincided with Dylan's and Lennon's greatest commercial successes, so it is reasonable to assume they would have been familiar with the issues he encountered, although perhaps not the vocabulary he used. As a Marxist, Denisoff primarily valued protest songs that promoted class consciousness or mobilised collective action, and he documented how the growth of commercial popular music undermined this format. This functional approach predated the rise of postmodern, postcolonial and intersectional analyses in the social sciences over subsequent decades. In popular music studies, for example, it was superseded by Phillip Tagg's (1987) work on semiotics and Simon Frith's (1989) work on song lyrics. Today Denisoff's research is sometimes dismissed as an overly reductive class analysis, although his output combines well with newer methods and is still consistently cited in post-millennial publications on protest music including David Boucher and Gary Browning's (2004) *The Political Art of Bob Dylan*, Jonathan C. Friedman's (2013) *Routledge History of Social Protest in Popular Music* and Ian Peddie's (2006) *The Resisting Muse: Popular Music and Social Protest*.

Of course, Denisoff was much closer to the founding traditions of 1960s protest music than any contemporary researchers or scholars. Evangelical Protestantism, trade union campaign songs and the civil rights movement were only a generation or so away from his own lived experience and, indeed, that of Dylan and Lennon. As a result Denisoff understood this music from a narrower and more immediate perspective than later theorists, and categorised it according to how effectively it met its main purpose of persuasion and propaganda. He identified six important functions of protest songs:

1. The song attempts to solicit and arouse outside support and sympathy for a social or political movement.
2. The song reinforces the value structure of individuals who are active supporters of the social movement or ideology.
3. The song creates and promotes cohesion, solidarity and high morale in an organisation or movement supporting its world view.
4. The song is an attempt to recruit individuals for a specific social movement.
5. The song invokes solutions to real or imagined social phenomena in terms of action to achieve a desired goal.
6. The song points to some problem or discontent in the society, usually in emotional terms.

(adapted from Denisoff, 1968: 229–30)

Denisoff classified protest music in three forms, corresponding to various combinations of these criteria. 'Magnetic songs of attraction', also called 'propaganda songs', satisfied all six precepts and encouraged listeners to participate in protest movements. Magnetic songs attracted new adherents, created a feeling of solidarity, encouraged social cohesion and promoted class consciousness via their straightforward ideology and performance rituals. He found high concentrations of magnetic material in American labour movement songbooks from the first half of the twentieth century, and in later works published by the Student Nonviolent Coordinating Committee and the African-American civil rights movement. 'Union Maid' (1940) and 'We Shall Overcome' (1948) are typical examples that presented catchy and uncomplicated melodies in a major key, alongside easily assimilated lyrics that engaged an audience while communicating political ideas.

Second was the 'rhetorical song', which merely described a social problem and invited indignation in the listener. For Denisoff, the rhetorical format fulfilled only the sixth and final precept for a propaganda song, that is, 'point to some problem or discontent in the society, usually in emotional terms' (Denisoff, 1968: 229). These compositions might cover a range of social issues, but invariably failed to prescribe any ideological or organisational remedy. Rhetorical songs were commonly less straightforward than magnetic songs, often with more complicated melodies and more ambiguous lyrical metaphors. As a result, rhetorical songs offered less direct means of transmitting information or mobilising political resistance.

They displayed individual dissatisfaction or alienation but presented no collective solutions and suggested no action. Rhetorical anti-war hits such as Creedence Clearwater Revival's 'Fortunate Son' (1969) or Barry McGuire's 'Eve of Destruction' (1965) insisted that something must be done but did not outline any collective action.

Denisoff (1968: 245) identified 'a marked decline in the magnetic propaganda song and a rise in the rhetorical song' during the 1960s that correlated with a drop in traditional class-based campaigns over previous decades. Rhetorical songs, he deduced, were now the dominant protest category. Furthermore, as these compositions displaced their magnetic predecessors, Denisoff predicted the emergence of an even more ineffectual style – a self-centred and tokenistic format, entirely inward looking and absent of any collective acknowledgements. Citing Bob Dylan's withdrawal from overtly political material as a significant influence in this development, Denisoff concluded: 'rhetorical songs are rapidly being replaced by *songs of symbolic introspective protest*' (Denisoff (1968: 247, my italics). This introspective trend was also noticed by Jerome Rodnitzky, who expanded on Denisoff's critique by decrying the new fashion for 'hazy' existential 'mood songs' expressing non-specific lifestyle issues:

> Originally growing out of a concrete situation that called for redress, protest songs are now more likely an expression of an individual life-style. Instead of calling attention to specific evils, they radiate general alienation and a hazy non-conformist aura and content. Listen to the most popular songs of Bob Dylan, Paul Simon, or even the Beatles. They have become lost in an existential haze. In attempting to be all things to all people, the compositions become do-it-yourself protest songs. One can read whatever one wants into the lines. Stance had become more important than goals. *The message song has become the mood song.* (Rodnitzky, 1969: 44, my italics)

While Denisoff himself only really discussed the first two modes of magnetic and rhetorical compositions in his original typology, this chapter also includes his and Rodnitzky's introspective 'mood song' as a third form of protest music.

R. Serge Denisoff: Adaptations and the 'Movement Artist'

Over the years since Denisoff's original research in the late 1960s, many scholars have adapted his categorisations or employed similar functional methods to evaluate protest music from various genres and causes. David E. James' (1989) content analysis of twenty anti-Vietnam war lyrics described them as 'essentially idealist' and bolstered Denisoff's concern over the popularity of rhetorical protest compositions. Charles Stewart et al.'s (1984) study of political rhythm and blues found that it rarely contained anything other than rudimentary information, and was only effective in making simplistic arguments to a sympathetic audience. David Boucher (2004b) renamed Denisoff's three classifications as 'finger-pointing' (magnetic), 'emotional' (rhetorical) and 'hallucinatory' (intro-spective) and used this framework to survey a wide range of protest songs across all the subjects cited in Bob Dylan's catalogue. Although Stewart and Boucher found issues with Denisoff's original model, their work still points towards the basic conclusion that rhetorical protest songs can function effectively in mobilising campaign support.

What follows refines Denisoff's criteria to enhance their relevance and usefulness by widening the scope of his analysis in three ways:

1. Denisoff's output concentrated exclusively on his two most familiar song types (magnetic or rhetorical) and disregarded his third intro-spective category because its message was too diluted to function as effective protest, whereas this book employs all three of the song types he theorised.
2. It also adds two new classifications for those compositions that connect adjacent categories. These are 'magnetic–rhetorical' and 'rhetorical–introspective'. Strung together, these song types form a continuum:

    • magnetic
    • magnetic–rhetorical
    • rhetorical
    • rhetorical–introspective
    • introspective

3. Finally, it synthesises Denisoff's analysis with Ron Eyerman and Andrew Jamison's (1998) work on social movements and the 'move-ment artist'.

Eyerman and Jamison's analysis of songwriters and social movements is possibly the best-known revision of Denisoff's work. It followed Wayne Hampton's (1986) study of social influence in protest music, which argued that Denisoff, Rodnitzky and others had overlooked the ongoing impact of an artist's cultural capital. For Hampton, 'guerrilla minstrels' such as Dylan and Lennon provided a common bond of hero worship that helped small groups form cohesive political campaigns. Here the relationship between the personal biography of a songwriter and the abstract values of their fans functioned as a vector for allegiance, authority, identity and leadership. As John Street (2002: 437) neatly summarised it: 'causes need representatives'. Eyerman and Jamison developed this role into the figure-head of a 'movement artist' whose output embodied 'exemplary action':

> The exemplary action of music and art is lived as well as thought: it is cognitive, but it also draws on more emotive aspects of human conscious-ness. As cultural expression, exemplary action is self-revealing and thus a symbolic representation of the individual and the collective which are the movement. It is symbolic in that it symbolises all the movement stands for, what is seen as virtuous and what is seen as evil. (Eyerman and Jamison, 1998: 23)

For Eyerman and Jamison, protest music is inscribed in the collective cultural memory via exemplary action in creative work of the movement artist. They called this form of dissemination 'cognitive praxis' and sug-gested a three-stage model for how it might work: *context*, the opportunity for collective learning; *process*, how artists challenge dominant aesthetic norms; and *knowledge*, new values and heightened shared consciousness. Bob Dylan, they argued, was the paradigmatic movement artist: someone whose protest songs 'provided a musical variant of critical social theory, mixing into the political discourse a new kind of insight . . . and proclaim-[ing] a poetic truth' (Eyerman and Jamison, 1998: 124).

In what follows, Denisoff's analysis is synthesised with Eyerman and Jamison's theorisation of the movement artist to explain the divergence in Dylan's and Lennon's anti-war protest music. It is suggested that Eyerman and Jamison were in fact quite wrong to characterise Dylan as an exemplary movement artist. He was a reluctant participant whose actions on behalf of the anti-war cause lasted only a year, after which he retreated into highly introspective material. The second half of this chapter shows how John Lennon became far more committed to the role of movement artist, although he also struggled with the conse-quences this entailed.

Bob Dylan's Anti-War Protest Music

'What comes out of my music is a call to action', Dylan declared in a 1963 interview with radical newspaper *National Guardian* (Heylin, 2000: 127). He employed similar terms during a mid-1980s television interview: 'The real protest songs were written really in the thirties and forties. "Which Side Are You On?", mining type songs, union kind of songs. That's where the protest movement developed from. There's still a strain of that type of thing in what I do, it's just more broad now' (Jarosinski, 2006: 891). Yet none of Dylan's anti-war compositions meet Denisoff's definitions for entirely magnetic songs. As Table 3.1 shows, most are on the rhetorical spectrum. Two early peace songs are magnetic–rhetorical compositions, but neither was released on Columbia Records. The effectiveness of his protest music raised Dylan's profile as a movement artist, but his subsequent abandonment of this form in favour of almost entirely introspective songs provides a measure of his determination to relinquish this role.

Anti-war songs were a consistent thread in Dylan's early output. He satirised Cold War civil defence preparations, censured militarism and wrote about actual or threatened conflicts. The timescale in Table 3.1 suggests Dylan's formative protest period of writing magnetic–rhetorical and rhetorical peace songs was surprisingly brief, lasting a little over a year. When we consider the dates of his earliest recording of each composition, all were initially put to tape during the twelve months between April 1962 and April 1963. Dylan published his first peace song, 'I Will Not Go Down under the Ground', in *Broadside #3*, April 1962. His last explicitly rhetorical anti-war composition, 'With God on Our Side', was written only a year later and first performed during his concert at New York Town Hall in early April 1963.

Table 3.1 *Typology of Bob Dylan's anti-war songs*

Category	Title	Recorded
Magnetic–Rhetorical	'Let Me Die in My Footsteps'	April 1962
	'Ye Playboys and Playgirls'	November 1962
Rhetorical	'Blowin' in the Wind'	May 1962
	'Cuban Missile Crisis'	November 1962
	'Long Ago Far Away'	November 1962
	'John Brown'	February 1963
	'Masters of War'	April 1963
	'Talkin' World War III Blues'	April 1963
	'With God on Our Side'	April 1963
Rhetorical–Introspective	'A Hard Rain's a-Gonna Fall'	December 1962
	'Chimes of Freedom'	July 1964
Introspective	'Gates of Eden'	January 1965
	'Tombstone Blues'	August 1965
	'Highway 61 Revisited'	August 1965

Dylan's final two 1960s peace songs, 'Tombstone Blues' and 'Highway 61 Revisited', were composed and recorded in rapid succession for the album *Highway 61 Revisited* (1965). They marked a significant departure from his magnetic–rhetorical and rhetorical songs of April 1962 to April 1963. Besides the obvious difference that Dylan had recorded with a backing band, 'Tombstone Blues' and 'Highway 61 Revisited' employed complex allegories to disguise their anti-war argument. This introspective approach first appeared in his material as early as 'A Hard Rain's a-Gonna Fall' (1962), which attracted significant attention for its distinctive poeticism. He returned to this format with 'Chimes of Freedom' on *Another Side of Bob* Dylan (1964). This album also signalled Dylan's abandonment of rhetorical protest music and his abdication from the movement artist role, as outlined in the track 'My Back Pages'. By the time the album *Highway 61 Revisited* was released his retreat was such that the symbolic ambiguity of 'Tombstone Blues' and 'Highway 61 Revisited' almost entirely obscured their peaceful message.

Dylan's Magnetic Songs, 1962

Originally titled 'I Will Not Go (Down under the Ground)', the song that became 'Let Me Die in My Footsteps' (1962) was one of the first protest compositions Dylan wrote in New York (Heylin, 2010a). It was recorded with John Hammond for the release of *The Freewheelin' Bob* Dylan (1963) but was then removed from the album and replaced by 'Masters of War'. 'Let Me Die in My Footsteps' criticised the logic of Cold War civil defence, arguing that should a nuclear attack happen there was no possibility of escape from the reality of mutually assured destruction. This was a common theme in Dylan's early songs such as the lost 'Strange Rain' (1962) and 'Ye Playboys and Playgirls' (1962). It also appeared in his later album artwork when a community fallout shelter programme sign, common on public buildings in the United States during the Cold War era, featured in the items surrounding Dylan on the sleeve of *Bringing It All Back Home* (1964).

'Let Me Die in My Footsteps' displayed two noticeable magnetic elements. First, it used a simple and inviting strophic format, with short verses followed by its sing-along title refrain. Second, the lyric also outlined a problem in the form of the nuclear threat, then offered a solution as Dylan imagines how economic reform and radical demilitarisation might correct the mistakes of the past. However, the call to action in 'Let Me Die in My Footsteps' failed to meet two of Denisoff's criteria for a fully magnetic protest song: it privileged the situation of the individual over the collective and its solution focused on a romanticised view of nature rather than class conscious exemplary action.

Dylan's individualism might seem like a minor detail but it is a consistent and important theme in his output, and one that will recur in Chapter 5. Here, it was expressed through his conspicuous use of the first-person 'I' and 'mine', rather than 'we' and 'our', during the song's narrative – which clearly prioritised the needs of a singular protagonist over any broader collective interests. This remarkably consistent approach was employed in many later peace compositions, including 'Ye Playboys and Playgirls' (1962), 'John Brown' (1962), 'Masters of War' (1963), 'A Hard Rain's a-Gonna Fall' (1962) and 'Talkin' World War III Blues' (1963). Dylan explained his specific use of the first-person perspective in 'Let Me Die in My Footsteps' as an 'ironic' rather than a 'radical' comment on idealised notions of American domesticity. The song explored a moral dilemma in which the protagonist's natural inclination to protect their immediate family conflicted with a wider community cohesion: 'Bomb shelters divided families [so] a song about the futility of fallout shelters was not that radical. It's not like I had to conform to any doctrine to do it. The song was *personal and social at the same time*, though. That was different' (Dylan, 2004a: 271, my italics). He subsequently revisited this conflict between kinship and society in another anti-war song, 'Highway 61 Revisited', which repurposed the Old Testament story of Abraham and Isaac as an allegory for parental sacrifice during the Vietnam war.

The other weak magnetic element in 'Let Me Die in My Footsteps', the lack of *solution* for the problem it described, was an appeal to a romanticised vision of rural America. This was also clearly at odds with Denisoff's imperative for class mobilisation. The song started promisingly with a call to arms inspired by Dylan's great influence, Woody Guthrie, that clearly identified with the values cultivated by traditional songs of attraction:

> There's always been people that have to cause fear
> They've been talking of the war now for many long years
> I have read all their statements and I've not said a word
> But now Lawd God, let my poor voice be heard
> (Bob Dylan, 'Let Me Die In My Footsteps')

Yet it concluded by turning towards the power of nature and the grandiose American landscape, urging listeners to immerse themselves in the beauty of nature, invoking images of mountain streams, canyons and waterfalls, wildflowers and meadows, 'out in the country where the land meets the sun' (Bob Dylan, 'Let Me Die In My Footsteps' 1963). This strong preference for romantic pastoralism over the class struggle constitutes another core theme in Dylan's work, one that ultimately defined his worldview. It is examined in more detail in Chapter 5.

'Ye Playboys and Playgirls' (1962), Dylan's second early magnetic–rhetorical protest song, also protested Cold War civil defence policies. In the second verse, the protagonist refuses entry to a door-to-door nuclear fallout shelter salesmen. Much like the seminal 'Blowin' in the Wind' (1962), 'Ye Playboys and Playgirls' critiqued a range of political issues including Jim Crow, anti-communism and militarism. It is notable that 'Blowin' in the Wind' preceded 'Ye Playboys and Playgirls' by only six months, given that each proffered such a different style of protest. While 'Blowin' in the Wind' represented Dylan's first genuinely *rhetorical* composition, 'Ye Playboys and Playgirls' was his final and most complete attempt at a traditional, sing-along, *magnetic* style of protest.

Dylan performed 'Ye Playboys and Playgirls' at the 1963 Newport Folk Festival as part of the Topical Songs and New Songwriter's Workshop hosted by Pete Seeger (see Figure 3.1). It was subsequently released by Folkways Records. Dylan and Seeger's session drew the largest crowd of that year's event, around 500 people, and the recording captured their performance of the song's repetitive lyrics and its memorable, simple refrain. Denisoff (1968) argued that civil rights era magnetic protest songs were commonly adapted from spirituals, and 'Ye Playboys and Playgirls' achieved instant familiarity due to its strong resemblance to the melody and arrangement of 'This Little Light of Mine' (1920) and 'Down by the Riverside' (Trad., 1918). In this context, 'Ye Playboys and Playgirls' sat squarely in the collective hootenanny tradition; the workshop audience was immediately able to join in as Seeger harmonised over Dylan's lead vocal and encouraged them to participate: 'You all can sing this with us even if you've never heard it before', he exclaimed as Dylan struck up the chords, 'because only one line changes in each verse' (Lerner, 2007).

The sing-along format of 'Ye Playboys and Playgirls' introduced another important magnetic element: the song's attempt to solicit support by engineering an active moral consensus among its listeners. Here, a solution to the problems raised came in the form of communal resistance and potential civil disobedience. The strophic form of the composition invited Dylan's audience to participate actively in unison and roused those present into collective solidarity, loudly declaring their defiance against institutional racism and

Figure 3.1 Bob Dylan and Pete Seeger perform at the Topical Songs and New Songwriter's Workshop, Newport Folk Festival, 28 July 1963. (© Shangri-La Entertainment)

Cold War militarism.[1] As *Broadside* observed: 'Its tune catches whole crowds easy, and the words come right along from the feeling' (Dunson, 1963: 10). Although much like 'Let Me Die in My Footsteps', 'Ye Playboys and Playgirls' did not precisely conform to all of Denisoff's magnetic criteria; not least because as with so many of Dylan's other protest songs it remained couched in the subjective experience of a protagonist using first-person singular pronouns to sing about the threat to 'his' world, 'his' house, 'his' road and 'his' freedom.

Nevertheless, this song remains Dylan's most conspicuous rallying cry and marked his zenith as a composer and performer of mass action propaganda music. Seeger's obvious enthusiasm for 'Ye Playboys and Playgirls' – he even compared the composition favourably to 'We Shall Overcome' – indicated its potential as a magnetic social movement anthem. Yet the fact that Seeger admired this song so much may also explain why Dylan discarded it so decisively and so rapidly. He never recorded 'Ye Playboys and Playgirls' in a studio, has not performed it onstage since 1963 and did not publish it in the first edition of his definitive

---

[1] Chapter 6 examines some of the psychological mechanisms underlying collective participation in sing-along songs such as 'Ye Playboys and Playgirls'.

collection *Lyrics 1962–2001* (Dylan, 2004b). Nor was it included in the authoritative documentary on Dylan's Newport Folk Festival performances, Murray Lerner's (2007) *The Other Side of the Mirror: Bob Dylan Live at the Newport Folk Festival*, even though that film includes three other contributions from that year's Songwriter's Workshop. On his first hearing, Seeger exclaimed 'Ye Playboys and Playgirls' would be 'sung by a million people before the year is out' (Dunson, 1963: 10). Dylan, who quickly began to outgrow his formative influences and adopt a much less magnetic and more conspicuously rhetorical tone, ensured this did not happen.

Dylan's Rhetorical Songs, 1962–1963

Rhetorical compositions describe a problem but offer no solutions. Denisoff saw these protest songs as less effective because they did not inspire mass mobilisation. Dylan's rhetorical compositions remain, however, some of his more powerful and best-known protest songs. Typically less didactic than his more straightforward magnetic lyrics, this style encouraged Dylan's creative expression to flourish, and his compositions reached a much wider audience as a result. Here, I consider the masterful series of rhetorical anti-war songs written and recorded in just two short years at the height of Dylan's involvement in the Greenwich Village folk revival scene during 1962–3: 'Blowin' in the Wind', 'Masters of War', 'With God on Our Side', 'Talkin' World War III Blues' and 'A Hard Rain's a-Gonna Fall'.

Peter, Paul and Mary's version of 'Blowin' in the Wind' (1962) became Dylan's breakthrough song and his greatest commercial success. With a melody taken from the African-American spiritual 'No More Auction Block', 'Blowin' in the Wind' conformed to some elements of magnetic songs by invoking the familiarity of old gospel tunes. Yet, by posing a long series of unanswered questions in a similar manner to Pete Seeger's 'Where Have All the Flowers Gone?' (1955) and by refusing to offer any solutions to these dilemmas, it also constituted Dylan's most distinctive early *rhetorical* composition. James Dunlap saw the insistent questioning of 'Blowin' in the Wind', and Dylan's inability or unwillingness to suggest any answers, as indicative of his inherent distrust of organised politics. 'Dylan's phrasing', he argues, 'implies a teleological view of history' where society is moving resolutely in a predetermined direction towards a final cause; but this song offers no class-based analysis, proposes no collective solutions and makes no call for programmatic change in the form of a 'Marxist-styled revolution with rules that one could articulate' (Dunlap, 2006: 562). Instead, its proposals are nebulous and only perceived via Dylan's instinctive and subjective individual intuition.

If the problem–solution formula of magnetic songs limited their potential popularity, 'Blowin' in the Wind' invited more open interpretations. The absence of answers in its lyrics may have left politically motivated listeners underwhelmed, but it also encouraged a wide variety of readings that gave the song a huge commercial potential. Almost anyone could perform 'Blowin' in the Wind' without appearing too radical. As a result, Elvis Presley, Cliff Richard and the Foggy Mountain Boys – to cite just three examples – recorded it during the 1960s.

Peter, Paul and Mary's 1963 version was an immediate and enormous hit, selling over 320,000 copies in its first two weeks to become to become the fastest-selling single in the history of Warner Bros. Records: 'Peter, Paul and Mary sang it everywhere they went, and they went everywhere' (Scaduto, 1996: 135). In their live shows Peter Yarrow habitually introduced 'Blowin' in the Wind' as a song written by 'the most important folk artist in America today', whose lyrics contained nine questions that would define the fate of that generation (Sounes, 2011a: 140). In so doing, he may have sought to emphasise the magnetic attraction of the composition, even though its lyric suggested no solutions to the issues raised. Dylan himself vacillated between promoting it as a peace anthem then insisting that it should not be interpreted as such. At a 1962 Gerde's Folk City performance, he said: 'This here ain't a protest song or anything like that, cause I don't write protest songs . . . I'm just writing it as something to be said, for somebody, by somebody' (Dylan in Heylin, 2010a: 78). Later that same year, in an interview for *Sing Out!* magazine, Dylan mused:

> like a restless piece of paper it's got to come down some time . . . but the only trouble is that no one picks up on the answer when it comes down so not too many people get to see it and know it . . . then it flies away again. I'm only 21 years old and I know that there's been too many wars. (Heylin, 2010a: 79)

Although it was a rhetorical composition, 'Blowin' in the Wind' could still prove an effective device for mobilising social movements. Duane R. Fish saw its unanswered questions as a source of *strength* rather than weakness because this form reflected the same problems it was trying to describe. Dylan's rhetorical technique of repeatedly posing moral dilemmas while refusing to provide any solutions expressed his own stance on these issues: 'Asking the questions and noting that there are no answers, reinforces claims concerning the war's futility' (Fish, 1994: 124). For David Boucher

(2004b) the considerable appeal of 'Blowin' in the Wind' lay in Dylan's capacity to contrive non-specific images then refuse to elucidate their meaning. This fuelled the imagination of his audience where a more magnetic and literal message might have foreclosed it. Others characterised Dylan's strategy as 'the effectiveness of moving from the particular to the general' (Gill and Odegard, 2004: 23). While his subject-specific anti-war protest song 'Cuban Missile Crisis' (1962) became less relevant once that event had passed, the message of 'Blowin' in the Wind' remained sufficiently flexible to sustain its relevance even as the political context evolved. This codified Dylan's new aesthetic of epistemological ambiguity – as confirmed in his analogy of justice as 'a restless piece of paper' – and established a predilection for elastic interpretations of truth and language that would soon entirely displace his old moral certainties. 'Blowin' in the Wind' was not only Dylan's first and most significant rhetorical composition, it also lay the groundwork for increasingly playful and ambiguous introspective protest songs yet to come.

'Masters of War' (1963) was released on *The Freewheelin' Bob Dylan* in the place of 'Let Me Die in My Footsteps' (Heylin, 2010a). The song's inspiration was President Eisenhower's farewell address, which cautioned against unfettered militarism: 'the song has got nothing to do with being anti-war. It has more to do with the Military Industrial Complex that Eisenhower was talking about' (Dylan in Heylin, 2010a: 119). Although essentially rhetorical in structure, 'Masters of War' also presents the problem–solution binary found in Denisoff's magnetic song typology. In this case, if taken literally, the 'solution' to militarism is to depose those responsible. This is one of Dylan's most sustained and vituperative anti-war compositions and a defining oppositional song from his early protest period.

Christopher Butler compared 'Masters of War' to 'angry' song precedents such as Merle Travis's 'Sixteen Tons' (1946), arguing that its language is both intensely polemical and elegantly artful. For Boucher the song represents an expression of controlled rage, a 'venomous attack' on the industrialists, militarists and politicians who choreograph Armageddon from the safety of comfortable chairs behind expansive corporate desks: 'an expression of utter contempt for the evil inflicted on the world by these men' (Boucher, 2004b: 157). As one of Dylan's most direct and emotional statements, its impact on his audience was immediate and profound, as *Broadside* noted at the time:

> Gil [Turner, MC, Gerde's Folk City] took out his six-string Gibson, handed it over to Bob Dylan, saying how Bob's new song 'Masters of War' was one

of the best Bob had ever written. I kept on thinking that he had written a lot
of good ones, some that had real lyric poetry, like 'Blowin' in the Wind' and
'Hard Rain's a-Gonna Fall' ... and I waited for the images of rain and
thunder and lightning to come out in great spectacles, but no, this time
there was a different kind of poetry, one of great anger, accusation, just
saying who the masters of war are, without compromising one inch in its
short sharp direct intensity. (Dunson, 1963: 10)

Like 'Blowin' in the Wind', 'Masters of War' offers a genuinely forceful
and affecting *rhetorical* song. Perhaps this is why it was re-imagined by
others as a *magnetic* composition – most notably when the GI Movement,
one of the more successful examples of social activism during the Vietnam
era, reprinted the lyrics as propaganda literature for mass distribution
among troops and support staff (Cortright, 2005). Dylan has also revived
the song at culturally important shows, such as the 1991 Radio City Music
Hall Grammy Lifetime Achievement Award concert that coincided with
the outbreak of the first Gulf War and his 1994 tour date in Hiroshima.

'With God on Our Side' (1963) presented another polemic against
militarism, this time contextualised via earlier conflicts such as the
American Indian Wars of the eighteenth and nineteenth centuries,
the Great War (1914–18) and the Second World War (1939–45). As
with 'Masters of War' this song was structured around a subjective
first-person framework. The first verse alone contains five first-
person singular pronouns. However, it also invokes the magnetic
elements of identification with others by incorporating a more plural
title and refrain, 'With God on *Our* Side'. This changed the perspective of the original version, from *Broadside* #27 June 1963, which
was called 'With God on *Your* Side' – a rare example of Dylan
invoking a plural possessive pronoun to persuade his audience that
'they, too, were implicated in wrongful thinking' (Dunlap,
2006: 570).

'Talkin' World War III Blues' (1963) was one of four talking blues
songs that Dylan recorded in the year-long sessions for *The Freewheelin'
Bob Dylan*, but it was the only track in this format that made it to the
album. Once again, the lyric's first-person perspective indicated Dylan's
preference for individualised narratives over songs of collective solidarity.
In 'Talkin' World War III Blues' the protagonist's Cold War nuclear
nightmare causes a psychiatrist to diagnose him as insane; but he then
recounts such a compelling account of this dream that it triggers the
doctor's own paranoid fantasy. This tale inverted the traditional relationship between caregiver and patient and, like the unanswered

questions in 'Blowin' in the Wind', offered another early example of Dylan's fluid approach towards knowledge and power. The song's self-deprecating and absurd humour softened its dark end-of-the-world psychosis, while its dreamlike symbolism pre-empted Dylan's subsequent turn towards increasingly chaotic and hallucinatory images. Far removed from traditional protest music, 'Talkin' World War III Blues' contained elements of mid-1960s post-acid kaleidoscopic surrealism, even though his first experience with LSD was 'still a year away, to the day' (Heylin, 2010a: 142).

'A Hard Rain's a-Gonna Fall' (1962) traversed a similarly post-apocalyptic landscape. Derived from an Anglo–Scottish border ballad, 'Lord Randall' (Trad.), the song sat squarely in the folk revival tradition; however, its distinctive and adventurous imagery represented a significant development in style and marked the first appearance of a genuinely *introspective* form. Chronologically, this was a surprisingly early song, composed some time before 'Talkin' World War III Blues'. As such, 'A Hard Rain's a-Gonna Fall' provided the first conceptual pivot point in Dylan's evolution from rhetorical protest to more oblique mood songs. It comprised 'a series of disconnected, enigmatic images' that created a 'panoptic' vision 'evoking global destruction' and 'metaphorical disasters' (Marqusee, 2005: 65). Thomas O. Beebee (1991: 29) suggests 'A Hard Rain's a-Gonna Fall' synthesised a new hybrid, 'the apocalyptic ballad'. According to Dylan, this kaleidoscopic collage was inspired by compiling arresting opening lines for songs he would never have the time to write (Shelton, 1986). The dislocated juxtapositions and intense subjective visions they invoked seemed, for some, designed to fashion a 'derangement of the senses' (Curtis, 1987: 152). Boucher (2004b: 161) found the lyrics too unfocussed to carry any meaningful connotation: 'it is doubtful that he had any intention to arouse any particular emotion in his audience to any practical effect'.

The more powerful Dylan's images, the more they obscured any political significance. Nevertheless, his abstractions became increasingly daring as rhetorical protest songs segued into rhetorical–introspective, then fully introspective, material. Any possibility of a 'message' became progressively more diluted, and any advocacy for protest activities increasingly incomprehensible. Dylan's first rhetorical–introspective song, 'A Hard Rain's a-Gonna Fall', foreshadowed this movement towards increasingly abstract forms.

Dylan's Introspective Songs, 1964–1965

If Eyerman and Jamison regarded Dylan's early Newport Folk Festival appearances as defining moments in exemplary action, the continuing popularity of his protest material certainly lived on well beyond his own desire to inhabit that role. Stevie Wonder's version of 'Blowin' in the Wind' (1966) became the first Top 10 Motown hit composed by a white artist, Huey Newton assembled the first issues of *The Black Panther* newspaper while listening to *Highway 61 Revisited*, Julius Lester incorporated Dylan's lyrics into *Look Out Whitey! Black Power's Goin' Get Your Mama!* (1968) and P. F. Sloan appropriated Dylan's folk-rock style for 'Eve of Destruction' (1965) – which made history as the first anti-war protest song to reach number one on the US Hot 100 (Doggett, 2007).

For some, including Dylan's producer Bob Johnston, the potency of Dylan's material inspired messianic devotion: 'I truly believe that in a couple of hundred years they'll find out he was a prophet … I think he's the only prophet we've had since Jesus' (Sounes, 2011a: 229). Dylan, however, found such comparisons tiresome. 'Being noticed can be a burden', he explained later, 'Jesus Christ got himself crucified because he got himself noticed. So, I disappear a lot' (Dylan in Gill, 1998: 37). After writing a dozen peace songs in the twelve months from April 1962 to April 1963 he abruptly stopped composing this material, abandoned the role of 'movement artist' and moved towards more introspective styles. The November 1963 assassination of President John F. Kennedy further dissuaded any activity that might position him as a cultural figurehead. Three weeks after this incident, Dylan revealed his new worldview in a speech at the National Emergency Civil Liberties Committee annual dinner: 'There's no black and white, left and right for me anymore. There's only up and down, and down is very close to the ground. And I'm trying to go up without thinking about anything trivial such as politics' (Dylan in Shelton, 1986: 200).

From this point, Dylan adopted the disconnected and introspective lyrical stance he first initiated in 'A Hard Rain's a-Gonna Fall'. His next album, *Another Side of Bob* Dylan (1964), featured predominantly love songs. The one overtly political composition, 'Chimes of Freedom', constituted Dylan's 'last great protest song' (Marqusee, 2005: 99) and demonstrated his command of rhetorical and introspective forms. Here, Dylan's protagonist was caught in a heavy storm in which the thunderclaps and bolts of lightning seemed to illuminate the plight of soldiers, refugees, prisoners and other marginalised groups and, in so doing, heralded new possibilities for social justice. This composition aside, fully introspective mood songs now dominated Dylan's songwriting. 'Gates of Eden', the only song on *Bringing It All Back Home* (1965) that discussed 'war', 'peace' or 'soldiers' did so in an entirely abstruse manner – mingling these terms with images of seagulls and beaches, cowboys and hunters, in a dense but meaningless collage. Ironically, Dylan's sleeve notes for this album contain his earliest direct reference to the Vietnam conflict.[2] They demonstrate the concerns he felt at being identified as a movement artist, describing a scene where the protagonist is confronted by a lynch mob with burning torches who scream at him and blame him for the anti-war protests.

'Tombstone Blues' on *Highway 61 Revisited* (1965) was Dylan's first electric peace song. It dramatically extended the graveyard imagery employed in 'Masters of War', using a metaphorical device that invoked the horrors of any conflict and implied criticism of those who might profit from it. Yet 'Tombstone Blues' was also so intensely allegorical that its meaning seemed entirely fluid by comparison. The most impactful sections appeared to accuse President Lyndon Johnson of callously escalating the war in Vietnam: 'The Commander-in-Chief answers him while chasing a fly / Saying, "Death to all those who would whimper and cry"' ('Tombstone Blues'). The sometimes coded and occasionally random references to historical and literary characters in songs on *Highway 61 Revisited* are difficult, if not impossible, to decipher. Other inhabitants of 'Tombstone' included Paul Revere's horse, Jezebel, Jack the Ripper, the ghost of Belle Starr, John the Baptist, the King of the Philistines, Galileo, Delilah, Cecil B. DeMille, Ma Rainey and Beethoven. In that context it is possibly futile to debate whether the reference to the 'Commander-in-Chief' alluded directly to President Johnson or if this was simply another character pulled from Dylan's stream-of-consciousness lyrics. Nonetheless, it is significant that these chaotic verses, where 'church, state, college and commerce collude to squander both the country's history and its future' (Gill and Odegard, 2004: 84), encouraged vigorous discussion about their meaning precisely as the conflict in Vietnam intensified.

As with all introspective songs, any understanding of 'Tombstone Blues' as an anti-war composition required some effort on the part of Dylan's audience as it necessitated a close reading of his lyrics – which, of course,

---

[2] Dylan did not use the word 'Vietnam' in any song until two obscure 1980s compositions. The unreleased 'Legionnaire's Disease' (1981) briefly mentions an uncle who served in the war, and his eponymous theme song for *Band of the Hand* (1986) contained a line honouring Vietnam veterans in reference to the film's central character.

explains its popularity among scholars. Boucher (2004b), for example, analysed the song as a surreal catalogue of historical, biblical and cinematic moments involving the nightmarish transformation of figures from American history and culture. Neil Corcoran likened it to Picasso's paintings of Nazi occupied Paris: 'I have not painted the war ... but I have no doubt that the war is in ... these paintings I have done' (Picasso, in Corcoran, 2002: 160). Once the listener became open to such possibilities, Dylan's complex layers of imagery revealed another significant injustice – the forced conscription of young African-American soldiers in a war of colonial oppression:

> The king of the Philistines his soldiers to save
> Puts jawbones on their tombstones and flatters their graves
> Puts the pied piper in prison and fattens the slaves
> Then sends them out to the jungle
>
> (Bob Dylan, 'Tombstone Blues')

David Boucher and Ellen Willis, writing almost forty years apart, argued that Dylan's oppositional tactics had evolved by the time of *Highway 61 Revisited* such that he was now protesting not just through the *content* of his work, but also via its *form*: 'Dylan became self-consciously poetic, adopting a neo-beat style loaded with images. Though he had rejected the traditional political categories, his new posture was if anything more scornful of the social order than before ... Aesthete not activist, but still oppositional, Dylan's work still bristled with messages' (Willis, 1967). Boucher (2004b: 15) later wrote: 'What I want to suggest, then, is that there is a point at which Dylan ceases to be a craftsman, ceases to have a preconceived idea with a determinate purpose, ceases to express his emotion, which was largely anger, *by* writing songs, and came to express it instead *in* writing songs.' Mark Polizzotti agreed that 'Tombstone Blues' was a clear departure in style, but he also noted the ideological continuity in its suspicion of, and resistance to, capricious corporate and state control. As such, it remained equally as valid as any of Dylan's earlier protest music, except in this song his moral opposition was now conveyed more by 'mood' and 'imagery' than by direct appeals to collective action (Polizzotti, 2006: 243).

'Highway 61 Revisited', Dylan's second introspective song on this album, used the Binding of Isaac, a familiar Old Testament story from Genesis 21–22, as a metaphor for domestic intergenerational conflict during the war in Vietnam. When God demanded that Abraham sacrifice his only son, Abraham's willingness to perform this supreme act of faith confirmed his position as the patriarch of Judaism, Christianity and Islam.

Dylan's re-telling of the tale in 'hip patois' offered an imaginative contemporaneous interpretation of this ancient archetypal narrative in the context of events on the home front (Heylin, 2010a: 257). On 28 July 1965, following an intense three-week debate in Congress and the media, President Johnson increased the size of active United States fighting forces to 125,000, doubled the military draft to 35,000 per month and dramatically extended his Operation Rolling Thunder bombing campaign (Buzzanco, 1996). Written in the run up to a recording session that occurred five days after these events, 'Highway 61 Revisited' appears to have been conceived as a direct response to the unprecedented controversy around a rapidly escalating commitment of troops and military resources. It seems Dylan viewed the looming conflict in Vietnam as another instance of mass paternal filicide, where those fathers who served in the Second World War and the Korean War would now forfeit their own children in the ultimate test of loyalty to the nation-state. This 'sacrificial identity' ritual recurred periodically throughout United States history and has manifested, in some form, in almost all enduring civilisations (Marvin and Ingle, 1996; Roskin, 1974):

> God said to Abraham, 'Kill me a son'
> Abe says, 'Man, you must be putting me on'
> God says, 'No'
> Abe says, 'What?'
> God says, 'You can do what you want, Abe, but . . .
> Next time you see me coming you better run'.
> Abe says, 'Where you want this killing done?'
> God says, 'Out on Highway 61'.
>
> (Bob Dylan, 'Highway 61 Revisited' 1965)

For Corcoran (2002) this message was directly analogous to Wilfred Owen's poem 'The Parable of the Old Man and the Young' (1918), in which Abraham *ignored* the angel's command not to slay his slay his child and the sons of Europe were annihilated in the Great War as a result. Clinton Heylin (2010a) and Mike Marqusee (2005) found the key to this interchange in Kierkegaard's *Fear and Trembling* (1843), where Abraham's impossible moral dilemma invites Dylan to evaluate 'the individual's relationship to the absolute', and to critique 'the inauthentic social and spiritual existence of bourgeois Europe' (Marqusee, 2005: 179). Echoing the message of earlier rhetorical songs such as 'Masters of War', the denouement of 'Highway 61 Revisited' exposed an unholy collusion between politicians, industrialists and media:

Now the rovin' gambler he was very bored
He was tryin' to create the next world war
He found a promoter who nearly fell off the floor
He said I never engaged in this kind of thing before
But yes I think it can be very easily done
We'll just put some bleachers out in the sun
And have it on Highway 61

(Bob Dylan, 'Highway 61 Revisited', 1965)

By setting the parable on Highway 61 Dylan directed his audience's attention towards the cultural spine of the United States. The road on which Bessie Smith suffered her fatal automobile collision ran adjacent to Elvis Presley's teenage home in the housing projects of Memphis, crossed the intersection where — according to blues mythology — Robert Johnson 'sold his soul' to the Devil, and was the route north taken by hundreds of thousands of African Americans during the Great Migration of the 1930s and 1940s. This distinctive location grounded the song's introspective allegory in a genuine historicity. As such, according to Dave Harker, Dylan's rejection of magnetic and rhetorical folk protest music and his abnegation of movement artist status could equally signify the reclamation of his personal authenticity. Rather than a cultural betrayal, it was 'the *opposite* of selling out' (Harker, 1980: 132, my italics). Dylan's audience was now more mature and independent-minded, his influences more reflective of his own musical interests and his electric message heard by a new audience of working-class teenage rock and roll enthusiasts as a result. Yet his introspective lyrical approach faced considerable resistance from folk enthusiasts. When challenged on the substance of his new material during his 1966 World Tour, Dylan angrily and repeatedly claimed he still sang protest songs – only in a more creative form: 'These are all protest songs now, *come on!*' On the same tour, this time in interview, he affirmed: 'All my songs are protest songs, every one of them. That's all I do is protest' (Dylan in Scorsese, 2005).

The lyrics of 'Tombstone Blues' and 'Highway 61 Revisited' proved sufficiently intriguing to facilitate long-standing discourse over their meaning. The fractured imagery required listeners to engage in greater depth when compared with the overt claims of magnetic songs. It also transcended their immediate cultural and political context of time-bound events and identifiable individuals. This defiantly introspective style drew audiences into the work but, like the repeated questions of 'Blowin' in the Wind', it implied a wide range of connotations with no solutions. Where the nuclear bunkers of 'Let Me Die in My Footsteps' drew attention to one specific threat – the dangers of Cold War militarism – the graveyard imagery of 'Tombstone Blues' invited the audience to contemplate mortality itself.

In this sense 'Tombstone Blues' and 'Highway 61 Revisited' are, perhaps, best understood as signifiers of the greater foundational shift in Dylan's epistemology at this time. His refusal to accept the role of movement artist coincided with his overt rejection of 'truth' or 'justice' – concepts that constitute the raison d'être of political activism – in favour of what David Hume called 'Universal Doubt', a form of Cartesian scepticism where even the notion of 'definition' itself becomes problematic (Schmidt, 2003). 'Tombstone Blues' decried 'knowledge', or any form of certitude or conviction, as a 'useless' and 'pointless' cause of pain and insanity. Pressed on this issue in *Don't Look Back* (1966), Dylan retorted: 'Truth is just a plain picture of a tramp vomiting, man, into the sewer ... Each of us really knows nothing, but we all think we know things. But we know nothing' (Dylan in Pennebaker, 1967). Later, in *Chronicles: Volume 1*, he concluded: 'It was pointless to think about. Whatever you were thinking could be dead wrong' (Dylan, 2004a: 35).

John Lennon's Anti-War Protest Music

This section discusses John Lennon's anti-war songs with reference to Denisoff's magnetic, rhetorical and introspective typology. Mapped against these classifications, the trajectory of Lennon's protest music reveals a near mirror image to that of Dylan's. The previous section showed how Dylan retreated from magnetic–rhetorical, through rhetorical, to entirely introspective coded anti-war protest songs. Lennon, in contrast, moved through Denisoff's categories in the *opposite* direction (see Table 3.2). His earliest anti-war songs appeared as generalised and introspective protest music on mid-1960s Beatles albums. These were followed by more specific rhetorical compositions that led to explicit attempts at magnetic mass mobilisation during his solo career, at which point Lennon enthusiastically embraced the role of movement artist theorised by Eyerman and Jamison. In August 1966, during a Beatles' press conference in New York, Lennon fielded an unknowingly prescient question: 'You seem to be doing a Bob Dylan in reverse. That is, you became popular playing rock and roll and now you seem to be doing a lot more folk rock' (Goodden, 2014i). Indeed, precisely at the time when Dylan rejected the mantle of campaigning spokesperson, Lennon adopted that position.

Table 3.2 *Typology of John Lennon's anti-war songs*

Category	Title	Recorded
Introspective	'The Word'	November 1965
	'Tomorrow Never Knows'	April 1966
	'Happiness Is a Warm Gun'	September 1968
	'The Ballad of John and Yoko'	April 1969
Rhetorical	'Come Together'	July 1969
	'I Don't Wanna Be a Soldier Mama . . .'	February 1971
	'Mind Games'	July–August 1973
Rhetorical–Magnetic	'All You Need Is Love'	June 1967
	'Happy Xmas (War Is Over)'	October 1971
Magnetic	'Give Peace a Chance'	June 1969
	'Imagine'	May–June 1971
	'Bring on the Lucie (Freda Peeple)'	July–August 1973

Lennon's Introspective Songs, 1965–1969

Rubber Soul's 'The Word' (1965) was Lennon's first musical statement in favour of peace. As a dance song from a beat group it was an atypical protest composition – although, by citing the 'good book' as its source of moral authority, it also employed the gospel tropes Denisoff identified as a characteristic of propaganda music. Here, Lennon synthesised two familiar concepts of 'love' as a word (signifier) and as an emotion (affect) with one of the key messages from *The King James Bible* Gospel of John – which, in its opening sentence, defines God as 'the Word' ('In the beginning was the Word, and the Word was with God, and the Word was God') then later also as 'Love' ('God is Love', John 4:8, 4:16). The result was a deceptively simple appeal to Christian *agape* – a selfless, unconditional regard for one's fellows: 'On one issue, at least, the New Testament message is clear and consistent: faced with the threat of physical violence, Christians must not reciprocate, even to the point of death' (Desjardins, 1997: 18).

As the first song in which the Beatles expressed any understanding of 'love' beyond the romantic and sexual context of teenage courtship rituals and physical desires, 'The Word' established a theme that was subsequently explored in 'Tomorrow Never Knows' and 'All You Need is Love'. It hypothesised a problem and suggested a solution via collective action, whereby merely articulating the word 'love' became a cathartic act of in-group solidarity that emancipated the listener and unified them with others who were doing the same. Yet the brevity of the lyrics and ambiguity of their message also identified 'The Word' as an entirely introspective composition whose countercultural and political connotations have only been acknowledged in retrospect:

> In effect it marks the climax of the group's marijuana period: a song predicting Love Militant as a social panacea and the accompanying rise of the hippie counterculture. In this, the Beatles were ahead of the game. In November 1965, the counter-cultural lifestyle was still the preserve of an LSD-using elite in California and London's Notting Hill. Even the word 'hippie' had yet to be coined, while the Summer of Love was still eighteen months away. (MacDonald, 1994: 143)

The Beatles' next album, *Revolver* (1966), was bookended by two remarkably uncompromising songs: Harrison's 'Taxman' and Lennon's 'Tomorrow Never Knows'. The latter drew on Timothy Leary and Richard Alpert's *The Psychedelic Experience: A Manual Based on the Tibetan Book of the Dead* (1964), a guide for attaining enlightenment using meditation and hallucinogenic drugs. Here, Lennon's advocacy for LSD as a means of personal and social advancement sought to puncture the materialism of mainstream Western culture. Unlike the New Testament *agape* of 'The Word', 'Tomorrow Never Knows' was ultimately rooted in the Nyingma school of Tibetan Buddhism. This universalist perspective defined love as an ever-present totalising force that exists 'everywhere' and in 'everything' and as such it can be read as the follow-up to 'The Word', a second gesture of abstract introspective protest. This ongoing preoccupation with love as something performative, the embodiment and enactment of peace, became a consistent theme in Lennon's output over the ensuing years and constituted the core message of his magnetic call to action in songs such as 'All You Need Is Love', 'Give Peace a Chance', 'Instant Karma! (We All Shine On)' and 'Imagine'.

Prior to the release of *Revolver* Lennon's press interviews became an opportunity for him to expound on this position, presenting love and peace as synonymous terms and imperative political goals: 'I'd been singing about love anyway – which is just another word for peace' (Lennon in Fawcett, 1976: 45). Such conversations now became magnetic gestures of protest in which he outlined problems and offered solutions. The most notorious, with the *Evening Standard*'s Maureen Cleave, compared the cultural impact of the Beatles with the declining influence of Christianity: 'Christianity will go. It will vanish and shrink ... We're more popular than Jesus now' (Cleave, 2006: 88). This comment caused significant controversy when published in the United States five months later, but it was only one of several overtly radical assertions during this period. Foremost in Lennon's mind was the need for the Beatles to issue a definitive anti-war statement during the run up to their 1966 World Tour. He privately seethed when the band's manager, Brian Epstein, instructed them simply not to answer any media questions on the escalating conflict in Vietnam: 'you can't just keep quiet about everything that's going on in the world unless you are a monk' (Leaf and Scheinfeld, 2007). As he later explained:

> On our first tour there was an unspoken thing that Mr Epstein was preventing us from talking about the Vietnam War and before we came back the second time to America George and I said to him 'We don't go unless we answer that question: what we feel about the war' . . . because we were being asked about it all the time. (Lennon in Metzinger, 2017)

Meanwhile the band spoke through their album sleeves. Two months prior to *Revolver,* Capitol Records issued a new compilation album for the North American market, *Yesterday and Today* (1966). The artwork pictured the Beatles draped in raw meat and broken dolls and was quickly withdrawn after complaints. Today, it is widely known as their infamous and very collectable 'butcher cover'. Lennon and McCartney may or may not have conceived of the gruesome image as a symbolic protest against the mounting death toll in South East Asia – it could just as easily have been inspired by their distaste for Capitol's release strategy – but they quickly characterised it as such. For Lennon the sleeve was 'as relevant as Vietnam' (Wiener, 1991: 17), while McCartney proclaimed it as 'our comment on the war' (Norman, 1981: 259).

Events came to a head in August 1966 when Lennon's 'we're more popular than Jesus' comments were reprinted in the debut issue of North American teen magazine, *Datebook*. Lennon received numerous death threats as a result, and with their inner circle increasingly worried about an assassination attempt the band were required to travel in a bullet-proof limousine during the United States leg of their world tour. In southern towns Beatles albums and singles that had spectacularly dominated the *Billboard* chart and overturned all previous sales records were now piled up and burned in the street, while new releases were boycotted by local radio stations. Their one appearance in the Deep South, at the Mid-South Coliseum in Memphis, was picketed by the Ku Klux Klan. In a heartstopping incident during their second set a loud 'Cherry Bomb' firecracker was thrown at the band seven minutes into their performance. As press officer Tony Barrow recalled: 'everybody, all of us at the side of the stage, including the three Beatles on stage, all looked immediately at John Lennon. We would not at that moment have been surprised to see that guy go down' (Gould, 2007: 346–7; also, Spangler, 2019b).

Three days later, at a press conference on their arrival in New York, the band finally and unequivocally shattered their public silence on the war in Vietnam.

> The first questioner asked them to comment on any aspect of the Vietnam conflict. They answered in unison. 'We don't like war, war is wrong', several times in a row. *John later gave his own brief and trenchant answer to the question: What did they think about the war? 'We think of it every day. We don't like it. We don't agree with it. We think it's wrong'.* (Wiener, 1991: 17, my italics)

This statement came at the high point of public opprobrium over Lennon's 'more popular than Jesus' controversy, at a time when many Americans still expressed solid approval for the looming Vietnam conflict in opinion polls. That Lennon chose to double-down with this intervention so soon after the Memphis firecracker incident demonstrated a new readiness to embody 'exemplary action' (Eyerman and Jamison, 1998) regardless of the consequences. As Eric Hobsbawm reflected: 'most British people at the time would have said they thought the war in Vietnam was wrong, but very few would have said *we think about it every day*. That was remarkable' (Wiener, 1991: 17–18). Yet, unlike his earlier off-the-cuff 'Jesus' comment, this bold declaration for peace passed almost entirely unnoticed in the media, receiving only minor coverage in local press. The New York *Daily News*, for example, devoted six full pages to coverage of the band's press conference but only one sentence on Lennon's courageous statement, while *Newsweek* and *Time* entirely ignored his opinions on the matter (Wiener, 1991: 17–18).

Immediately following the 1966 World Tour, Lennon accepted the role of Musketeer Gripweed in *How I Won the War* (Lester, 1967). His portrayal of this character further substantiated his position as a movement artist and a leading advocate for peace. Lennon repeated his controversial stance on class, contemporary culture and the Vietnam conflict during another highly politicised magazine interview while on the film's set in Almería, Spain. This text, published in *Look Magazine*, combined the same elements of stating a problem, proposing a solution and calling for collective action as any overtly magnetic protest song:

> The last generation might have been just like today's young adults, he maintains, had it not had to fight the war. 'If they said, "Fight the war

now," my age group would fight the war. Not that they'd want to. There
might be a bit more trouble gettin' them in line – because I'd be up there
shouting, "Don't do it!"'. (Lennon in Evans, 2004: 187)

Lennon's Rhetorical Songs, 1967–1969

'All You Need Is Love' (1967) was the first time Lennon's anti-war politics
appeared in any form of rhetorical–magnetic composition. Commissioned
as the British contribution to *Our World*, the first live global satellite
television broadcast, the band's performance was seen by a portion of
what was then the largest television audience in history: up to
500 million people (MacFarlane, 2013). Given the multinational viewers
and the short timeframe of the Beatles' segment, 'All You Need Is Love'
required a simple and direct message, which presented an excellent opportunity for a lightly coded magnetic protest song. The chorus opened with
an anthemic mantra, five words repeated twice over four bars using a one
note melody, whose directness announced his resolute and straightforward
collective solution. This was augmented by a sing-along performance with
participation from other movement voices such as Mick Jagger and
Graham Nash. 'All You Need Is Love' conveyed what had now become
a consistent message in Lennon's output: that by enacting peaceful behaviour one might embody anti-war sentiment. A powerful statement of
exemplary action, it marked his international recognition as a popular
music movement artist.

In May 1968 Lennon and McCartney travelled to New York to conduct
the press conferences that launched Apple in the United States. When
asked about Vietnam for WNET radio, Lennon replied forcefully: 'It's
another piece of insanity. It's another part of the insane scene. It's just
insane. It shouldn't be going on. There's no reason for it – just insanity'
(Lennon in Wiener, 1991: 74). As McCartney tried to haul the interview
back to its original purpose, Lennon introduced, for the first time,
a concept that shaped his output for the next four years – bringing the
psychology of marketing into protest music: 'We're gonna package peace
in a new box' (Wiener, 1991: 74). The following week, on his return to the
UK, Lennon began his relationship with Yoko Ono. This partnership
introduced two significant new elements to his anti-war campaign. First,
Lennon decoupled his reading of universal love from its connection with
consciousness-raising drugs and moved it back towards the New
Testament gospel doctrine of *agape* – as originally envisioned in 'The

Word'. Second, inspired by Yoko's artistic input, Lennon expanded his creative palette into avant-garde events and media happenings. Lennon and Ono initially found their voice as movement artists with the release of *Unfinished Music No. 1: Two Virgins* (1968), the first of several projects that involved wilfully undermining Lennon's self-image and popular position as a Beatle. Here, he embraced the high art experimentalism of *musique concrete*, quite literally the antithesis of that which had made him so successful, in an unlistenable album with an exceptionally unflattering image on the cover (Blaney, 2005).

Using avant-garde happenings as a template for exemplary action, he and Ono now became salespeople for the concept of peace: 'We're trying to make Christ's message contemporary. What would He have done if He had advertisements, records, films, TV and newspapers?' (Lennon in Hopkins, 1987: 101). This was very different to the angry but overlooked anti-war remarks Lennon had made two years earlier while promoting the *Revolver* album. Instead, it involved a more impactful form of performative protest designed to generate worldwide media coverage, the 1969 Bed-In for Peace protests in Amsterdam and Montreal:

> we knew whatever we did was going to be in the papers. So we decided to utilise the space we would occupy anyway by getting married, with a commercial for peace and also a theatrical event. The theatrical event we came up with which utilised the least energy with the maximum effect was to work from bed and what we virtually had was a seven-day press conference in bed. The first day they fought at the door to get in thinking there was something sexy going on, and they found two people talking about peace. Reporters always have five minutes with you or ten minutes with you. We let them ask anything for as long as they wanted for seven days, and all the time we just kept plugging peace; and the story that came out was 'John and Yoko do Bed-In for Peace'. We were just promoting peace like you promote any product. They promote war: 'Join the Marines!' We were promoting peace. (Lennon in Snyder, 2008)

This strategy drew on the 1960 civil rights movement sit-ins in Greensboro, North Carolina, the 1964 Berkeley Free Speech Movement and the 1967 Human Be-In at Golden Gate Park, San Francisco. After overcoming two false starts, a refused American visa and an abandoned Bahamas bed-in, Lennon and Ono worked surprisingly diligently. Photographer Gerry Deiter, granted round-the-clock access in Montreal, observed how Lennon's publicist Derek Taylor ensured a constant stream of media as groups of reporters were ushered into the hotel room at fifteen minute intervals from 9 a.m. to 9 p.m.: 'I don't recall there ever being fewer than a dozen to two dozen people in the room at one time. Two film crews going at all times and a dozen photographers' (McGrath, 2007). Even Lennon's fierce critic Albert Goldman (1988) calculated that 150 journalists attended the Montreal event every day. Lennon and Ono also made over 350 telephone calls to radio stations across the United States. Photographer David Fenton acknowledged Lennon and Ono's uniquely creative approach to campaigning: 'There had never been anything like it. It was completely original. The conscious use of one's myth to project a political, social and poetic goal' (Leaf and Scheinfeld, 2007).

Here, Lennon and Ono aligned with Eyerman and Jamison's (1998: 23) ideal of the 'self-revealing' movement artist whose values are embodied in their work. Unfortunately the bed-ins also met with ridicule in the British press, where Lennon and Ono inadvertently enhanced their reputation as pampered celebrities almost entirely disconnected from reality. *The Daily Mail* crowned Lennon 'Clown of the Year', one popular columnist dismissed his and Ono's work as 'the most self-indulgent demonstration of all time', while *The Sunday Express* mocked the pair as 'the outstanding nutcases of the world' (Hopkins, 1987: 100). This last comment may also refer to their 'ACORN PEACE' stunt in the weeks between their two international bed-in protests. Lennon and Ono asked their staff to send a pair of acorns, 'two living sculptures', to every world leader in the name of 'world peace'. Spring is, of course, entirely the wrong season for gathering nuts and these ambitious plans left their team with an almost impossible task, thus demonstrating that exemplary action must at least have *some* basis in real life for it to be effective.

Nevertheless, Lennon and Ono persevered, decorating their Amsterdam and Montreal hotel rooms with advertising slogans such as 'BED PEACE' and 'HAIR PEACE' that combined avant-garde art with ingenious puns. Later that year they developed this concept further, commissioning billboards in eleven cities worldwide to announce: 'WAR IS OVER! (IF YOU WANT IT) Happy Christmas from John & Yoko'. Placing political posters in spaces more typically reserved for consumer goods constituted an innovative form of dissemination that promoted progressive values by using street media against itself (Eyerman and Barretta, 1996: 505–6). If the phrase did not inspire people to create their own slogans it would, at least, promote discourse in the public square: 'We're selling it like soap, you know, and you've got to sell and sell until the housewife thinks "Well, there's peace or war – that's the two products"' (Lennon in Leaf and Scheinfeld, 2007).

Lennon and Ono also released an anti-war protest song after each bed-in event: 'The Ballad of John and Yoko' and 'Give Peace a Chance'. Lennon was so eager to release 'The Ballad of John and Yoko' (1969) his recording featured the only two Beatle band members available in the studio: himself and McCartney (Goodden, 2014 j). The composition was a 'ballad' in the traditional meaning of the term, a heroic story focussed on a central dramatic event – in this case the media attention given to the couple's wedding and honeymoon bed-in. The song's anti-war message employed self-referential wordplay that punned on his and Yoko's desire for 'peace' as simultaneously (1) an end to war and (2) a period of respite from the relentless media attention. 'The Ballad of John and Yoko' is significant because it was recorded and released only three years after Lennon's 'bigger than Jesus' comment had caused the singer to fear for his life. Once again, Lennon invoked His name, this time not as a digression in a media interview but as a profane exhortation of angry irritation ('Christ!') emphasised as the first word of refrain that, as if to accentuate the vulnerability Lennon felt as a movement artist, also ended with a bold crucifixion metaphor. This provocative phrase was excised from the single's eventual title, which was originally 'The Ballad of John and Yoko (They're gonna crucify me)', but it received a widespread radio ban nonetheless (Goodden, 2014 j). Despite the inevitable lack of air play the release still managed to reach number eight in the Billboard Hot 100 chart, demonstrating Lennon's substantial cultural capital and the potential in his future campaigns.

Lennon's Magnetic Songs, 1969–1973

The second release associated with Lennon's bed-ins, 'Give Peace a Chance' (1969), was his first solo single and his first fully magnetic anti-war protest song (see Figure 3.2). Much like 'All You Need Is Love', it was a simple and repetitive statement of exemplary action that urged listeners to disregard their differences and unite behind the cause of peace: 'In my secret heart I wanted to write something that would take over "We Shall Overcome" . . . I thought, why doesn't somebody write one for the people now? That's what my job is, our job is' (Lennon in Wiener, 1991: 97). The gospel inspiration, the song's conspicuous use of 'we' rather than 'I', its simple chord structure, the sing-along chorus and the accompanying choir all provided strong magnetic elements. As a collective promotion of progressive values, 'Give Peace a Chance' exemplified cognitive praxis and demonstrated Lennon's true potential as a movement artist. For Denisoff, it constituted the definitive magnetic anti-war protest song of the late 1960s:

Figure 3.2 John Lennon and Yoko Ono, 'Give Peace a Chance', Room 1742, Queen Elizabeth Hotel, Montreal, 1 June 1969 (© Pictorial Press Ltd.)

> Only John Lennon's 'Give Peace a Chance', a chant put to music, has actually had any success in the American political arena, with marchers singing the piece at anti-war rallies. Significantly, 'Give Peace a Chance' structurally is the only current political song which is based on the more traditional format of protest songs, being repetitive, easy to sing, and stressing movement solidarity. (Denisoff, 1983: 38)

That such an unequivocally magnetic song enjoyed chart success, reaching number two in the UK Singles Chart and number fourteen on the Billboard Hot 100, confirmed the potency of Lennon's message. In November 1969, it contributed to a historically important mass mobilisation when 500,000 anti-war protesters, the largest demonstration ever held in Washington, DC at that time, converged at the Washington Monument during the Moratorium to End the War in Vietnam. As the crowd accompanied Pete Seeger's rendition of 'Give Peace a Chance' he improvised taunts towards the Nixon administration, some of whom were observing the event from the vantage point of the White House: 'Are you listening Nixon?', 'Are you listening Agnew?', 'Are you listening in the Pentagon?'. Lennon pointed to this in an interview with Gloria Emerson from the *New York Times*: 'What were they singing at the Moratorium?

They were singing a happy-go-lucky song which happens to be one I wrote, and I'm glad they sang it. And when I get there I'll sing it with them' (Leaf and Scheinfeld, 2007). *Newsweek* magazine also confirmed the magnetic attraction of 'Give Peace a Chance': 'Now it will serve as the centrepiece for sing-ins at shopping centers planned in Washington and will join the list of carols to be sung in projected nationwide Christmas Eve demonstrations . . . the peace movement has found an anthem' (Wiener, 1991: 97).

John Dean, the President's senior legal advisor, acknowledged the composition's effectiveness when discussing these events some years later:

> Nixon would put out the line during these demonstrations that he was watching a football game or something like that. He was very concerned with the demonstrations. They were making a definite impact inside the White House. With 'Give Peace a Chance' I remember photographing a million people at a demonstration singing it with their hands up, and that song became the national anthem of the anti-war movement in the way that the folk song 'We Shall Overcome' became the national anthem of the Civil Rights Movement before that. (Leaf and Scheinfeld, 2007)

The success of 'Give Peace a Chance' encouraged Lennon to write more protest music. 'Come Together' (1969) originated as conceivably the most useful form of magnetic propaganda any movement artist could produce: a campaign theme for Timothy Leary's run against Ronald Reagan as Governor of California. It was eventually issued, alongside Harrison's 'Something' (1969), as a double-A-side single in Britain and the United States. Banned by the BBC, 'Come Together' only reached number four in the UK. It was positively received among North American audiences, however, and the single quickly moved to number one on the Billboard Hot 100. Macdonald (1994) saw the song's stream-of-consciousness lyrics as a significant revolutionary statement in themselves, one that rejected prevailing morals and behavioural norms and foreshadowed a new era of postmodern relativism.

As the decade closed, Lennon, rather than Dylan, was recognised as the voice of his generation when *Rolling Stone* declared him 'Man of the Year' and Desmond Morris nominated him ATV's 'Man of the Decade'. These awards inspired another ambitious attempt at exemplary action as Lennon declared 1970 'Year One' of a New Age of Peace and announced plans for the Mosport Park Peace Festival in Toronto. This event would then transform into a world tour and mobilise an International Peace Vote:

'We aim to make it the biggest music festival in history' (Lennon in Wiener, 1991: 128). Mosport represented a model for how a movement artist might inspire collective mobilisation. Hundreds of radio stations in the United States and Canada signed up to the festival's 'Peace Network', which dispersed regular 'Peace Network Reports' and special 'Peace Messages' from Lennon and Ono. Listeners were asked to share details of local activism – 'demonstrations, draft resistance, benefit concerts, film showings, poster contests' – that could then be broadcast nationwide. Meanwhile. the promoters seemed to lose track of the event itself as, while vacillating over a basic pricing strategy, they dreamed up the fanciful gimmick of flying Lennon into the venue via an 'air car' (Wiener, 1991: 129–30). Abandoned amid the ensuing organisational chaos, Mosport Park Peace Festival became an unfortunate missed opportunity in the struggle to build a movement.

The following year, Lennon rebounded with 'Imagine' (1971), his most commercially successful release as a solo artist, a near straightforward magnetic composition and a paradigm of exemplary action. The song suggested that social problems could only be fully solved by rejecting ideologies of religion, property and nationhood. It used collective phrases such as 'we' and 'come and join us' to offer a simple argument for in-group solidarity by synthesising the biblical Brotherhood of Man doctrine with 'virtually the Communist manifesto' (Lennon in Blaney, 2005: 83). 'Imagine' drew on ideas raised in Ono's instructional avant-garde art book *Grapefruit* (1964). Rather than performing peace through embodied acts of love, as in 'The Word' or 'All You Need Is Love', 'Imagine' simply asked listeners to *visualise* social reform. This, like the unanswered questions of Dylan's 'Blowin' in the Wind', allowed the song to be performed safely by a wide range of artists, despite its radical agenda. Lennon also camouflaged his potentially seditious message with a simple and restrained melody. Such factors helped 'Imagine' become popular music's most subversive classic. It is still performed regularly at significant public occasions, including the 2012 and 2020 Olympic Games ceremonies, and immediately before midnight on New Year's Eve in Times Square, New York City, every year since 2005 –6. Curiously, David Archuleta's popular rendition of the song in the 2007 *American Idol* final omitted the line asking listeners to imagine no religion, which demonstrates the ongoing cultural sensitivities around that subject in the United States.

'Imagine' was followed by another successful anti-war protest song, 'Happy Xmas (War Is Over)' (1971). This developed Lennon's imaginative peace campaign from two years earlier: 'I was sick of 'White Christmas' [and wanted] something that would last forever' (Blaney, 2005: 101). The lyrics advocated for collective empathy as a strategy to overcome fear and oppression, while the arrangement reinforced this magnetic appeal. After opening with the intimacy of a whispered greeting to Lennon and Ono's children, it built towards a loud communal sing-along. Like 'Give Peace a Chance' this used a hypnotic refrain that superimposed a phrase coined by Lennon and Ono in their 1969 billboard campaign ('War is over, if you want it') over a melody shared by the 'Hare Rama' mantra, which originated in the *Kali Santarana Upanishad* (Beck, 2006; Urish, 2007).

Encouraged by his success as a movement artist, Lennon then doubled down with *Some Time in New York City* (1972), a project constructed entirely around overtly magnetic and rhetorical protest music. This release fared extremely poorly – not, perhaps, because of *what* Lennon said but because of the *way* he said it. While 'Imagine' cloaked its subversive intent as a beguiling thought experiment, unabashed propaganda songs such as 'Attica State' alienated all but a core audience of committed activists. Greil Marcus recoiled at the album's 'horrendous, witless politics' while *Rolling Stone*, once a pillar of support, lambasted it as 'simply a set of injustices clumsily . . . shouted at us in the tone of a newsboy . . . so embarrassingly puerile as to constitute an advertisement against itself' (Wiener, 1991: 217). The visceral reaction to *Some Time in New York City* demonstrated the impossibility of presenting a collection of old-fashioned magnetic compositions to an audience more familiar with 1960s rhetorical or introspective styles. In that sense, it confirmed the arrival of the postmodern, relativist epistemology Lennon had anticipated two years earlier in 'Come Together', his stream-of-consciousness campaign song for Timothy Leary.

Speaking in defence of the album, Yoko Ono presented an argument for the couple's strategy as movement artists that could have come directly from one of Denisoff's many textbooks or articles on protest songs:

> Music was once separated into two forms. One was court music, to entertain the aristocrats. The other was folk songs, sung by people to express their emotions and their political opinions. But lately the folk songs of this age, pop song, is becoming intellectualised and is starting to lose the original meaning and function . . . We went back to the original concept of folk song. Like a newspaper, the function was to present the message accurately and quickly. (Ono, in Hopkins, 1987: 161)

Nevertheless Lennon persevered in promoting *Some Time in New York City* on television and other media, single-handedly trying to foment a cultural and political revolution during the run up to the 1972

Presidential election. This has since been acknowledged as one of the most overtly radical acts by any major popular music artist (Doggett, 2007; Goldman, 1988). Earlier that year Lennon was notified of his pending deportation by the Immigration and Naturalization Service. His residency in the United States now dependent on the tenuous hold of a sixty-day rolling visa and a long series of legal appeals, he and Yoko Ono had also been under surveillance by the Federal Bureau of Investigation for the previous nine months (Goldman, 1988; Lifton, 2015). Once again, a bold exemplary action now threatened significant personal consequences. As close friend, Elliot Mintz, observed: 'I thought about how much the political climate had changed since the sixties; I thought, "They are taking a real chance this time. And they are not afraid". I was overwhelmed by their dedication to the issues they believed in' (Wiener, 1991: 245). In August 1972 Lennon gave his final full-length concert, a benefit for disabled children at Madison Square Garden. Wearing a green US Army shirt, he performed a rousing 'Come Together' adding improvised calls of 'Stop the war!' and closed the show with his magnetic anti-war song 'Give Peace a Chance'. Here, accompanied by the 20,000-capacity audience, Lennon repeated his iconic refrain with further cries of 'No more war!' as Stevie Wonder ad-libbed onstage beside him. The event, screened as an ABC TV special, offered a final public celebration of his work as a movement artist (Dysinger and Gebhardt, 2011).

The sleeve of Lennon's next album, *Mind Games* (1973), showed him walking away from Ono and his campaigning past. Lennon even changed the name of the title song, first intended as another magnetic protest anthem, from 'Make Love Not War' to 'Mind Games'. (If you hum those words over the melody, it fits perfectly.) This more introspective style proved popular and as a result *Mind Games* (1973) was received as a return to form. Nonetheless, elements of Lennon's original message remained subtly concealed in the work. It contains an unusually heavy emphasis on the drawn-out word 'love', making a universalist claim for the power of this phenomenon that had been consistent in his work since 'The Word'. Furthermore, the song's original title and chorus refrain, the popular 1960s anti-Vietnam war slogan 'make love not war', remained clearly audible in the fade-out. During media interviews to promote this album, Lennon explained how this composition articulated his continuing struggle for peace:

> There's no new myth there. It's the same thing but it's called *mind games*. Whenever people say 'What do you mean peace? Are you ever going to get it? Isn't it naïve?' and all the rest of the shit. The answer is that we didn't fly

for thousands of years but we talked about it among many, many other dreams. So whatever we project we get, so I try to keep on projecting the dream of peace and love, or whatever the cliché is, because I prefer that. (Lennon in Breschard and Snyder-Scumpy, 1974: 47, my italics)

Lennon later defined his basic approach to protest music by paraphrasing Dylan's famous comment '*all* my songs are *protest* songs', saying 'all *my* songs are *peace* songs' (Snyder, 2008, my italics). Interestingly, *Mind Games* contained one last genuinely magnetic anti-war composition. 'Bring on the Lucie (Freda Peeple)' had a sing-along chorus and a lyric firmly rooted in collective interests whose verse used the word 'we' multiple times to invoke group solidarity. Given that his new album's title track had been effectively de-radicalised, 'Bring on the Lucie (Freda Peeple)' retained a startlingly unequivocal anti-war position. Lennon punctuated the song's final chorus with a loud exhortation for peace demanding an immediate end to the killing that echoed his cries of 'No more war!' from the stage of Madison Square Garden the previous year. Its bold imagery of a murderous government literally sliding in the blood of their victims demanded that those in power should act morally and reproached them for their crimes. In a typically magnetic stance, 'Bring on the Lucie (Freda Peeple)' called for direct exemplary action against corruption, militarism and other forms of oppression, while exhorting its audience to find their own voice. Nonetheless, Lennon finally abandoned the role of movement artist during his eighteen-month 'lost weekend' separation from Ono in 1973–5. His closing comment on peace campaigns appeared in 'Scared', from *Walls and Bridges* (1974). Effectively a farewell to protest, Lennon emphasises his vulnerability as a political figurehead by alluding to the Roman Catholic 'bell, book, and candle' excommunication ritual. A near perfect mirror of Dylan's 'My Back Pages', the song even closes by quoting his famous 'Like a Rolling Stone' chorus lyric.

Conclusion: Lennon as Exemplary Movement Artist

Lennon's introspective peace songs began with 'The Word' and 'Tomorrow Never Knows'. Chronologically, these compositions intersected with Dylan's retreat from the role of movement artist, which Lennon assumed in his place. Over the ensuing years his anti-war songs moved from introspective through to rhetorical and magnetic forms and, unusually, Lennon enjoyed significant success with three rhetorical–magnetic and magnetic anti-war songs – 'Give Peace a Chance', 'Imagine' and 'Happy Xmas (War

Is Over!)' – at a time when these styles were increasingly unfashionable. His cultural capital as a Beatle also meant that the media often took great notice whenever he and Ono engaged in distinctive exemplary actions. As such, both came to embody the movement artist role. Lennon's 1966 statements against the war, the 1969 bed-in protests and billboard campaigns, the contribution made by his peace songs to momentous events such as that year's Moratorium to End the War all demonstrated the possibilities for collective mobilisation through protest music. Things did not always work out, of course, as the failed venture of the Mosport Park Peace Festival demonstrated, but Lennon also showed courage when he came under pressure – especially during the Beatles' final tour of the United States. Eventually, after becoming aligned with pockets of opinion not shared by his mainstream audience or supporters in the media, he stepped away from public activism – just as Dylan had done a decade earlier.

Ultimately Lennon conceded that his enthusiasm for magnetic propaganda songs limited his creativity: 'It almost ruined it, in a way. It became journalism and not poetry ... I think I found out it's a waste of time' (Lennon in Hammill, 1975). Having once, in 1969, declared he was going to 'change people's heads', Lennon eventually determined that: 'It's no good telling people anything, they have to find out' (Lennon in Snyder, 2008). This conclusion, that change must come from within and that consciousness is the only effective instrument of change, constitutes a core theme of the remainder of this book. Poignantly, during his retirement, Lennon missed several opportunities to play precisely the kind of concerts with Bob Dylan that he had once worked hard to facilitate. These included Phil Ochs' 'An Evening with Salvador Allende' in New York (1974), and Dylan's own 'Night of the Hurricane' benefits to aid Rubin Carter in New York City (1975) and Houston (1976). Nevertheless, the fact remains that Lennon and Ono used their movement artist status to campaign against the conflict in Vietnam more consistently and with more success than most, regardless of the risks involved. Historians generally agree that such forms of activism bolstered the media's opposition to the war, and that this contributed to increasing public disenchantment, so it seems reasonable to conclude that their efforts helped bring the possibility of peace onto the political agenda. In so doing, Lennon bequeathed a legacy of unusually magnetic protest anthems, some of which are still performed live and broadcast to huge international audiences half a century later.

John Lennon and History

Overview: 'Always Historicise!'

This chapter, along with Chapter 5, is inspired by Fredric Jameson's (1981: 9) famous exhortation: 'Always historicise!'. They draw on his work as America's leading Marxist literary critic to widen the perspective on Dylan and Lennon, which pulls outwards from songs protesting a single event in history to encompass the broader subject of history itself. Both artists grounded their creative output in the experiences of their youth and their own cultural contexts, incorporating or alluding to an array of historical characters, events and literary sources. Chapter 4 discusses Lennon's use of imperial tropes from the Victorian and Edwardian era. Chapter 5 examines Dylan's wide-ranging references to nineteenth- and early twentieth-century North American or European authors and artefacts.

Jameson adhered to Marx's concept of historical materialism: that history is experienced on an individual basis via the necessity of class struggle, then shaped on a grand scale by the evolution of economic systems – otherwise known as 'modes of production'. He applied this model to literary theory using German philosopher Hans-Georg Gadamer's *Horizontverschmelzung* (1965), or 'the fusion of horizons'.[1] This is the premise that subjective individual experiences are determined by that which may be perceived from any given vantage point. Gadamer envisioned three concentric perceptual horizons: individual narratives, collective action and periodic epochs. These categories provide a framework to evaluate the historical references in Dylan's and Lennon's output.

---

[1] For readers unfamiliar with the concept, a class by Yale University Professor Paul Fry (2009) offers an accessible introduction: https://youtu.be/GQvp5zoZbvo.

Jameson interpreted Gadamer's *first horizon* as politically symbolic individual acts: incidents, texts or artworks that precipitate broader social movements. He viewed all cultural artefacts 'from the literary institutions of high modernism all the way to the products of mass culture' (Jameson, 1981: 80) as historicised texts, the instinctual responses of artists to their social and economic conditions. For Jameson the relevance of any artwork or utterance at this level was revealed overtly in its *content* and unconsciously in its *form*. Here, the structural contradictions in an artefact are particularly important because they expose its ideological tensions: the class antagonisms of capitalism, intrinsic to 'the circumstances of any work, to which it is – simultaneously – both an expression and a reaction' (Jameson, 1981: 82).

This broader context of class conflict constitutes Jameson's second horizon, where cultural artefacts from the first horizon combine and contribute to the frictions between workers, capitalists and the state. Jameson coined the phrase 'ideologeme' to signify 'the smallest intelligible unit' of this discourse (Jameson, 1981: 76). Examples of ideologemes include pseudo-ideas, 'an abstract value, an opinion or prejudice', and proto-narratives, an individual utterance contributing to more complete texts (Jameson, 1981: 87). These function as a type of cultural raw material that, when assembled into more cohesive expressions of collective interest, reveal the antagonisms inherent in any economic system. As Marx and Engels' (1848: 1, my italics) *Communist Manifesto* famously declared: '*The history of all hitherto existing society* is the history of class struggles.'

Jameson's *third horizon* turns towards this grand vision, the known history of all humanity, via the mode of production. Modes of production are historical epochs defined by how they produce and distribute the material goods necessary for sustenance and survival. They transcend politically symbolic acts (horizon one) and class discourse (horizon two) and constitute the defining element of Marx's materialist conception of history. Marx theorised six broadly chronological modes of production according to their economic and social structures: Neolithic kinship groups, early Asiatic societies, slaveholding oligarchies in classical Greece and Rome, European feudalism, capitalism, and communism. Each engendered cultural and social relations aligned with its economic underpinnings: magic and myth, kinship, sacred religious rites, early city state politics, feudal dominion, commodity fetishism and collectivisation. As competing modes of production emerge and override each other in this broad third horizon, they interact with and become evident in the individual cultural artefacts and collective class antagonisms of horizons one and two.

Here, Jameson turned to Raymond Williams' notion of 'dominant', 'emergent' and 'residual' modes of production to elucidate the mechanics of this process (Williams, 1977: 121–7). A *dominant* structure is the prevailing mode of production at any given time. *Residual* influence is that which sustains from older modes, often as anachronisms retained in the infrastructure of current social order. *Emergent* ideas and practices are those created by groups and individuals that challenge dominant systems, sometimes even foreshadowing new modes of production. During the 1960s, these took the form of the civil rights movement, alternative lifestyles and the counterculture, or the revolutionary New Left (Jameson, 1981). In this chapter and in Chapter 5, I juxtapose Jameson's three horizons against the context, content and form of Dylan's and Lennon's historicity, using Williams's concept of emergent and residual modes of production to highlight periods of conflict and change.

The dominant mode of production during Dylan's and Lennon's formative and breakthrough years is best described as Fordist industrial capitalism: the prolonged post-war demographic and economic boom that saw significant growth in automobile production, urbanisation, consumer products and mass media outlets, reaching its apogee sometime between the late 1950s and the mid-1960s. Fordism provided the market for new forms of youth culture including, of course, the enormous upsurge in folk and popular music that swept Dylan and Lennon to international prominence (Hesmondhalgh, 1996). However, as economic growth stalled in the late 1960s, then ground to a halt with the 1973 oil crisis, capitalism segued into the globalised *post-Fordist* mode of production we experience today. This economic shift prompted its own cultural realignment, too, as twentieth-century modernism morphed into contemporary postmodernism (Jameson, 1991). Here and in Chapter 5, I show how Dylan's and Lennon's affinity for history enhanced their awareness of, and their ability to articulate, the profound social changes that occurred during this time.

Introduction: John Lennon and History

Lennon's interest in history stemmed from his post-war childhood in a highly literate, aspiring middle-class household in suburban Liverpool. His self-produced school magazine *The Daily Howl* included references to 'Winston Crutchill' and Queen Ann (Harry, 1964). The creative strategies Lennon adopted as a composer and writer built on this affinity and resulted in some of his most impactful and influential releases. It was evident in the wide range of characters from current events, the recent past and more remote periods in his lyrics, poetry and prose. His songs alluded to significantly more historical events than McCartney's but fewer than Dylan's (see Table 4.1 and Tables 5.1, 5.2, 5.3 and 5.4 in Chapter 5). Many of these appeared in the Dylan parody material Lennon recorded at home in the late 1970s, which was posthumously released on the box set *John Lennon Anthology* (1998).

This section maps the historical references in Lennon's literature and lyrics against Jameson's three hermeneutic fields. The first horizon, individual artefacts and utterances, is used to discuss the numerous Victorian imperial tropes in his songs and texts, focussing on the poetry and prose of *In His Own Write* (1964) and *A Spaniard in the Works* (1965), the conceptualisation of *Sgt. Pepper's Lonely Hearts Club Band* (1967), and his contribution to that album's famous closing song 'A Day in the Life'. The second horizon of class antagonism explores Lennon's Irish ancestry, his fascination with the Second World War, plus the vivid allusions to northern working-class heritage throughout his poetry and prose and in Beatles compositions such as 'A Hard Day's Night' and 'For the Benefit of Mr Kite!'. Jameson's third horizon, modes of production, is used to discuss Lennon's rejection of the materialist conception of history and his consistent commitment to human consciousness as the ultimate driver of social progress. I conclude that Lennon was philosophically more Hegelian than Marxist. He saw *ideas* as the primary catalyst of change, not the materialism of class politics or economics, a worldview heavily influenced by neo-Vedantic and Vedic philosophy.

Walter Bryce Gallie (1956) defined the philosophy of history as an 'essentially contested concept' and Lennon's engagement with this theme, not least in his musical and textual borrowings from the Indian subcontinent, necessitates the negotiation of two problematic subject areas: the colonial legacy of the British Empire, and the acts of appropriation committed by the Beatles. That history is ubiquitous in popular culture is self-evident from the statues in our shared spaces, the subjects on school and university curricula and the socio-economic structures that govern our existence. Scratch any surface almost anywhere in the United Kingdom, however, and its colonial past peeks through. One example is in Eloise Knapp Hay's choice of authors for her dual biography discussed in Chapter 1. E. M. Forster excoriated racism and repression in the Raj but stopped short of overtly endorsing the Indian Independence Movement. Rudyard Kipling, moreover, was admonished as a writer who actively

Table 4.1 *Historical figures in Lennon's lyrics, prose and poetry, 1964–86*

	Lennon's Beatles songs
North America	Richard A. Cooke III (Bungalow Bill), Edgar Allen Poe, Captain Marvel, Moondog, Muddy Waters
Europe	The Duke and Duchess of Kirkaldy (fictional), The English Army, Pablo Fanque, John Henderson, The House of Lords, The King and Queen, William Kite, Louis XIV (The Sun King), King of Marigold (fictional), Zanthus (Henry the Horse)
Worldwide	Chairman Mao
Religious figures	Jesus Christ ('Ballad of John and Yoko'), Lady Madonna (McCartney first, then Lennon), Mother Mary (McCartney's only other historical reference)
	Lennon's Beatles period prose/poetry
In His Own Write (1964)	Fredastaire (Fred Astaire), Enig Blyter (Enid Blyton), Uncle Tom Cobra (folksong character Uncle Tom Cobley), Prevelant Ze Gaute (Charles de Gaul), Disraeli Hands (Benjamin Disraeli), Duke of Edincalvert (Duke of Edinburgh), Captaive Flint (Captain Flint), Small Jack Hawkins (Jack Hawkins), Madhalf Heatlump who only had one (Adolf Hitler), Jumble Jim (Jungle Jim), Harry Lime, Harrassed Macmillion (Harold Macmillan), The Piltdown Retord (Piltdown Man), Priceless Margarine (Princess Margaret), Large John Saliver (Long John Silver), Friendly Trumap (Freddie Truman, cricketer), Queen Victorious (Queen Victoria)
A Spaniard in the Works (1965)	Alibabba (Ali Baba), Dr (not the) Barnardo (Thomas John Barnardo), Harrybellfonte (Harry Bellafonte), breakfast of bogard (Humphrey Bogart/Dirk Bogard), Rice Krustchovs (Nikita Khruschev), de Arch bitter of Canterbubble (The Archbishop of Canterbury), Benjamin Distasteful (Benjami Disraeli), Sir Alice Doubtless-Whom (Sir Alec Douglas-Hulme), Father, Alecguinness (Alec Guinness), Harrods McMillion (Harold MacMillan), Eric Morley, Jack the Nipple/Jock the Cripple (Jack the Ripper), Mickey Most, Richard the Turd (Richard III), Snore Wife and some several dwarts (Snow White and the Seven Dwarfs), Doctored Whopper (Dr Who), Harassed Wilsod (Harold Wilson)
	Lennon's post-Beatles songs
North America	Bob Dylan, Alan Ginsberg, John F. Kennedy, Timothy Leary, Norman Mailer, Richard Nixon, David Peel, Popeye, Elvis Presley, Henry Rockefeller, Jerry Rubin, John Sinclair, Tommy Smothers
Europe	British Brigands, Tommy Cooper, Druids, The Emperor, Hitler, Old Mother Hubbard, The IRA, Princes, Princesses, Derek Taylor

Table 4.1 *(cont.)*

Religious figures	Buddha, Jesus Christ, The Angel of Destruction, Krishna, St Paul

Lennon's post-Beatles songs (released posthumously)

Lennon's own songs	Rupert Bear, Buddha, Jesus Christ, George Formby, Dr Henry Jekyll, Mona Lisa, Virgin Mary, Mickey Mouse, Nazis
Bob Dylan parody songs	Judy Garland, Karl Marx, Mohammed, Pam Nixon, Richard Nixon, Peter Mark Roget, Deng Xiaoping

Yoko Ono Songs on joint Lennon/Ono albums

Lenny Bruce, Eldridge Cleaver, Angela Davis, Charles Manson, Chairman Mao, Marilyn Monroe, Richard Nixon, The Pope, Queen of England, Henry Rockefeller, Jerry Rubin, Raquel Welch

Lennon's Post-Beatles prose/poetry

Skywriting by Word of Mouth (1986)	Allah, Thomas (the Apostle), Lady Astor, Brigitte Bardot, Batman, Wallace Beery, Candice Bergen, Leonardo (Leonard) Bernstein, Buddha, Sonny Bono, Michael Caine, Rory Calhoun, Glen Campbell, Truman Capote, Al Crapp (Al Capp), Cher, Jesus Christ, (Winston) Churchill, Esoteric (Eric) Clapton, Norman (William) The Conqueror, Alice Cooper, Johnny Dankworth, Rennie Davis, Boris (Doris) Day, Joe DiMaggio, Marcel Duchamp, Bob Dylan, Albert Einstein, President Eisenfront (Eisenhower), Anita Ekberg, Errol Flynn, Fuckminster Buller (Buckminster Fuller), Greta Garbo, Paul Gaugin, Allen Ginsberg, Hermann Goering, David and Goliath, Elizabeth Gould, Billy (the) Graham, Juliette Greco, Rosie (Rosey) Greer, Dick Gregory, Pearl Harbour, Earnest Hemmingway, Alfred Hitchcock, Adolf Hitler, Abbie Hoffman, Robbing (Robin) Hood, Howard Hughes, Mick Jagger, Bianca Jagger, Elton John, Jasper Johns, John F. Kennedy, Evel Knievel, Cleo Lane, King Lear, Timothy Leary, Richard Lester, Liberace, G. Gordon Liddy, Merrill Lynch, alley mgraw (Ali MacGraw), Karl Marx, Virgin Mary, Perry Maisonette (Mason), Charlatan the Great (Charlotte of Mecklenburg-Strelitz), Yehudi Menuhin, Moses, Milarepa, John Mitchell, Mohammed, Dame Roberta Morely (Robert Morley), Napoleon, (Emperor) Nero, Anthony Newlywed (Newley), Paul Newman, Huey Newton, Isaac Newton, Richard Nixon, Larry (Laurence) Olivier, David Peel, (Pablo) Picasso, Elvis Presley, Pythagoras, Robert Redford, Jerry Rubin, the Good Samaritan, Mary Queen of Scots, Bobby Seale, Hail(e) Selassie, (William) Shakespeare, Siddhartha, John Sinclair, Barbara Stanwick, Liz Taylor, St Thomas, Hunter S. Thompson, Strom Thurmond, Spencer Tracy, Rudy Vallée, Vincent Van Gogh, Barbara Walters, Rabbit Warren (Chief Justice Earl Warren), Arthur Yanov, Maharishi Mahesh Yogi

represented and legitimised the British Empire (Said, 2005). More recently, the controversy over the UK Home Office's hostile treatment of the Windrush generation (Williams, 2020) had an unexpected connection to Lennon. Trinidadian Harold Phillips, better known as 'Lord Woodbine', was a close associate of the Beatles who arrived in the United Kingdom on HMT *Empire Windrush* in 1948. Phillips' role is under-represented in most accounts, but he ran two nightclubs in Liverpool where various early iterations of the band appeared and regularly socialised with the group. He also travelled to Hamburg with the Beatles and was sufficiently involved with them to be mistaken for their manager (McGrath, 2010a).

Some of Beatles' most challenging postcolonial commentary occurred in January 1969 at Twickenham Studios during writing sessions filmed for what became *Let It Be* (1971). The original title song for this project, 'Get Back', was itself first conceived as an extemporised recording known as 'Commonwealth'. Had that name stuck, it is tempting to imagine that the band's final album might also have been called *Commonwealth*. McCartney's stream-of-consciousness lyrics referenced the Kenyan Asian refugee crisis, Enoch Powell's recent 'Rivers of Blood' speech and the Commonwealth Immigrants Act 1968. His intent was quite clearly to critique Powell and others hostile to immigration; however, egged on by Lennon, his words sound scatological and insensitive – much like the latter's poetry and prose: 'Don't dig no Pakistanis taking all the people's jobs . . . You'd better get back to your Commonwealth homes' (Lewisohn, 2004: 166). Lennon's backing vocal, a sharp rising atonal 'Yes?' in response to McCartney's call of 'Commonwealth!', was modelled on Peter Sellers' brownface role as an Indian doctor in the movie *Goodness Gracious Me* (1960). Lennon's amusement is clear from his audible laughter during the improvised dialogue:

McCARTNEY: I went to Pakistani, I went to India, I've been to old Calcutta and I've had enough of that. I'm coming back to England town.

LENNON: Yes! (laughing) Welcome!
McCARTNEY: And dirty Enoch Powell and he's had enough of Parliament.

(Anon., 2018)

Cultural appropriation and cultural imperialism, the assimilation and exploitation of marginalised and colonialised cultures, are complex and significant concerns. Questions have been raised around the Orientalism in many Beatles recordings, of course, plus McCartney's ska pastiche 'Ob-La-Di,

Ob-La-Da' (1968) and Lennon's reggae song 'Borrowed Time' (1984) – although, if intended as such, that title does work as a clever self-referential pun. A meaningful analysis of the moral implications in Lennon's output is beyond the scope of this book. That is not to minimise the issue, however, as decolonising the curriculum is a pressing matter in the academy and challenging cultural appropriation is a key component of that task. Current thought is probably best represented by Kathryn B. Cox (2017) who shows how the Beatles exploited and minimalised Indian classical music by using its long-standing and sophisticated ancient heritage as a backdrop for their dilettante alternative lifestyles. Earlier scholars such as David Reck (1985) drew on Edward W. Said's *Orientalism* (1978) to argue it was inevitable that Western perceptions of the East should be romanticised as information about these traditions arrived only sporadically, usually in waves associated with influential individuals or major overseas events. In what follows, I acknowledge that ethical ambiguities and aesthetic complexities are layered through all globalised cultural forms (Born and Hesmondhalgh, 2000; Rogers, 2006).

Lennon's First Horizon: Imperial Artefacts

As Eric Hobsbawm (1987) noted in *The Age of Empire: 1875–1914*, in the 1960s Victorian and Edwardian Britain was still comparatively recent. This section discusses Lennon's references to Britain's colonial legacy in the context of Jameson's first horizon, the field of politically symbolic individual utterances. It outlines two parameters that shaped his cultural context: the residual influence of Whiggism in post-war education and the legacy of imperialism in British children's literature. It then compares Lennon's historical references in his nonsense poetry to Lewis Carroll's depictions of cultural differences in the Victorian era. Finally, it shows how Lennon's affinity with Britain's imperial heritage was expressed in his contribution to the sleeve artwork of the Beatles' *Sgt. Pepper's Lonely Hearts Club Band* and in the narrative of its famous closing song 'A Day in the Life'.

The Whig interpretation of history was the predominant perspective in British culture and education from the 1688 Glorious Revolution to the mid-twentieth century. Derived from the Protestant reformation, the Enlightenment, English parliamentary values and colonial expansion, it regarded the British Empire as a positive global force that inspired and motivated economic and social progress worldwide. Over almost three centuries of economic, political and technological ascendancy, this outlook fostered a distinct sense of natural superiority in nationhood, class privilege, Protestant Christianity and economic liberalism. As the British version of Manifest Destiny, the 'Whig consensus' is one of the defining western-centric ideologies that underpin twenty-first century discourses around White Privilege and White Fragility (DiAngelo, 2018; McIntosh, 1988). Although fragmented by the Great War and twentieth-century modernism, the residual influence of Whiggism sustained well into the 1950s, a world still populated by men and women born and raised in the late Victorian and Edwardian era. This, perhaps, is what Lennon's school friend Pete Shotton (1984: 49) was referring to when his memoir described their Quarry Bank school masters as 'mired in the Victorian academic tradition'.

Lennon was a voracious reader with an appetite for literature 'like an insatiable physical hunger' (Norman, 2009: 47). From the age of five he lived with maternal aunt and parental guardian Mary 'Mimi' Smith at her 'Mendips' home in the suburb of Woolton. A socially conservative matriarch figure who has been compared to Charles Dickens' Betsey Trotwood (Norman, 2009: 23), Smith's well-stocked domestic bookshelves were populated with a range of archetypal imperialist Whig histories typical among aspiring middle-class households at the time. These included a complete set of the revised fourteenth edition of *Encyclopaedia Britannica* plus gold-embossed and leather-bound collections of Winston Churchill's four-volume *A History of the English-Speaking Peoples* (1956–8) and six-volume *The Second World War* (1948–53), all of which were well used by Lennon (Coleman, 1984; Kenny, 2015; Lewisohn, 2013; Sullivan, 1995). Curiously, given his Irish ancestry and surname, John Winston Lennon was christened with a middle name honouring the arch-Whig wartime prime minister. This was despite the fact that at the time of his birth, in October 1940, Churchill had been in office for only five months and was still considered a controversial appointment. It may seem remarkable today, but the strong working-class tradition of taking a notable colonialist's surname for your own child's middle name dated back to the Second Boer War (1899–1902), when the most popular choices were Redvers (after Major-General Sir Redvers Buller) and Baden (after Lieutenant General Robert Baden-Powell). Others referenced famous battles such as Mafeking and Bloemfontein, and the practice was almost as widespread among daughters as it was among sons (Nickerson, 2012).[2]

---

[2] The author's own father was born in a working-class district of Sheffield and never visited Africa or had any connection to the continent but was given the middle name Rhodes, after notorious imperialist Cecil Rhodes, for much the same reason.

'Imperial nostalgia' (Lorcin, 2013), the longing for a lost colonial order, was a common theme in Lennon's childhood reading. This included the works of A. A. Milne, Kenneth Grahame, Edward Lear and Robert Louis Stevenson. Arthur Ransome's *Swallows and Amazons* (1930), W. E. Johns' *Biggles* (1932–68), Enid Blyton's *The Famous Five* (1942–63) and Hugh Lofting's *The Story of Doctor Doolittle* (1920) were cherished texts, but his favourite was Richmal Crompton's *Just William* (1922) series: 'It was all imagining I was *Just William*, really' (Kenny, 2015: 75). William led his school friends on make-believe escapades that included a big game hunt and doing their bit to support the war effort. Crompton's narratives reflected her own social context: the waning British Empire. In a world populated by archetypal postcolonial characters such as the bluff figure of Colonel Fortescue, Lennon identified with the protagonist's audacious humour and his insights into the challenges of gang leadership. William even inspired him to join the Scout Movement – a youth organisation founded to foster the 'imperial ideal' by the 'Hero of Mafeking', retired army general Robert Baden-Powell (Norman, 2009; Shotton, 1984; Warren, 1986).

Lennon also gorged on boys' short-story periodicals. Popular during the 1950s prior to the rise of children's television, these tuppeny magazines had a significant impact on young male imaginations – largely by promulgating imperialist ideology via tales of colonial 'derring-do'. They lamented Britain's declining global influence and celebrated the achievements and grandeur of the past (Boyd, 2002; Williams, 1951). Publications such as *Rover*, *The Wizard* and *The Hotspur* included the adventures of Ruthless Ruff, a Great War flying ace; Blazing Ace of Spades, a fighter pilot during the Second World War; Wilson the Wonder Athlete, mountaineer and Ashes-winning England cricket captain; Bill 'The Wolf of Kabul' Sampson, a British imperial intelligence agent. These figures personified the resilience and stoicism of the British 'stiff upper lip' (Norman, 2009). George Orwell's essay 'Boys' Weeklies' critiqued the publications that 'festooned' every small newsagent's shop 'from floor to ceiling':

> England is always right and England always wins ... The King is on his throne and the pound is worth a pound. Over in Europe the comic foreigners are jabbering and gesticulating, but the grim grey battleships of the British Fleet are steaming up the Channel and at the outposts of Empire the monocled Englishmen are holding the n—rs at bay. (Orwell, 1940)

Eagle was the only illustrated comic book tolerated by Mimi Smith in Lennon's adopted home. Characters included Luck of the Legion, a British member of French colonial forces in North Africa; Storm Nelson, who patrolled the Caribbean; and Special Agent Harris Tweed, a monocled British government spy. Its most famous strip featured space explorer Dan Dare: Pilot of the Future. Dare wore a uniform styled in 1940s British Army khaki, retained a faithful batman, reported to his grey-haired moustachioed superior Sir Hubert Guest, an obvious postcolonial archetype, and captained an Interplanetary Space Fleet that resembled a unit from the British Expeditionary Force or Royal Flying Corps. Such images seem archaic from a twenty-first century perspective, not least because the only female character of note is botanist Professor Peabody, yet the immense popularity of this cartoon strip was also entirely based on its appeal to post-war British imperial nostalgia. There can be little doubt of the ongoing influence of such material throughout Lennon's childhood and in his future work. It is present in his famous nostalgia song 'Strawberry Fields Forever' and also as an aside in the first bridge section of 'She Said She Said' – where the protagonist echoes Orwell's 'England is always right' by emphasising and repeating how, when he was a boy, everything was somehow just 'right': 'I just always found that when I was writing, I would always drift back into childhood. It would come out whether I liked it or not. I mean, it's just a fact that that's what makes you what you are, childhood. There's no getting away from it' (Lennon in Spangler, 2019c).

Victorian children's author Lewis Carroll was a lifelong influence on Lennon: 'I always admit to that because I love *Alice In Wonderland* and *Alice Through the Looking Glass* . . . I usually read those two about once a year, because I still like them' (Lennon in Harry, 2000: 833). As a youth he became obsessed with *Alice*'s imaginary world and could recite *Jabberwocky* from memory (Shotton, 1984). The opening line of 'Lucy in the Sky with Diamonds' was drawn directly from 'All in the Golden Afternoon' the preface poem in Lewis Carroll's *Alice's Adventures in Wonderland* (1865). Here the author rows along the Isis section of the River Thames with his young muse. It features prominently in many illustrated reprints of the book and the definitive feature film version, Walt Disney's 1951 animation. As Lennon acknowledged: 'It was Alice in the boat, I was visualising that' (Harry, 2000: 574). The metre of this song is noticeably Carrollian, as is the first line of 'I am the Walrus', which recalls the rhythm of Alice's court evidence in *Adventures in Wonderland*: 'I gave her one, they gave him two, You gave us three or more; They all returned from him to you' (Haigha, 2017). Lennon's combination of perplexing syntax and semantic contradictions also echoed Carroll's style. The famous whimsy of Lennon in a garden waiting for the English sun but sitting, inevitably, in warm summer rain resembles the wordplay of Carroll's 'Jam to-morrow and jam yesterday – but never jam to-day' (a pun on the Latin *iam*, meaning 'now' in future or past tenses) and his inverse logic that five nights five times hotter than a single night 'must be five times as cold for the same reason' (Richards, 1993).

Lennon's and Carroll's wordplay revealed more profound parallels between Victorian and post-war attitudes to foreign territories. In some ways, Carroll's inner fantasy world was a response to unprecedented advances in organic taxonomy brought about by explorers, geographers and naturalists – the nineteenth-century version of Dan Dare's Professor Peabody – returning home with a wealth of previously unknown species data, and the new and totalising explanation for the origin of life offered by Charles Darwin's theory of biological evolution. Together, these discoveries significantly redrew all pre-existing knowledge of flora and fauna beyond the shores of Europe and undermined any possibility of existence for the fictional animals in heraldry, folklore and mythology. A trained mathematician and logician, Carroll's response was to reimagine his own natural environment. Like Lennon, he explored this in a series of hand-made teenage periodicals, *The Rectory Magazine*. Later, professional illustrators John Tenniel and Henry Holiday would redraw his fantasy creatures in familiar depictions of the Bandersnatch, Jabberwock and Snark – synthesising recognisable animal shapes into bizarre new forms and, in so doing, replicating wider anxieties over the existential significance of Darwin's tree of life (Dunn and McDonald, 2009; Richards, 1993).

A century later the grotesques sketched by Lennon to illustrate *The Daily Howl, In His Own Write* (1964) and *A Spaniard in the Works* (1965) invoked similar concerns. In *The Daily Howl* Mr Klink's feet and hands were interchanged, Frank Einstien's [sic] baby was preposterously over-sized, while Eric Hearble woke up one morning 'with an abnorman fat growth a bombly on his head'. Just as Carroll's Victorian monsters signified a response to the new Darwinian taxonomy, Lennon's distorted forms invoked a postcolonial aversion towards foreign bodies. In 'On Safairy' Jumble Jim and the Whide Hunter explored 'the mighty jumble' seeking 'poisonous snacks' and 'rhinostrils and hippoposthumous' (Lennon, 1964: 62–3). In 'Treasure Ivan' the one-legged pirate captain Large John Saliver and his shipmate Blind Jew sailed to 'a sudden Isle far across the ocean' (Lennon, 1964: 42). Unhappy Frank 'left the country and settled down in another country which he did not like half as much as his dear old home in England' (Lennon, 1964: 72). By situating so many of these crude portrayals in distant lands, Lennon correlated his distaste for their appearance with a distinct unease over their alien unfamiliarity. Such misgivings were a common thread in popular geopolitical novels at the time. Anthony Burgess' *The Malayan Trilogy* (1964), David Caute's *At Fever Pitch* (1961), Alan Sillitoe's *Key to the Door* (1961) and Paul Scott's *The Jewel in the Crown Quartet* (1966) all revealed their own apprehensions about Britain's waning international influence.

Even the title of Lennon's second book, *A Spaniard in the Works* (1965), was based on a pun entirely suffused with ancient colonial prejudices. It combined the common English idiom 'to throw a spanner in the works' with a historic British animosity towards the competing Spanish Empire. The Black Legend (*La Leyenda Negra*) was a xenophobic trope that demonised Iberians as inherently cruel, immoral, untrustworthy and dim. It originated during the sixteenth-century Spanish Inquisition and Anglo–Spanish war, a period of religious friction and imperial rivalry that culminated in the attempted invasion of England by King Phillip II's Armada in 1588. Lennon's title story included extended wordplay on this pejorative stereotype. He envisioned 'a garlic eating, stinking, little yellow greasy fascist bastard catholic Spaniard' who moves to Scotland: 'Jesus El Pifco was a foreigner and he knew it. He had imigrateful from his little white slum in Barcelover' (Lennon, 1965: 13). Given the huge potential North American market for Lennon's book it must have been a source of frustration for his publishers that the idiom 'to throw a spanner in the works' was an exclusively British English expression at that time. The North American English variant, to throw 'a monkey wrench in the works', only became popular after the success of Edward Abbey's *The Monkey Wrench Gang* (1974), an environmental novel that argued for widespread industrial sabotage.

The commercial and creative high-water mark of the Beatles' *Sgt. Pepper's Lonely Hearts Club Band* (1967) saw the historical and imperial artefacts in Lennon's prose, poetry and film work redirected into his musical output. Here, the Beatles synthesised their northern English childhood nostalgia with postcolonial tropes, low brow popular entertainment, high culture Western classical music, avant-garde experimentalism, adventurous studio effects and traditional Indian instrumentation. Lennon's contributions included 'Lucy in the Sky with Diamonds' discussed above, plus 'A Day in the Life' and 'Being for the Benefit of Mr Kite!', two songs that feature in the remainder of this chapter. *Sgt. Pepper's* originated with Paul McCartney's idea for a fictional Edwardian marching band. The title offered a pun on the salt and pepper condiments he found on the return flight from a 1966 safari holiday at Treetops Hotel, in the newly independent Republic of Kenya.[3] Sgt. Pepper was represented on the album's sleeve insert as a Kitchener-esque figure taken from Peter Blake's extensive collection of military cigarette cards: dashing Boer War cavalry officer Lieutenant General Sir James Melville Babington of the Queen's Royal Lancers (Goodden, 2014a). The sleeve artwork of *Sgt. Pepper's* entirely repurposed the upright, straight-backed martial image of Kitchener and Babington as burlesque jesters, restyling their soldierly demeanour in conspicuously inappropriate colours. In 1963, the Beatles' manager, Brian Epstein, had launched the band's Parlophone career in distinctive black and grey Edwardian collarless suits. Four years later, the Beatles now reinvented postcolonial chic in *Sgt. Pepper's* vibrant satin uniforms (Whiteley, 2003).

This vogue for colourful military tunics originated with fashion boutiques such as the appropriately named 'I Was Lord Kitchener's Valet', who had supplied Eric Clapton, Mick Jagger and Jimi Hendrix with distinctive antique cavalry jackets earlier that same year. Here the Beatles and others caricatured residual Victorian and Edwardian values at a time when these mores faced significant pressures from the counterculture during the 1967 Summer of Love. The trend was one example of a profound shift in popular attitudes, a comprehensive 'generational replacement' that occurred as emergent 1960s youth cultures usurped the social codes of their parents – in this instance by remodelling longstanding military traditions even as the extreme privation and sacrifice of two world wars persisted in living memory (Abramson and Inglehart, 1986). Lennon demonstrated his commitment to documenting these changes by comparing his stance on current affairs with that of his writing partner: 'Paul said, "Come and see the show". I didn't. I said, "I read the news today, oh boy"' (Lennon in Burger, 2016: 40).[4]

A closer look at the *Sgt. Pepper's* sleeve artwork reveals that it is saturated with multi-layered colonial tropes. Lennon and McCartney only proposed around twenty of the sixty-six figures featured on the cover but these included Johnny Weissmuller, whose presence reflects the near universal appeal of Edgar Rice Burroughs' Tarzan character at that time. The most consequential figure in the story of decolonisation, Mahatma Gandhi, may have been hidden in the photomontage – but the band did also approve, or at least acquiesce in, the inclusion of two men who personified British

[3] Fourteen years earlier, at the same resort, then in 'The Colony and Protectorate of Kenya', Princess Elizabeth heard news of her father King George VI's death and her succession to the throne.

[4] Given McCartney's contributions also included poignant teenage runaway narrative and the 1967 Ivor Novello award-winner 'She's Leaving Home', Lennon's comment seems entirely unfair.

imperial nostalgia: explorer Dr Henry Livingstone and British colonial army officer T. E. Lawrence (Lawrence of Arabia). These individuals are frequently overlooked in even the most well-informed critical commentary on this famous image. Ian Inglis (2008: 93), for example, inventoried Blake's tableau as 'movie stars ... artists ... sportsmen ... gurus ... comedians ... writers ... singers ... philosophers and scientists'; while Sheila Whiteley (2008: 11) catalogued them as 'famous figures past and present – philosophers, artists, painters, writers, film stars, comedians and, at Harrison's request, a number of Indian gurus'.

The album's closing song, 'A Day in the Life', offered further multi-layered references to class, colonialism and social change. It began by recounting the death of Guinness heir Tara Brown, a prominent member of The Protestant Ascendency, the Anglo–Irish ruling class who prospered greatly from the British state's benevolence prior to the 1916 Easter Rising and 1921 partition. Lennon then alluded to a war movie in which the 'English Army' achieved another victory. Given the prevalence of such films in British picture houses throughout the 1950s and 1960s – whether in successful Second World War titles such as *The Bridge on the River Kwai* (1957), *Ice Cold in Alex (1958)* and *Guns of Navarone* (1961) or in post-imperial tales of conflict such as *Lawrence of Arabia* (1962), *Guns at Batasi* (1964) and *Zulu* (1964) – this familiar image must have epitomised the sense of colonial nostalgia among his audience. Indeed, the line para-phrases both the title of Richard Lester's ironic black comedy *How I Won the War* (1967) and its rousing eve-of-battle speech in which company commanding officer Lieutenant Goodbody admonishes Lennon's character, Musketeer Gripweed, for the poor condition of his regimental cap badge:

> Your badge represents the *regiment* and the regiment represents all of us. You. Me. All of us here today. A dirty badge is a *disgrace!* It represents your fathers, mine, his before that. It represents battles fought and won years ago. Battles fought so that we could live as we wanted to ... it represents *tradition*, Musketeer! (Lester, 1967)

The song's final verse cited a *Daily Mail* article expressing concern about the poor condition of the nation's highways: 'There are 4,000 holes in the road in Blackburn, Lancashire' (Kennedy, 1967). A cotton town founded by artisan hand-loom operators, Blackburn became 'the weaving capital of the world' following the advent of industrialised power looms supplied by the import of raw textiles from British colonies (Abram, 2014). Lennon's gritty image of northern potholes was then juxtaposed with a more grandiose vision, London's Royal Albert Hall. This expansive building was designed and constructed by Captain Francis Fowke and Major-General Henry Y. D. Scott, two Royal Engineers chosen because of their reputation as the architects who 'built the Empire' (Williams, 2010). An exceptionally large venue for its time, the auditorium had a capacity of around 4,000, which – perhaps knowingly, perhaps coincidentally – was the same as the number of holes in Lennon's imagined Blackburn.

The Royal Albert Hall was the venue where, four months earlier, Lennon saw Bob Dylan perform his memorable shows with the Hawks on the evening of their limousine journey together through London. As one of many public monuments and memorials commissioned to memorialise Queen Victoria's royal consort Prince Albert, its prominence in the song exemplified Lennon's affinity with Britain's imperial history. The image of 'holes' rather than people filling the structure drew the attention of his audience to its empty grandiosity, inviting them to pause and contemplate the human cost in territories such as the Indian subcontinent: the thirty-five million lives lost due to famine during British colonial rule, the sacrifices on behalf of the Indian Independence Movement, the casualties among British Army and British Indian Army recruits (Tharoor, 2017). Whatever Lennon's intention, this melancholic connection between potholes in a northern mill town road and the empty seats in a monument to imperialism certainly resonated with other elements of his colonial nostalgia.

Lennon's Second Horizon: Class Antagonism

> I was always political in a way, you know. In the two books I wrote, even though they were written in a sort of Joycean gobbledegook, there's many knocks at religion and there is a play about a worker and a capitalist. I've been satirising the system since my childhood. I used to write magazines in school and hand them around. I was very conscious of class, they would say with a chip on my shoulder, because I knew what happened to me and I knew about the class repression coming down on us.
>
> (Lennon in Spangler, 2019c)

This section considers Lennon's historicity according to Jameson's second horizon: class discourse. Lennon expressed his class consciousness from an early age, principally in his desire to avoid exploitative labour. As such music, art and literature became Lennon's principle means of escape from this reality. Later, he engaged in different types of class discourse at various times throughout his career. During the Beatles early years, Lennon expressed the antagonisms he could not yet voice in song via his prose and poetry. Overtly class-conscious protest music eventually materialised in his solo compositions 'Working Class Hero' (1970) and 'Power to the People' (1971). The section traces the development of his class consciousness up to that point. It begins with the hardships experienced by Lennon's Irish migrant forebears and the working-class nostalgia of 'In My Life' (1965). It then considers his morbid fascination with the Second World War, and the cynical sense of humour displayed in his published poetry and prose. It closes by examining Lennon's introduction of politically ambiguous working-class tropes in 'A Hard Day's Night' (1964) and 'Being for the Benefit of Mr Kite!' (1967).

The experiences of Ireland's colonial population following the sixteenth-century Tudor conquests were not entirely dissimilar to those of subjugated nations further afield. Their proximity to the mainland, however, also allowed more than one and a half million Irish migrants to pass through the port of Liverpool between 1845 and 1855 – most to escape the hardship of the Great Famine. Many journeyed on to the United States, Canada or Australia. Others, such as Lennon's great-grandparents, James Lennon and Jane McConville, remained in the city of Liverpool under conditions of extreme poverty. A quarter of Liverpool's population was Irish-born at this time. After his visit to the city in the early 1840s, Frederic Engels described these migrant communities as almost wholly 'uneducated and immoral . . . having grown up almost without civilisation, accustomed from youth to every sort of privation, rough, intemperate and improvident', existing in 'especial filth and especial ruinousness':

> The worst dwellings are good enough for them; their clothing causes them little trouble, so long as it holds together by a single thread; shoes they know not; their food consists of potatoes and potatoes only; whatever they earn beyond these needs they spend upon drink. What does such a race want with high wages? The worst quarters of all the large towns are inhabited by Irishmen. (Engels, 1892: 92)

Lennon was named after his Irish paternal grandfather, John (Jack) Lennon. Born in Liverpool in 1855, Jack resided in Toxteth, adjacent to the docks, where he worked as a shipping clerk and labourer. Here, according to Engels, 50,000 people lived in squalid proletarian courtyard housing: 'narrow, dark, damp, badly-ventilated cellar dwellings' (Engels, 1892: 32). Jack's first wife perished in the Walton Workhouse and eight of his fifteen children did not survive infancy. In 1921, when Jack died of sclerosis, he was buried in an unmarked common grave in Anfield Cemetery (Wheeler, 2005).

Some events in the timeline of Lennon's career as a Beatle align poignantly with his family's Irish heritage. Just prior to the release of their debut single 'Love Me Do' in September 1962, John, Paul and George stood for their first photo session with Ringo in front of the abandoned Liverpool Bonded Tea Warehouse at Stanley Dock. This location, the site of a nineteenth-century Catholic enclave 'hard by the docks' where new Irish migrants found their first tenement housing in 'a city within a city', would certainly have been familiar to Lennon's great-grandparents (Kenny, 2015: 27). A significant proportion of the UK's tea imports also passed through the same warehouse in thousands of packing cases from China and India, meaning it was also, in all likelihood, the source of the tea-chest bass played by Len Garry in Lennon's first band, the Quarrymen. Three years later, in May 1966, on the British leg of his world tour, Bob Dylan was photographed by Barry Feinstein on the same patch of waste ground with the same warehouse building as a backdrop. The following week, he and Lennon met in London and filmed the infamous drunken limousine conversation discussed in Chapter 2.

The living conditions endured by James Lennon, Jane McConville and their children in Liverpool undoubtedly qualified for what contemporary sociologists call 'generational poverty', a scenario that renders families ill-equipped to rise above their circumstances. Jack's son Alfred, John Lennon's father, spent many years in leg irons as a boy due to rickets. He bore the physiological markers of this underdevelopment as an adult, with a shortened stature and pronounced limp. Born illegitimate with his parents not yet married, then a significant social stigma, Alf was only eight when his father died (Lewisohn, 2013). Raised in the Blue Coat School, a charitable institution for the betterment of orphans, Alf spent much of his life working for the British Merchant Navy. As such, his story duplicated a familiar Victorian literary trope: the 'foundling-turned-seaman'. Here, an abandoned child finds work in the merchant navy, sails abroad to numerous colonial ports, and helps build an empire constructed around the model of an idealised Victorian family that they themselves could never hope to experience (Peters, 2000). Frederic, the apprentice boy in Gilbert and Sullivan's *The Pirates of Penzance* (1879), was a variant of this character.

Indeed, Alf Lennon spent most of 1940 – the year of John's birth – at sea. By then the British Merchant Navy had grown to be the world's largest merchant fleet. Servicing a classic thalassocracy, a sea-based empire, it carried a third of global ocean-going tonnage and employed 200,000 sailors, over 70 per cent of whom were from the British working class (Carr, 1945). Thousands of vessels traversed routes to the world's ports and harbours – from Aden to Zanzibar – where they loaded, unloaded, refuelled and resupplied goods. In this way the fate of thousands of ordinary merchant seamen such as Alf Lennon was inextricably bound to the economics and geopolitics of Britain's colonies in what was, even at its best, a genuinely hazardous occupation.[5] Merchant seamen had higher casualty rates than coal miners, quarry workers and active military service personnel (Fink, 2011). Alf Lennon endured many personal hardships, including three terms of imprisonment, and was absent for much of John's early childhood. In these chaotic circumstances, the longest time that John, Alf and Julia Lennon lived as a nuclear family was for a period of only *eighty days* (Lewisohn, 2013). As Mimi Smith later explained following her adoption of John: 'Our house was a lot quieter than the places he'd been living in and we could give him some stability. He'd had a bit of a bumpy ride up till then' (Norman, 2009: 30).

Despite these disadvantages, the Lennon 'family myth' retained strong musical traditions. At some point in the late nineteenth century it is possible that John's grandfather, Jack Lennon, fled the grinding poverty of Liverpool Docks to perform in the United States with Andrew Robertson's Colored Operatic Kentucky Minstrels (Wheeler, 2005). This was not such an unusual occurrence given the number of Irish migrants who found similar work but, if true, it had significant cultural ramifications. Jack's son Alf taught his wife, Julia, to play the banjo. Julia then instructed their son John on the instrument; Lennon openly acknowledged that he first learned to play a guitar in standard E, A, D, G, B, E tuning[6] only after meeting Paul McCartney in July 1957. As Henry W. Sullivan (1995: 64) noted, this family history 'provided a signpost for the teenage Lennon to follow, a potent precedent for looking to the United States for self-definition in the art of singing black music to a strummed accompaniment'. That the grandson of a former blackface minstrel became popular in North America by singing 'Twist and Shout', an English-accented

---

5 The principal role of the British Navy was to protect this valuable merchant fleet, far more so than fighting with enemy ships or conducting blockades (Jackson, 2006).

6 In her memoir, Lennon's sister Julia Baird (2007: 88) vividly describes their mother, Julia, teaching John to play the mother-of-pearl backed banjo (handed down from John's grandfather Jack after one of his overseas trips). She does not disclose whether this was a four-string or five-string instrument, but each has a different standard tuning (C, G, B, D and G, D, G, B, D) to the typical acoustic guitar.

performance that soon became better known than the original Isley Brothers' hit, exemplified the literary trope of historical irony (Ritter, 1986).

As a British artist enjoying global success, Lennon remained conscious of his northern working-class heritage: 'the first thing we did was to proclaim our *Liverpoolness* to the world' (Lennon in Spangler, 2019c). This theme, like others, appeared in his literature before it was announced in his music. 'Liddypool' from *In His Own Write* appraised nineteenth-century public spaces in the city, including the Queen Victoria Monument in Derby Square and the Walker Art Gallery: 'We are not happy with her Queen Victorious Monologue, but Walky Through Gallery is goodly' (Lennon, 1964: 48). It was also represented in *A Hard Day's Night* (1964), when Lennon described George Harrison as a 'Scouse of distinction!'.

The first reference to Liverpool in his music was 'In My Life' from *Rubber Soul* (1965) as Lennon looked back to the environs of his childhood.[7] The earliest iteration of this song recalled familiar nineteenth-century sights visible from his regular journey on 'the number 5 bus route into town' such as the Old Dutch Café, Childwall Abbey Hotel, St Columba's Presbyterian Church, Picton Clock Tower and the Liverpool Overhead Railway – strongly associated with the city's working-class culture – which appeared in the original lyric as 'the Docker's Umbrella that they pulled down' (Goodden, 2014f). These distinctly localised images and personal memories were ultimately edited from the final version of Lennon's song, but the work still hinted at its genuine historicity by noting how some places have changed, some have stayed the same and others are gone forever.

Jameson (1981: 102) defined history as a collective struggle, 'that which hurts', and the shared suffering of the Second World War retained a strong residual presence in the cultural and social fabric of 1950s working-class Liverpool. Lennon did not shirk from the collective anguish of these memories. At Liverpool College of Art, which he attended from 1957–60, at least one of his sketchbooks contained illustrations of Lennon giving a straight-armed Nazi salute to a crowd shouting 'Heil John' (Butler, 2018). His biographical account of the Beatles in *Mersey Beat* magazine recounted their first visit to St Pauli, Hamburg: 'the Gestapo had taken my friend little George Harrison (of speke) away because he was only twelve and too

---

[7] Dylan's early composition 'Liverpool Gal' describes his time with artist Pauline Boty during his first visit to London in November 1962 and has nothing to do with Merseyside or the Beatles, or Liverpool itself.

young to vote in Germany; but after two months in England he grew eighteen and the Gestapoes said "you can come"' (Lennon, 1961). From Hamburg itself, in a letter home to Harrison's mother, he wrote: 'We've moit stag yet another moons in Hitlar [we might stay another month in Hamburg]' (Davies et al., 2012: 33).

Meanwhile the Beatles' performances in Bruno Koschmider's Indra and Kaiserkeller club venues were famously enlivened by the proprietor's instructions to 'mach shau' (make a show) and attract customers, causing Lennon to devise a provocative routine in which he goose-stepped across the stage while berating those present as 'Nazis . . . Hitlerites . . . German spassies' and 'fucking ignorant German bastards' (Norman, 2009: 202; Spitz, 2006: 217). As Pete Best recalled, Lennon routinely 'played the idiot who shouted his mouth off and yelled obscenities' while in Hamburg (Best and Doncaster, 1985: 24). He also regularly used the straight-armed Nazi salute while performing, a gesture punishable in West Germany by up to three years in prison at this time. Kaiserkeller employee Horst Fascher remembers Lennon's regular 'Heil Hitler' greetings: 'He'd pull out a black comb and pretend it was a moustache . . . people laughed' (Allert, 2009: 94; Crossland, 2006).

Many well-regarded academics and biographers have overlooked or excused Lennon's boorishness. Ian Inglis regarded his 'irritability, anxiety, restlessness and disorientation' as a symptom of amphetamine abuse (Inglis, 2012: 38). Philp Norman suggested his behaviour could not have been sufficiently insulting so as to provoke a serious response from the audience. This seems unlikely given the violence endemic to St Pauli's night-time economy and the feelings of those present who must have remembered the Royal Air Force's 1943 destruction of Hamburg during *Operation Gomorrah*. This reduced more than half of the city to rubble, caused 80,000 casualties and was the heaviest aerial bombardment in military history at that time. For Norman (2009) the acquiescence of his audience indicated that Lennon's actions were either misunderstood or somehow accepted as playful. Some witnesses were less forgiving, however. Kaiserkeller employee Horst Fascher recalled physically intervening, on stage and off, to defend Lennon on numerous occasions: 'John's big mouth, bigger than any musician I ever met, got me into trouble a few times' (Crossland, 2006).

Lennon was not the only 1960s British celebrity to have mocked Hitler in this way, of course. Others included Peter Sellers, Spike Milligan and Keith Moon. Nonetheless, his culturally insensitive gestures persisted for quite some time – even through to the height of Beatlemania. In 1964 he

Figure 4.1 John Lennon and Paul McCartney greet thousands of fans packed in Town Hall Square, Melbourne with a Nazi salute, 15 June 1964. Lennon mimes a Hitler moustache with his fingers. (© News Ltd / Newspix)

was filmed and photographed performing a straight-armed Nazi salute before a huge throng of Beatles fans at two major public events (see Figure 4.1). The first, at the Southern Cross Hotel in Melbourne in June, even prompted some of his over-excited band mates to participate (Baker, 1996). Then, in July at a civic reception in Liverpool Town Hall for the northern premier of *A Hard Day's Night*, Lennon shouted 'Sieg Heil!' as he gestured to the crowd below. This time, however, he was immediately chided by Ringo (Anon., 2015).

It is important to acknowledge the facetious irony in Lennon's actions on these occasions. Indeed, when confronted by what appeared to be a genuinely fascist motif his response was visceral shock and outrage. In February 1964, during the Beatles' first visit to the United States, the band were captured by news cameras as they emerged from the service elevator backstage at a major New York venue, either Carnegie Hall or CBS-TV

Studio 50 (now The Ed Sullivan Theater). Lennon walked into frame, surrounded by reporters, and joked about their circumstances, then was visibly taken aback at the sight of what looked like a large white swastika daubed high on a matt black wall above. Noticeably upset, his train of thought entirely derailed by the striking image, Lennon gesticulated towards it and insisted it be recorded on film:

REPORTER: Apparently, it's as posh as the elevators at the Plaza.

LENNON: Oh, I don't know, it compares very favourably . . . [Looks up, turning to address the camera.] Hey! Look at that! [Points upward.] Stamp that out! Go on! [Motions at the camera to capture the swastika.] *Stamp it out!*

(Anon., 2011)

Examined more closely the graffito was in fact a left-facing *sauwastika* (卐), a Sanskrit symbol familiar to Buddhist and Hindu culture. Lennon's instinctive reaction demonstrated his genuine sensitivity to the consequences of fascism and the recent experience of the Second World War.

The misfortunes visited upon working-class Britain during that conflict featured prominently in Lennon's literature. *In His Own Write* featured three overt examples, each a framing device for the ongoing narrative. In 'A Surprise for Little Bobby', he wrote: 'It was little Bobby's birthmark today and he got a surprise. His very fist was jopped off, (The War) and he got a birthday hook!'. This was followed immediately by 'Halbut returb (A Play)' which begins 'Fourteen yearz now I halb been wading for sweet Halbut to return from the wars' (Lennon, 1964: 70–1). In a biographical postscript on the back cover, 'ABOUT THE AWFUL', Lennon repeats the family myth that he was born during the Liverpool Blitz: 'I was bored on the 9th of Octover 1940 when, I believe, the Nasties were still booming us led by Madalf Heatlump (Who only had one)' (Lennon, 1964). Allusions to wartime suffering also appeared in The Beatles' first two films, although here they were diffused with satire – a common working-class coping strategy (Mäkelä, 2004; Sullivan, 1995). Lennon impersonated a German submarine captain while clowning in a bathtub in *A Hard Day's Night*: 'Guten Morgen, mein Herr! [Enter George Harrison] Ah zee filthy Englander. Guten Morgen!'. In a moment of slapstick he then vanished under the soap suds to the consternation of his manager. The military humour in *Help!* included two bumbling scientists complaining about their equipment as 'useless ex-Army rubbish' while elsewhere the film contained comedic interventions by the Scots Guards Pipes and Drums, the Queen's Guard and the Ghurkha Regiment.

Perhaps Lennon's most sustained class discourse appears in the form of his interview statements and his written publications. As a youth, his chief concern was how to avoid exploitative labour, an existence he dismissed at the time as 'Brummer striving' (Lewisohn, 2013: 8). 'I wanted to be rich' he explained 'because I was relatively poor and I thought rich would sort of get you out' (Lennon in Burger, 2016: 123). Numerous indications of this preoccupation appear in his media interactions, even dating back to his first attempt at writing a band biography for *Mersey Beat*: 'Ambition: To be rich!' (Lennon, 1961). Similar anxieties were repeated in early Beatles interviews which, due to their unprecedented international success, included many questions about money, or the lack of it. A 1964 Sydney press conference contained a typical exchange on this subject:

Q: Are you individually millionaires yet?
JOHN: No, that's another lousy rumour. I wish we were. (*laughter*)
Q: Is Brian Epstein a millionaire?
JOHN: No, even he's not one, poor fellow.
Q: Where does all the money go?
JOHN: Well, a lot of it goes to Her Majesty!
GEORGE: *She's* a millionaire! (*laughter*)

(Lennon in Spangler, 2019a)

The controversial 1965 interview with London *Evening Standard* journalist Maureen Cleave that caused such an outcry in the United States is discussed in Chapter 6, but it is worth noting here how the debate over Lennon's 'bigger than Jesus' comment obscured his articulate remarks on class antagonism elsewhere in the same conversation:

> I often think that it's all a big conspiracy, that the winners are the Government and people like us [the rich] who've got all the money. That joke about keeping the workers ignorant is still true; that's what they said about the Tories and the landowners and that; then Labour were meant to educate the workers but they don't seem to be doing that any more. (Cleave, 2006: 88)

Poetry and prose became an important outlet for Lennon at this time, principally because this longer form of expression facilitated the kind of challenging subject matter – including complex characters, extended metaphors and lewd wordplay – that could not be incorporated in song lyrics. Well-known politicians were lampooned with double entendre toilet humour in 'We must not forget … the general erection' (*A Spaniard in the Works*). 'Scene three Act one' (*In His Own Write*) lambasted social and political institutions such as the negotiations between bosses and union officials – 'a scruddy working clog, cap in hook what is gesticulated greatly but humble toward a big fat catipalyst boss':

FATTY: It's harf parst three Taddpill and the men haven't done a strike. Why can't we settle this here and now without resorting to a long union discussion and going through all that bit about your father.

SCRUDDY: Why don't yer shut yer gob yer big fat get or I'll kick yer face in. Yer all the same you rich fat Bourgies, workin' uz poor workers to death and getting all the gelt and going to France for yer 'olidays.

(Lennon, 1964: 38–9)

Lennon's few references to prominent politicians in song lyrics offer an interesting comparison. His backing vocals for Harrison's 'Taxman' (1966) alluded to Labour Prime Minister Harold Wilson and Conservative Leader of the Opposition Edward Heath only by their surnames, whereas his poetry offered a more detailed political critique using imaginative images and increasingly complex wordplay: 'Harassed Wilsod ... pudding the Laboring Partly back into powell after a large abcess. This he could not have done withoutspan the barking of thee Trade Onions' (Lennon, 1965: 40) (see Figure 4.2). Such ideas migrated from his literature into his lyrics only after Lennon became an overtly magnetic political songwriter towards the end of the 1960s. His prose piece 'Koms der revolution', for example, predated 'Revolution' and 'Revolution 9' (1968) by three years: 'Quite orften I lose, but thats Socialism' (Lennon, 1965: 61).

Daily Howl character Fungus McDungheap and his 'National Health Scotch Specs' was another element of class discourse in Lennon's writing that pre-empted the issues he faced in public as a Beatle – in this instance his refusal to wear government-issue glasses during the first half of the band's career. This gesture can, like the Beatles colourful adaptation of military uniforms, be read as an example of 'generational replacement' (Abramson and Inglehart, 1986). In this case, it represents Lennon's resistance to an old-fashioned residual bureaucratic ethos, the emergent culture's rejection of parental impositions and working-class stigmatisation. A similar concern appeared in a moment of slapstick in *Help!* (1965) when Lennon jokingly fished a pair of familiar round National Health Service spectacles from his bowl of soup asking 'What's this? Glasses?'. Soon afterwards his adoption of exactly the same style of eyewear for *How I Won the War* (1967) marked a re-evaluation of his masculinity and his commitment to the aestheticisation of working-class culture (Mäkelä, 2004).

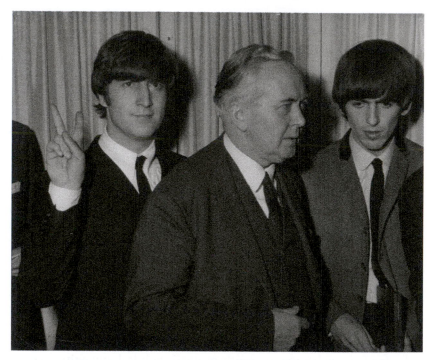

Figure 4.2 The Beatles receive the 'Show Business Personalities of 1963' Award from
Labour Party leader and Member of Parliament for their hometown Liverpool,
Harold Wilson, at the Dorchester Hotel in London on 3 March 1964. John Lennon
gives Winston Churchill's famous 'V for Victory' sign behind Wilson's back. (©
Keystone Pictures USA/ZUMAPRESS)

This relationship between class and fashion accessories in the form of
glasses, hats and jewellery is layered with meaning throughout Lennon's
personal history. In 1926, his father Alfred first met his mother, Julia
Stanley, while walking around Sefton Park lake. Alf was fifteen and having
recently left the local Blue Coats orphanage school, wore a bowler hat in
a misguided attempt to demonstrate a measure of sophistication. When
Julia mocked this pretentiousness, Alf responded by skimming his head-
wear across the water in a moment of romantic comedy that sparked the
beginning of their relationship (Sullivan, 1995). Later, in his own characteristically defiant expression of class consciousness at the 1963 Royal
Variety Performance, Lennon asked HRH the Queen Mother to 'just
rattle your jewellery' instead of clapping along. He said of the incident: 'I

was fantastically nervous, but I wanted to say something to rebel a bit' (Womack, 2016: 790).

Class politics was not a natural fit in the Beatles' early repertoire, but nonetheless Lennon's affinity for the subject encouraged him to contribute two songs concerning work and poverty. The first, 'Money (That's What I Want)', was a cover of the Berry Gordy/Janie Bradford complaint about their lack of earnings as songwriters. This reflected Lennon's own concerns that his band was not being properly paid for their engagements. As Larry Parnes, who employed the Beatles prior to their first Hamburg trip remembered, 'John comes on the phone and says, "Larry, where's the bloody money?" He was the spokesperson and he would always say the same thing, "Where's the bloody money?"' (Badman, 2009: 123). Indeed, Lennon was so unaccustomed to success that he struggled with the novelty of his first disposable income. McCartney recalled how, as the band started to generate a good income, Lennon's working-class heritage materialised in an obsession over what was then a relatively upmarket snack: 'He went mad on Jaffa Cakes! He went insane about them, gimme gimme gimme. And about a week later he couldn't look at one. For the rest of his life it was, "Don't talk to me about Jaffa Cakes"' (Bennahum 1991: 18).

The second, 'A Hard Day's Night' (1964), was one of the few early 1960s hit singles about the economic realities of working-class life. For James McGrath the artfulness of this composition lies in the manner in which it captures the defining factor of the proletarian experience: the reality of labour and its intrusiveness into daily life. Here, Lennon defiantly undermined the escapism in most romantic popular music of that era. The song's protagonist is caught between two commitments, his job and his partner, proving that 'money does matter' and 'the home is ruled from outside' (McGrath, 2010b). 'A Hard Day's Night' included the familiar idiom 'work like a dog', which means to labour extremely diligently yet still not make ends meet. It is another colonial trope dating back to Emanuel D'Aranda's *The History of Algiers and Its Slavery* (1666). Claiming the song as one of his own was clearly important to Lennon. When Dick Lester confirmed *A Hard Day's Night* as the title of their forthcoming movie he raced home to compose and complete the theme tune before his partner McCartney could do so (MacDonald, 1994). The song also offers more evidence of Lennon's preference for political engagement in his literature rather than his music at that time. Although its title 'A Hard Day's Night' is generally accepted to have been coined on 19 March 1964 by Ringo Starr in a radio interview at Twickenham Film Studios (MacDonald, 1994: 90) it was, in fact, already published in print in

Lennon's *In His Own Write*. Here, 'Sad Michael' includes the line: 'He'd had a hard days [sic] night that day' (Lennon, 1964: 35). So this phrase either originated with Lennon himself, or he must have heard Starr use the same figure of speech on an earlier occasion in order to include it in his book.

'Being for the Benefit of Mr Kite!' from *Sgt. Pepper's Lonely Hearts Club Band* (1967), offered another historicised depiction of class and labour. It was inspired by an 1843 poster advertising a fundraising event for William Kite, a popular horse rider at Pablo Fanque's Circus Royal. Equestrian circuses were founded in Britain after the Seven Years' War (1756–63) when returning cavalrymen sought employment as performers in travelling entertainment shows. Eight decades later they had become a strong cultural tradition, and William Kite one of the best-loved performers at Pablo Fanque's celebrated troupe. Lennon's song thus depicted the Victorian equivalent of a benefit concert for someone who worked in an industry that, itself, arose from a post-imperial labour surplus. Lennon often took great care to ensure accurate representation of his ideas, especially where they related to childhood experiences or class allegiances. When Abbey Road, engineer Geoff Emerick announced, '"For the Benefit of Mr Kite!" This is take 1', Lennon quickly corrected him with 'No. "*Being* for the Benefit of Mr Kite!"' (Lewisohn, 2004: 98) although he did change the horse's name from Zanthus to Henry, possibly for improved scansion and alliteration.

This brief studio exchange between engineer and musician offered a snapshot into the Beatles' recording aesthetic at this time, and demonstrated Lennon's deep appreciation for the history embodied within the work. He brought Fanque's circus poster into Abbey Road to show producer George Martin and, in a unique synthesis of nineteenth-century visual print and 1960s avant-garde recording techniques, requested a soundscape so convincing that listeners could 'smell the sawdust' (Martin and Pearson, 1994: 89) (see Figure 4.3). As Martin devised his inspired harmonium accompaniment, Emerick borrowed techniques from European *Musique Concrete* and cut up a tape recording of a calliope (a large fairground steam organ) then tossed them in the air before splicing them back together. Placed as the closing song on Side One, which had opened with the hum of an expectant theatre audience, 'Being for the Benefit of Mr Kite!' enhanced the blend of live and studio performance on this album (MacFarlane, 2013). Interestingly, when streamed or played on CD this arrangement creates a particularly affecting moment as the work now segues immediately into the dilruba, sitar, tabla and tambura of

Figure 4.3 A faithful recreation of the poster that inspired 'Being for the Benefit of Mr Kite!', created by Peter Dean and printed using the same methods available in 1843. Copies are available at https://kiteprint.com/ (© 2020 Kite.)

Harrison's 'Within You Without You'. This format unexpectedly juxtaposes the imagined soundscape of a Victorian fairground in industrial Lancashire against the authentic instrumentation of Hindustani devotional music.

Fanque's circus toured all over the United Kingdom but was best known in northern English factory towns, which is why Lennon's poster advertised an engagement in Rochdale. His regular benefit performances often included events to raise funds for professional circus performers and Fanque was renowned for this kind of philanthropy – although he also made history as Britain's first black circus proprietor, another hidden colonial legacy in Lennon's output (Turner, 2003). Lennon's meditation on this event, much like his earlier references to working-class tropes in 'A Hard Day's Night', foreshadowed the reorientation of his class-conscious output, which eventually migrated from his poetry and prose into his solo material.

In the mid-1960s Lennon's literature was his only means to communicate a political critique unsuited to pop music compositions: 'To express myself I would write *A Spaniard in the Works* or *In His Own Write*, the personal stories which were expressions of my personal emotions ... I'd have a separate songwriting John Lennon' (Norman, 2009: 358). Clearly, he was proud of these efforts. The opening scene of *Help!* shows Lennon choosing *A Spaniard in the Works* from the large bookshelf occupying the entire back wall of his apartment. He embraces it and kisses it affectionately, before reclining to read it on a sunken bed – where five other copies of the same book surround him on the mattress and twenty more are visible in the bedside bookshelf by his pillow, alongside a similar number of *In His Own Write*. Indeed, Lennon's poetry and prose offered an unlimited creative space that facilitated a wide-ranging and radical discourse, something that was not possible in his early recordings.

Curiously, this also elicited some of the Beatles' first positive responses from high-culture critics. Only three months after the very first musicological appreciation of their work – William Mann's 'What songs the Beatles sang' from *The Times*, 27 December 1963 – Lennon's poetry and prose was favourably compared to Edward Lear, James Joyce, Artemus Ward, Mark Twain, Brendan Behan, James Thurbur and Paul Klee in a range of high-culture magazine publications and academic outlets (Womack, 2016). The *Times Literary Supplement* acclaimed *In His Own Write* as 'worth the attention of anyone who fears for the impoverishment of the English language and of the British imagination' (Norman, 2009: 360). *Virginia Quarterly Review* affirmed: 'No one is writing satire today with the flair he has demonstrated in his first two books' (Sauceda, 1983: 5). As a result, Lennon's nonsense verse – produced years before his experimental studio arrangements, his Fluxus-inspired productions with Yoko Ono, or overtly 'magnetic' protest songs such as 'Working Class Hero' (1970) and 'Power to the People' (1971) – constituted his first genuinely class-conscious cultural artefacts *and* his first critically acclaimed revolutionary modern art.

Lennon's Third Horizon: Consciousness

Class politics was just one element of Lennon's personal value system. Another was an ongoing commitment to philosophical idealism inspired by his interest in Vedic thought[8]. Lennon's activism became more overtly radical during the second half of the 1960s but, ultimately, he determined *consciousness* as the defining factor in human progress. This section discusses this worldview in the context of Jameson's third horizon: historical epochs and their modes of production. The Beatles career spanned two of the most important economic and cultural developments in recent times: the shift from post-war Fordist mass production to contemporary globalised capitalism, and the final collapse of the British Empire. They were cultural trailblazers for these events in many ways. What follows draws together Jameson's Marxist historicism and Lennon's Vedic idealism using Henry W. Sullivan's (1995) analysis of the Beatles and postmodernity. It shows how Lennon's appropriation of Eastern traditions reoriented his perspective from a class analysis to one based on subjective consciousness, where spiritual growth superseded the physical realm of historical materialism: 'If we want to change the world we must first change the individual' (Lennon in Goldberg, 2010: 158)

Sullivan employed Lacanian psychoanalysis to analyse the Beatles' class politics and performance aesthetics during the economic and cultural developments of the 1960s. Like other scholars from the time – such as

---

[8] The word 'Vedic' is used here to denote the vast range of philosophies and spiritual practices drawn from the Vedas and known principally through the *Upanishads* (also known as the Vedānta), *The Bhagavad Gita*, *The Brahma Sūtras* and other canonical Hindu texts compiled in the northern regions of the Indian subcontinent mostly during the Iron Age (1500–200 BCE). Many gurus who influenced twentieth-century Western culture were Vendāntic philosophers and practitioners, including Swami Vivekananda and Maharishi Mahesh Yogi. Other schools included the Vaishnavite Hinduism practiced by A. C. Bhaktivedanta Swami Prabhupāda, founder of the International Society for Krishna Consciousness (ISKCON). This chapter and Chapter 5 use 'Vedic', taken from the oldest Sanskrit texts, as an umbrella term to connote the broad tradition in which these ideas stand.

Lawrence Grossberg (1984), Simon Frith (1996) and Theodore Gracyk (1996) – he sought to establish how popular music might diminish an individual's sense of alienation by providing a mechanism for their collective empowerment. In Lennon's case the arrival of rock and roll reoriented his directionless youthful energy towards a more purposeful organised group identity. Prior to this, as catalogued by school friend Pete Shotton, his juvenile subversive acts were best characterised as chaotic anti-social misdemeanours: trespass, vandalism, shoplifting, arson, street brawls, sexual harassment, bullying, truancy and absenteeism (Shotton and Schaffner, 1983; Sullivan, 1995). However, in 1956, Lennon's discovery of Elvis Presley gave life a new purpose and a new creative focus: 'Nothing really affected me until I heard Elvis. If there hadn't been an Elvis, there wouldn't have been the Beatles' (Wiener, 1991: 147). Indeed his most familiar axiom, 'Before Elvis there was nothing' (Mäkelä, 2004: 26) compared Presley's impact to that of a psychological rebirth by invoking the Old Testament creation metaphor of Genesis 1:1 ('in the beginning God created the heavens and the earth').

From a Lacanian perspective Sullivan (1995: 67) viewed Lennon's parents, Alf and Julia, as 'self-evident' subversives who consistently refused to submit to authority. Lennon's very conception was itself, a purposeful act of defiance on the part of his mother, whose unplanned wedding ceremony was in direct contravention of her father's wishes. 'There! I've married him!', she exclaimed, waiving her registry office certificate in the Stanley family home afterwards (Sullivan, 1995: 59). The dearth of paternal discipline during Lennon's early childhood, due to Alf Lennon's long absences overseas and his eventual abandonment of Julia and John, equated, in psychological terms, to an absence of 'Law-of-the-Father'. This manifested as narcissism and a disinclination to observe social norms. It also explained Lennon's audacity and creativeness: 'John lived in the Imaginary as if it were the Real', while also displaying symptoms of Lacanian perversion and male hysteria (Sullivan, 1995: 67). Sullivan points to a clear 'class cleavage' between the two maternal figures in Lennon's life as evidence of this alienation. While Mimi held bourgeois aspirations and ideals, Julia never escaped genuine poverty. Lennon duly 'oscillated between what the two women represented to him' in his behaviour, speech patterns and attitudes (Sullivan, 1995: 61). His resistance to Mimi Smith's house rules and traditionalism, his embrace of Julia's rebelliousness and working-class humour, all found expression in his struggle for empowerment via rock and roll music.

Elvis Presley's explosive impact on popular music in Western Europe coincided with the high-water mark of the British Empire and its first phase of postcolonial anxiety. The coronation of Queen Elizabeth II offered a brief false dawn in 1953 before the national humiliation of the Cyprus Emergency and Suez Crisis heralded the dramatic collapse of Britain as a world power in the second half of 1956 – precisely as Presley made his international breakthrough. Fredric Jameson (1984) has traced the origins of 1960s youth culture back to the global impetus for decolon- isation that occurred at this time. In France he observed how the arrival of rock and roll coincided with the Battle of Algiers in 1956–7. In addition to the problems in Suez and Cyprus, the United Kingdom also withdrew from Sudan, the Gold Coast and Malaya during this period. Yet while only three former colonies gained full independence in the 1950s, these events set in train almost ten times as many disestablishments in the 1960s – the same decade in which the Beatles rose to prominence as Britain's new international cultural ambassadors. The Beatlemania of 1963, for example, occurred as the British Empire dissolved in Borneo, the Colony of Jamaica, the Colony of Aden, South Yemen, Kenya, Singapore and Uganda; the 1964 'British Invasion' and the band's first world tour coincided with further disestablishments in Nyasaland, Rhodesia and The Crown Colony of Malta.

The Beatles' international success during a period of imperial disestab- lishment inevitably generated numerous ironic juxtapositions. The phrase the 'British Invasion', coined by Walter Cronkite on CBS Evening News on 7 February 1964, referenced profound historical connections between the United Kingdom and the United States forged in the Burning of Washington during the War of 1812 (Nachman, 2009). Capitol Records' ensuing promotion campaign across North America, 'The *Beatles* are coming!', recalled another familiar image from an earlier colonial conflict, the Revolutionary War. Paul Revere's midnight ride to warn the militia that 'The *British* are coming!' on the eve of the Battle of Concord in 1775 became internationally famous after its retelling in Henry Wadsworth Longfellow's poem 'Paul Revere's Ride' (1861). The band's unprecedented worldwide success was recognised in 1965 by the award of MBEs (Member of the Most Excellent Order of the British Empire). As Lennon observed at the time: 'I reckon we got it for exports' (Gleed, 2012: 166). Four years later, he returned the medal referencing a new postcolonial conflict: 'as a protest against Britain's involvement in the Nigeria–Biafra thing' (Greene, 2016: 61). The most poignant figure here is, perhaps, Lennon himself. With his mother deceased and his father lost overseas, he now embodied a celebrity version of the foundling-boy-turned-seaman trope that Alf Lennon had personified a generation earlier. Here, as the originator and leader of the Beatles, he became the unwitting global envoy of a culture in irreversible decline as Britain's residual economic and colonial influence gradually faded away.

Notwithstanding the long and indisputable catalogue of injustice and oppression suffered by denizens of the British Empire over the four centuries of its existence, the trade routes it established forged economic and cultural relationships that persisted for many years after the dissolution. Formally administered via the associations between countries belonging to the Commonwealth of Nations, these were also expressed in cultural and linguistic links – in the 'special relationship' between the United Kingdom and the United States, for example, or the various migration rights afforded to citizens of former colonies.[9] In their role as unofficial cultural envoys, the Beatles, the first globally recognised pop group in history, appropriated musical and visual tropes from several regions once occupied or administered as part of the Empire. These included rock and roll, soul and even country music from North America, Jamaican ska, plus their warm postcolonial nostalgia towards Britain's most populous and economically important former colony, the subcontinent of India.

Musical and textual borrowings from India were prevalent on every Beatles album from *Help!* (1965) onwards, commencing with the drone in 'Ticket to Ride'. These references began via the inept and patronising skits in their second movie, but evolved into more benign forms of Orientalism, introducing Indian music to fans who might not otherwise have heard it, in compositions such as Harrison's contribution to *Sgt. Pepper's Lonely Hearts Club Band*, 'Within You Without You'. Here, the Beatles contributed to the growing post-Christian awareness of Vedic and Vedantic traditions as an alternative to Western cultural and moral norms. This movement originated with international speaking tours from well-known Indian gurus Swami Vivekananda and Paramahansa Yogananda, who travelled across Europe and North America during the 1890s and 1920s (Reck, 1985). Indeed, the five Indian yogis on Peter Blake's *Sgt. Pepper's* sleeve depict the lineage Harrison discovered in Yogananda's best-selling book *Autobiography of a Yogi* (1946): Paramahansa Yogananda himself, his close friend and brother-disciple Swami Satyananda Giri, their guru Sri

---

[9] See Gascoigne, 2006; Gorra, 2008; Lalvani, 2016; Tharoor, 2017.

Yukteswar Giri, *his* guru Shyama Charan Lahiri, and *his* guru Mahavatar Babaji. Harrison later wrote 'Dear One' (1976) in honour of Yogananda.

Lennon's first mention of India, unsurprisingly, was not in his music but in his literature – the clumsy caricature of 'Indian Hump' from 'Neville Club' in *In His Own Write*. Richard Lester's second Beatles' film *Help!* offered an equally patronising and vulgar portrayal of South East Asian culture. The plot centred around a poorly constructed caricature of Thugs, a central Indian bandit tribe that worshipped Mother Kali, the Hindu goddess of destruction whose history dates from the thirteenth century. The following year, *How I Won the War* parodied colonial attitudes to indigenous populations in Colonel Grapple (Michael Hordern) and Lieutenant Goodbody's (Michael Crawford) dialogue about the 'wily Pathan'. This refers to the Pashtun tribes that inhabit the border zone between present-day Afghanistan and Pakistan, at one time the North-West Frontier Province of the British Raj and the setting for Kipling's 'The Ballad of East and West' (1889):

GRAPPLE: Never under-rate the wily Pathan . . . The Pathan lives in India. India is a hot, strange country. It is full of wily Pathans and they're up to wily things . . .

GOODBODY: Shall we be fighting him in this war, sir?

GRAPPLE: Of course we will, boy! The British Army's always fought the wily Pathan . . . How did you get into an OCTU [Officer Cadets Training Unit] not knowing history? God help your men!

(Lester, 1967)

Although the Beatles' appropriation of Eastern culture gradually evolved into more artful and empathetic forms, they initially seemed surprisingly naïve. In April 1965, while filming the Rajahama Indian restaurant sequence for *Help!*, George Harrison first heard the sitar music that subsequently became so important to their output: 'We were waiting to shoot the scene in the restaurant when the guy gets thrown in the soup and there were a few Indian musicians playing in the background. I remember picking up the sitar and trying to hold it and thinking, "This is a funny sound"' (Goodden, 2014d). Six months later he recorded his contribution to Lennon's 'Norwegian Wood (This Bird Has Flown)' (1965). Harrison's subsequent efforts to fuse Indian classical and Western popular music encompassed Beatles songs such as 'Love You To' (1966) and 'Within You Without You' (1967) as well as the first solo album from a Beatle, *Wonderwall Music* (1968), and his collaboration with Ravi Shankar on *The Concert for Bangladesh* (1971).

In August 1967, the Beatles attended Maharishi Mahesh Yogi's public lecture at the London Hilton (see Figure 4.4). It had an immediate and profound effect on Harrison and Lennon, and became the most culturally impactful event of its type since the tours of Swami Vivekananda and Paramahansa Yogananda decades earlier: 'The youth of today are really looking for some answers – for proper answers the established church can't give them, their parents can't give them, material things can't give them' (Lennon in MacFarlane, 2007: 77). *Time* magazine subsequently featured the Maharishi on its cover and *Life* proclaimed 1968 as 'The Year of the Guru'. Meanwhile the band visited India on a six-week trip described as 'the most momentous spiritual retreat since Jesus spent those forty days in the wilderness' (Goldberg, 2010: 7). Here, Lennon displayed an uncharacteristic evangelism, 'we're going to build a transmitter powerful enough to broadcast Maharishi's wisdom to all parts of the globe – right here in Rishikesh' (de Herrera, 2016: 238) and wrote an expansive collection of

Figure 4.4 The Beatles meet Maharishi Mahesh Yogi in London, 19 September 1967. (© Keystone Pictures USA)

songs about his experiences including 'Bungalow Bill', 'Maharishi' (subsequently released as 'Sexy Sadie') and 'India' (unreleased). Notwithstanding this prodigious musical output, the encounter held even greater spiritual consequences. Despite his subsequent disparagement of Maharishi Yogi, Lennon remained a practitioner of Transcendental Meditation and continued to disseminate his own version of Vedic philosophy throughout the 1970s:

> That's what the great masters and mistresses have been saying ever since time began. They can point the way, leave signposts and little instructions in various books that are now called holy and worshipped for the cover of the book and not for what it says, but the instructions are all there for all to see, have always been and always will be. (Lennon in Lennon et al., 1981: 110)

This was not Lennon's only experience of Eastern spirituality at that time. In 1968 a group of International Society for Krishna Consciousness (ISKCON) followers met with George Harrison while attempting to establish a presence in London. In 1969 ISKCON's founder Swami Prabhupāda and his devotees were accommodated by Lennon and Ono at their Tittenhurst Park home, four years before Harrison purchased what became the organisation's UK headquarters at Bhaktivedanta Manor (Cole, 2007). He also used the phrase 'Hare Krishna' in at least two songs, 'I Am the Walrus' (1967) and 'Give Peace a Chance' (1969), the latter accompanied by chanting and finger cymbal percussion from devotees of ISKCON Montreal. Lennon, Ono and Prabhupāda's conversations were eventually compiled into a book, *Search for Liberation: Featuring a Conversation between John Lennon and Swami Prabhupāda* (Lennon and Prabhupāda, 1981).

These strands of Vedic thought constituted the most consistent and significant philosophical influences of Lennon's late–Beatle period. Maharishi's school of Transcendental Meditation stemmed from his guru Brahmananda Saraswati's practice of Advaita Vedanta, in which knowledge of one's own soul (the true self) acquired through intensive meditation constituted the highest form of freedom and reality. Prabhupāda's doctrine was shaped by his interpretation of *The Bhagavad Gita*, a Sanskrit text in the Bhakti tradition of selfless devotion to Krishna as a path towards enlightenment. Crucially, each represented the exact opposite of historical materialism. Rather than *class consciousness*, both focused on internalised *subjective consciousness* as the source of their truth claims about the external world. This was, by definition, antithetical to the materialist outlook, and Lennon's position on the matter quickly became unequivocal. All the greatest accomplishments of science and culture, he claimed, were by-products of heightened self-realisation:

> many, if not all, great men and women were 'mystics' in a sense: Einstein, who at the end of his life remarked that if he had to do it over, he would have spent more time on the spiritual; Pythagoras and Newton were mystics. But the main point [is] in order to receive the 'wholly spirit', i.e., creative inspiration (whether you are labelled an artist, scientist, mystic, psychic, etc.) the main 'problem' was emptying the mind. (Lennon, 1986: 33–4)

While Jameson regarded competing and evolving modes of production as the determinant of social and ideological structures, John Lennon emphasised consciousness and *the spirit* as the ultimate drivers of human progress. As such, he was far more closely aligned with the Hegelian precept of absolute idealism than Marxist historical materialism. Like Hegel, Lennon essentially saw reality as a manifestation of spirituality, and all forms of historical development as a dialectical exchange between different modes of thought (Hegel, 1977). As he explained during a long interview with two Keele University students in December 1968:

WILES: When you look back do you think there's been this advance over the last few hundred years?

LENNON: I think it goes and comes, y'know. Cycles. Like all the astrologers and all those people say. We've been and fallen back. And I think it continues on that and that when the earth as a whole evolves to its full state of consciousness, there's a good chance it will just fall back into the crap again, y'know.

(Burger, 2016: 59)

Lennon considered consciousness as the grounds for all existence and the mind as the *only* effective agent of change. He actively pursued mechanisms to harness this power – such as LSD, Transcendental Meditation, Hari Krishna chanting, Primal Scream Therapy and the *yīn* and *yáng* of a macrobiotic lifestyle.

Indeed, this idealism remained Lennon's most consistent message. It appeared in the New Testament spirituality of 'The Word' (1965), the Tibetan Buddhist mantra of 'Tomorrow Never Knows' (1965), the anthemic 'All You Need Is Love' (1967), his imagined dialogue with Marxist demonstrators brandishing 'Mao Tse-tung's *Little Red Book* in the Beatles song 'Revolution' (1968), and through most of his post-Beatles output with Yoko Ono. Lennon and Ono spoke of generating world-wide 'absolute consciousness' during their 1969 Toronto bed-in for peace, while their Bagism protests that same year were based on the concept of 'total communication' (Bari, 2008; Burger, 2016). As discussed in Chapter 6, 'Across the Universe' (1969), 'Instant Karma! (We All Shine On)' (1969) and 'Mind Games' (1973) invoked various aspects of Vedic astrology, while 'Imagine' (1972) placed subjective thought at the forefront of protest and espoused the renunciation of all material 'possessions'. This technique, also used in the anti-war composition 'Happy Xmas (War is Over)' (1972), encouraged the audience to simply *visualise* peace rather than actively campaign for it, and presented this as a practicable strategy for limiting global conflict. For Lennon and Ono, it seemed, war could literally end *only if we want it enough*: 'Wishing is more effective than waving flags. It works' (Lennon in Davies et al., 2012: 359). Such statements may sound trite, but they accurately summarise Lennon's sincere faith in the power of ideas to determine economic, social and technological progress. Throughout his adult life he remained convinced that only consciousness could affect meaningful change: 'A dream you dream alone is only a dream. A dream you dream together is reality' (Lennon in Lennon et al., 1981: 15).

In many ways, these concepts aligned to the North American New Thought Movement, which postulates that God is everywhere and in everything, that humans are divine beings and that mental states manifest in real-world physical outcomes. This tradition continues in the contemporary publishing phenomena of Rhonda Byrne's popular self-help book, *The Secret* (2006) and it is tempting to imagine how Lennon might have responded to such pseudoscience had he been alive today. Since Lennon's death, Yoko Ono has continued to champion similar strands of activism. Her introduction to Peter Gabriel's performance of 'Imagine' at the opening ceremony of the 2006 Turin Winter Olympic Games was reproduced on her website to commemorate the International Day of Peace in September 2010: 'You may think: "Well, how are we going to get one billion people in the world to Think PEACE?" Because if one billion people in the world Think PEACE, we will get PEACE. Remember, each one of us has the power to change the world' (Ono, 2010).

Lennon and the Beatles were certainly positioned at an interesting historical juncture: they came of age during the post-war Fordist economic boom, but their international success coincided with the birth of the globalised economy and the collapse of the British Empire. Henry W. Sullivan positioned *Sgt. Pepper's Lonely Hearts Club Band* – with its combination of local and global, high art and low art – at a pivotal point between modernity and postmodernity. That this album so firmly cemented the band's position as postcolonial cultural ambassadors was due, at least in part, to Lennon's inventive synthesis of historicity and spirituality. Sometime during the mid-1960s, it seems, his visceral working-class Liverpudlian materialism melded with an innate desire for self-realisation and found its expression in songs such as 'The Word' and 'Tomorrow Never Knows'. Lennon's class consciousness always carried a note of experimentalism, as was evident in his grotesque school drawings and the abstract language games of his prose poems. Increasingly influenced by Vedic traditions, he eventually came to embody the long-standing ideological and methodological dichotomy between the New Left's historical materialism and the counterculture's esoteric hippie spirituality:

> radical politics has traditionally alternated between these two classical options or 'levels', between the image of the triumph of the collectivity and that of the liberation of the 'soul' or 'spiritual body' . . . The problem is not merely that of the respective priorities of these two 'levels', not merely interpretive and hermeneutic, but also practical and political, as the fate of the countercultural movement of the 1960s demonstrates. (Jameson, 1991: 59)

After the break-up of the Beatles, Lennon produced several examples of 'magnetic' revolutionary protest music, as defined by R. Serge Denisoff and discussed in Chapter 3. 'Working Class Hero' (1970) and 'The Luck of the Irish' (1972) articulated his Irish proletarian identity, while 'Power to the People' (1971) and 'Sunday Bloody Sunday' (1972) were fully realised mass-mobilisation propaganda songs. Some of these compositions were precipitated by Lennon's interview with Tariq Ali and Robin Blackburn for the International Marxist Group's *Red Mole* newspaper in March 1971, and his attendance at an anti-internment protest march in London in August of that year. In the aftermath of the 'Bloody Sunday' killings in January 1972 Lennon even met with Gerry O'Hare from the Irish Republican Army (IRA) to discuss a fundraising benefit show (Rogan, 2010). At this point, he briefly transitioned from pacifist anti-war campaigner to militant seditionist.[10] He subsequently characterised this period as a diversion into 'phony radicalism' (Spangler, 2019d). It certainly sat uncomfortably alongside the inveterate idealism of an artist whose greatest legacy remains the suggestion that change from within is a necessary precursor to all meaningful social progress. Chapter 6 examines Lennon's preference for the transcendent over the material in more depth, and explains the evolutionary psychology underlying it.

---

[10] In this context, the fact that Lennon's mother, Julia Stanley, survived an IRA gas attack at Liverpool's Trocadero Cinema in May 1939 gives rise to another historical irony. Few people are aware of the IRA's extensive terror campaign on the British mainland that year, although bombs exploded in British cities every few days for almost nine months. Lennon had apparently forgotten this element of his family history, too. Or perhaps he regarded the casualties as politically expedient.

CHAPTER 5

Bob Dylan and History

Introduction

Bob Dylan's career-defining output in the early and mid-1960s was shaped entirely by his affinity for the past. References to historical events and characters, both real and imaginary, are scattered throughout Dylan's work – possibly more so than any other popular music lyricist. They include archetypes from Biblical, Greek and Roman ancient worlds; medieval folkloric and Shakespearean characters; nineteenth- and twentieth-century philosophers; political leaders, writers and literary figures; fictional characters and Hollywood celebrities. Tables 5.1 and 5.2 list these citations, grouped by region and area of influence. While Dylan's British and European forebears are well established, his associations with influential North American cultural traditions has sometimes been overlooked. Consequently, as the previous chapter considered Lennon's British imperial legacy, this chapter focuses on Dylan's relationship with New England transcendentalism.

Transcendentalism was an intellectual and literary movement that grew from the Unitarian Church in New England during the early nineteenth century. Leading figures in the Transcendental Club in Cambridge, Massachusetts, included Ralph Waldo Emerson, Henry David Thoreau and Margaret Fuller. Put simply, the three most significant tenets of transcendentalism were:

1. a scepticism towards Christian orthodoxy inspired by the literature and philosophy of English and German Romanticism;
2. a sincere trust in self-reliance, subjective intuition and individual liberty;
3. an abiding belief in the power of nature, allied with an inherent scepticism towards industrial progress.

Table 5.1 *Historical figures in Dylan's lyrics, 1962–2000*

	United States
Political, economic history	John Jacob Astor, John Birch, Christopher Columbus, Walter Cronkite, Dwight Eisenhower, Barry Goldwater, Henry Hudson, Thomas Jefferson, John F. Kennedy, Henry Kissinger, Abraham Lincoln, Paul Revere, John D. Rockefeller, George Lincoln Rockwell, Theodore Roosevelt, Betsy Ross
Criminal justice, outlaws, old West	'Diamond' Jim Brady, Hollis Brown, Frank Dupree, Robert Ford, Pat Garrett, John Wesley Harding (Hardin), Jesse James, Billy the Kidd (William H. Bonney), Captain Kidd, Lone Ranger and Tonto (fictional), Billy Lyons, Henry Porter (Rawhide), Lillian Russell, Lee 'Stack-O-Lee' Shelton, Belle Starr, John B. Stetson, Donald White
Writers, Literary Characters	Captain Arab (Ahab), William Faulkner, F. Scott Fitzgerald, Erica Jong, Moby Dick, Camille Paglia, Tom Paine, Ezra Pound
Hollywood actors and characters	Ernest Borgnine, Yul Brynner, Richard Burton, James Cagney, Bette Davis, Cecil B. DeMille, Clark Gable, Errol Flynn, Sally Kirkland, Sophia Loren, King Kong, Peter O'Toole, Gregory Peck, Anthony Perkins, Henry Porter, Anthony Quinn, Elizabeth Taylor, Rudolph Valentino, (Brigitte Bardot, Anita Ekberg)
Biblical or religious figures	Abel, Abraham, Buddha, Cain, David, Delilah, Eli, Gabriel, Goliath, Good Samaritan, James (Jesus' brother), Jesus Christ, John the Baptist, John, Judas Iscariot, Lucifer, Luke, the Madonna, Mark, Mary, Mohammed, Noah, Samson, St Peter the Apostle, St Augustine of Hippo
Blues, country, rock, folk, jazz musicians	Bo Diddley, Tim Drummond, Terry Ellis, Richard Farina, Woody Guthrie, Saxophone Joe Henderson, Cisco Houston, Rock-a-Day Johnny, Robert Johnson, Alicia Keys, Lead Belly, George Lewis, Bascom Lamar Lusford, Taj Mahal, Blind Willie McTell, Charley Patton, Elvis Presley, Ma Rainey, Billy Joe Shaver, Sonny Terry, Big Joe Turner, Eric Von Schmidt, Neil Young
	Europe
Writers, literary characters	Madame Butterfly, Casanova, Desdemona, T. S. Eliot, Oliver Goldsmith, Sherlock Holmes, Hunchback of Notre Dame, Jack the Ripper, James Joyce, Juliet, Ophelia, Othello, Phantom of the Opera, Bertha Mason, Arthur Rimbaud, Romeo, William Shakespeare, Robert Louis Stevenson, Paul Verlaine,

Table 5.1 (*cont.*)

Politics	Napoleon Bonaparte, Charles De Gaulle, Adolf Hitler, Louie XVI, Karl Marx, Prince Phillip, Rasputin, Duke of Wellington
Scientists, philosophers	Charles Darwin, Albert Einstein, Friedrich Nietzsche, Wilhelm Reich
Children's stories	Cinderella, Robin Hood, Little Jack Horner, Little Bo Peep, Tom Thumb, Tweedle-Dee and Tweedle-Dum, Robin Hood

Table 5.2 *Historical figures in Dylan's prose and poetry, 1962–76*

The Times They Are a-Changin' (1964) 'II Outlined Epitaphs'	Charles Aznavour, Brendan Behan, William Blake, Bertolt Brecht, Ray Bremser, Lenny Bruce, Johnny Cash, Jesus Christ, Gertrude Stein, Cinderella, Paul Clayton, Miles Davis, Marlene Dietrich, Adolf Eichmann, Ludwig Erhard, Eddie Freeman, Allen Ginsberg, Woody Guthrie, Adolf Hitler, Harry Jackson, Lyndon Johnson, Joshua, Robert E. Lee, A. L. Lloyd, Dean Martin, Michelangelo, Henry Miller, Modigliani, Richard Nixon, Edith Piaf, Pete Seeger, The Rolling Stones, Joe B. Stuart, Elizabeth Taylor, Pancho Villa, Francois Villon, Muddy Waters, Yevgeny Yevtushenko, Emiliano Zapata
Another Side of Bob Dylan (1964) 'Some Other Kinds Of Songs . . .'	Lenny Bruce, Jesus Christ, Cinderella, Adolf Eichmann, Ludwig Erhard, Allen Ginsberg, Lyndon Johnson, Joshua, Dean Martin, Michelangelo, Henry Miller, Richard Nixon, Gertrude Stein, The Rolling Stones, Joe B. Stuart, Elizabeth Taylor, Pancho Villa, Emiliano Zapata
Bringing It All Back Home (1965)	Bach, Humphry Bogart, James Dean, Sleepy John Estes, Allen Ginsberg, Joe Hill, Norman Mailer, Jayne Mansfield, Mozart, Jack 'Murph the Surf' Murphy, Mortimer Snerd, The Supremes, Leo Tolstoy, Hank Williams
Highway 61 Revisited (1965)	Bach, John Cohen, Mozart, Friedrich Nietzsche, Orpheus, Quasimodo, Antonio Vivaldi
Tarantula (1965–6 pub. 1971)	Abraham, James Arness, King Arthur, James Baldwin, Jean Paul Belmond, Ingmar Bergman, Bluebeard, Lord Byron, James Cagney, Jesus Christ, (Emperor) Constantine, George Custer IV, Doris Day, Fyodor Dostoevsky, Dwight Eisenhower, J. Edgar Hoover, Charles de Gaulle, (General) Francisco Franco, George IV, Barry Goldwater, John Henry, Grace

Table 5.2 (*cont.*)

	Kelly, Ernest Hemmingway, Adolf Hitler, Homer, Job, Lyndon Johnson, Teddy Kennedy, T. E. Laurence (of Arabia), Huddie Ledbetter (Lead Belly), Robert E. Lee, Abraham Lincoln, Martin Luther, Mary Magdalen, Mary (Mother of Jesus), Groucho Marx, Mary, José Melis, Henry Miller, Agnes Moorehead, Arthur Murray, Nero, Donald O'Connor, J. C. Penny, Truman Peyote, Pinocchio, Romeo, Jane Russell, The Good Samaritan, Sammy Snead, Igor Stravinsky, Tarzan, Shirley Temple, Rudolph Valentino, George Washington
Planet Waves (1974)	Charles Baudelaire, 'Buddah', Dwight Eisenhower, Francisco Goya, Victor Hugo, Jacob, Joshua
Desire (1975)	Rubin Carter, Arthur Rimbaud, Leo Tolstoy

In this chapter, Fredric Jameson's three horizons of analysis provide a framework to explore the parallels between transcendentalism's core values and Dylan's appreciation of history. Jameson's first horizon, individual artefacts and utterances, is represented by Dylan's and the transcendentalists' shared enthusiasm for *literature*. Both drew on established literary traditions to inform their ideas, cited writers and characters from the past throughout their work and considered 'the poet' as a truth-teller, the conduit for our social conscience. This section examines the transcendental influences visible in Dylan's output, such as Emerson, Thoreau and Walt Whitman, plus another nineteenth-century writer connected to that tradition, Herman Melville. Jameson's second horizon of class discourse corresponds with Dylan's and the transcendentalists' deep-rooted commitment to *individualism*. This is, of course, a very different approach to this subject – as self-reliance and obdurate individualism is the *opposite* of in-group solidarity and collective action. Jameson's third horizon, the underlying mode of production, is manifest in Dylan's and the transcendentalists' shared attachment to *nature*, their pastoral romanticism and their visceral misgivings about industrial progress. The chapter closes with reference to Leo Marx's (2000) and Eric Lott's (1993) analyses of popular culture in North American at the time of the industrial revolution.

Dylan's First Horizon: Literary Artefacts

This section considers Dylan's and the transcendentalist's enthusiasm for literature in the context of Jameson's first horizon: individual utterances and artefacts. It discusses the parallels with North American transcendentalism that appear in Dylan's work – his habit of citing authors and literary characters in lyrics, his use of literature as a source of moral authority and validation, his struggle to accept the social responsibility born by writers, and the similarities between Emerson's (1844) concept of the 'The Poet' and Eyerman and Jamison's (1998) characterisation of Dylan as 'movement artist' discussed in Chapter 3. Critics have explored various literary influences in Dylan's output: premodern (Filene, 2000), English Romanticism (Beebee, 1991), French symbolism (Marqusee, 2005), modernism (Campbell, 1975; Marqusee, 2005), the beat poets (Gray, 2008) and postmodernism (Boucher, 2004b; Rocheleau, 2006). Recently, scholars have turned to Dylan's small-town Midwestern childhood and 1950s high school education to explore how this cultivated his appreciation of nineteenth-century North American literature (Clayton, 2009; Marcus, 2009; McCarron, 2017). Imre Saluszinsky (1992, 2001) and Mark Ford (2003), however, were the first researchers to notice correlations between Dylan and the transcendentalists:

> Above all, Dylan, as a poet is an American Romantic visionary, in the tradition of Emily Dickinson, Hawthorne, Whitman and Thoreau. In other words he is one more among the distinguished progeny of Ralph Waldo Emerson. *Dylan's debt to Emerson has hardly been noticed and yet he is a thoroughly traditional Emersonian transcendentalist.* (Saluszinsky, 1992, my italics)

British Dylan scholars have sometimes undervalued Dylan's North American literary heritage. Michael Gray (2008) suggests that they mistake the influence of nineteenth-century transcendentalism for that of eighteenth-century European Romanticism. This confusion is probably because the English Romantics were such an important resource for both Dylan and the transcendentalists, particularly in the context of their shared passion for literature and nature. Emerson only completed his first notable works after visiting Europe and meeting William Wordsworth, Samuel Taylor Coleridge, John Stuart Mill and Thomas Carlyle. Thoreau was hugely inspired by Wordsworth's philosophy of poetry, his position as a public intellectual and the value he ascribed to context, nature and literature. A voracious reader, Thoreau maintained detailed bibliographies that amounted to over two million words by the time of his death, many of which were used as citations in his own texts. *Walden*, for example, begins by referencing Hanno and the Phoenicians, Deucalion and Pyrrha, Sir Walter Raleigh, Hippocrates, Confucius and Charles Darwin (Thoreau, 1854).

Dylan's passion for literature is evident in his own copious references to influential writers, and in his relationship with cultural mentors such as Allen Ginsberg, Pete Seeger and Suze Rotolo. *Chronicles: Volume 1* established these literary bona fides with a seven-page review of the books Dylan read while staying at Ray Gooch's New York City apartment that listed European and Russian authors such as Nikolai Gogol, Guy de Maupassant, Victor Hugo, Charles Dickens, Sigmund Freud, Alexander Pushkin, Fyodor Dostoevsky and Leo Tolstoy. In the same work, Dylan also recalled in some detail how Rotolo introduced him to Lord Byron, Bertolt Brecht and Arthur Rimbaud. His reaction to the latter's '*Je est un autre*' was memorable: 'When I read those words the bells went off. It made perfect sense. I wished someone would have mentioned that to me earlier' (Dylan, 2004a: 288).

Yet despite this keenness to defer to his literary predecessors, and his clear appreciation of twentieth-century American sources, Dylan rarely acknowledged his transcendental heritage. Published interviews and writings from 1960–2006 reveal only one reference to Emerson and his protégé, the influential poet Walt Whitman,[1] during a *Rolling Stone Magazine* interview, and three oblique references to Whitman and Thoreau in *Chronicles: Volume 1* (Dylan, 2004a: 14, 103, 286; Jarosinski, 2006: 1385). Aside from these comments, Dylan did not discuss the transcendentalists in *any* of the media interviews he conducted from 1960–2006.[2] By comparison, he cited other well-known influences far more readily. For example, Arthur Rimbaud appears at least fifteen times in interviews over the same period (Jarosinski, 2006).

Notwithstanding this reluctance to recognise transcendentalist writers by name, it is inconceivable that Dylan was unfamiliar with their work. Greil Marcus (2009), David Pichaske (2010) and Sean Wilentz (2011) all postulate that he was certain to have a strong understanding of these ideas

---

[1] Emerson's ringing endorsement of Whitman's *Leaves of Grass* ('I greet you at the beginning of a great career') was in some ways analogous to Pete Seeger's early advocacy for Bob Dylan, not least because both relationships subsequently turned sour over artistic differences.

[2] A 1991 conversation published as 'Bob Dylan Breaks His Five-Year Silence' in Brazilian periodical *Zero Hora* contained the line, 'I'm in favour of the absolute freedom of the individual . . . Thoreau was right about that'; however, this later transpired to be a fabricated quote (Jarosinski, 2006: 1123).

given their ubiquity in secondary level education across North America during the 1950s. By the time Dylan entered the University of Minnesota he could hardly have avoided exposure to the core beliefs and principal texts familiar to every student of literature at that time. Indeed, *Chronicles: Volume 1* refers to precisely the period in which Whitman produced his first versions of *Leaves of Grass* (1855, 1860) and *Drum Taps* (1865) in a passage where Dylan describes searching for inspiration in the New York Public Library. Here, he discovered nineteenth-century essayists and public speakers, 'bearded ideologues of high abstraction' who understood 'American geography and religious ideals':

> I had grasped the idea of what kind of songs I wanted to write, I just didn't know how to do it yet . . . I couldn't exactly put in words what I was looking for, but I began searching in principle for it, over at the New York Public Library . . . I started reading articles on microfilm from 1855 to about 1865 to see what daily life was like. I wasn't so much interested in the issues as intrigued by the language and rhetoric of the times. (Dylan, 2004a: 84)

Transparent references to transcendentalism do eventually appear in three mid- and late-period Dylan compositions. The titles of 'Trust Yourself' (1985) and 'I Contain Multitudes' (2020) cite lines from Emerson and Whitman. The final verse of 'Cross the Green Mountain' (2003) written for Civil War movie *Gods and Generals* (2003) recasts a scene from Whitman's 'Come Up from the Fields, Father' (1865):

> A letter to mother
> Came today
> Gunshot wound to the breast
> Is what it did say
>
> But he'll be better soon
> He's in a hospital bed
> But he'll never be better
> He's already dead
>
> (Bob Dylan, 'Cross the Green Mountain')

> . . . come to the front door mother, here's a letter from thy dear son.
> . . . gunshot wound in the breast, cavalry skirmish, taken to hospital,
> At present low, but will soon be better . . .
> While they stand at home at the door he is dead already,
> The only son is dead.
>
> (Whitman, 1865: 21)

Much like Thoreau, Dylan has also consistently used conspicuous referencing of literary predecessors to bolster his own authenticity and authority.

These run from W. H. Auden to Yevgeny Yevtushenko and are found throughout Dylan's output from his earliest to his most recent releases (Roe, 2003). 'Desolation Row' (1965), famously, has one of the most fulsome *dramatis personae* in popular music. Its hallucinatory tableaux intermingled characters from ancient and modern history (Einstein, Nero), the Old Testament (Abel, Cain, Noah), Shakespeare and European folklore (Cinderella, Ophelia, Romeo), modernist writers from the earlier in the twentieth century (T. S. Eliot, Ezra Pound) and fictional creations of his own (Dr Filth). Dylan's most recent release *Rough and Rowdy Ways* (2020) contains an equally wide range of historical attributions – from jazz musicians to classical composers, biblical characters to Hollywood icons (see Table 5.3).

Table 5.3 *Historical figures in* Rough and Rowdy Ways *(2020)*

	Named individuals	Indirect references
'Murder Most Foul'	Dickie Betts, Patsy Cline, Nat King Cole, Tom Dooley, Pretty Boy Floyd, Glen Frey, Stan Getz, Don Henley, John Lee Hooker, Harold Houdini, Wolfman Jack, King James, Etta James, Lindon Baines Johnson, Buster Keaton, John F. Kennedy, Harold Lloyd, Lady Macbeth, Terry Malloy, Thelonious Monk, Marilyn Monroe, Jetty Roll Morton, Lindsey Nicks, Stevie Nicks, Scarlett O'Hara, Lee Harvey Oswald, Art Pepper, Carlie Parker, Oscar Peterson, Bud Powell, Jack Ruby, Uncle Sam, Bugsy Siegal, Guitar Slim, Carl Wilson	Louis Armstrong, Francis Barraud, George Bennard, Irving Berlin, Marlon Brando, Kirk Douglas, Clint Eastwood, Fred Ebb, John Kander, Stanley Marks, Junior Parker, Sun Ra, Jimmie Rogers, Frank Sinatra, Joe South, Robert Franklin Stroud, Larry Williams, Little Walter, Henry Clay Work
'I Contain Multitudes'	Ludwig van Beethoven, William Blake, Frédéric Chopin, Anne Frank, Edgar Allen Poe	David Bowie, Liam Clancy, Marcel Carné, Heraclitus, Ward Hill Lamon, Abraham

Table 5.3 (*cont.*)

	Named individuals	Indirect references
		Lincoln, Bob Luman, Mott the Hoople, Antoine Ó Raifteirí, Carl Perkins, Richard III, William Shakespeare, Howard Schwarz, Warren Smith, Gene Vincent, Walt Whitman
'My Own Version of You'	Marlon Brando, Julius Caesar, Sigmund Freud, St Jerome, St John, Władziu Valentino Liberace, Karl Marx, Al Pacino, St Peter, Leon Russell	Frankenstein, William Shakespeare, Mary Shelley, John Steinbeck
'Mother of Muses'	Calliope, Bernard Law Montgomery, George S. Patton, Elvis Presley, Martin Luther King, Winfield Scott, William Tecumseh Sherman, Georgy Zhukov	Homer's Odyssey, Mnemosyne
'Key West (Philosopher Pirate)'	Gregory Corso, Allen Ginsberg, Buddy Holly, Louie Jordan, Jack Kerouac, William McKinley, Harry S. Truman	Ponce de León

'Bob Dylan's 115th Dream' (1965) is possibly Dylan's most revealing and sophisticated song constructed around a single literary text. It made repeated allusions to Herman Melville's archetypal nineteenth-century American novel *Moby Dick* and the character of Captain Ahab ('Captain Arab'). F. O. Matthiessen (1941) coined the term 'American Renaissance' to define how nineteenth-century writers such as Melville explored 'the possibilities of democracy' in their work, suggesting that Ahab symbolised inherent contradictions in the 'heroic patriot' archetype. 'Bob Dylan's 115th Dream' extended this allegory by reimagining *Moby Dick* as a kaleidoscope of North American tropes – from Columbus and the Pilgrim Fathers to the Bowery slums – set in a future dystopia belaboured by haphazard communication failures and random acts of civil disorder – a bleak vision punctured only by his scatological humour. Dylan's most artful literary quip occurs when the protagonist returns to his ship, the Pequod, to find a parking ticket secured to the vessel's mast. This replaced the golden doubloon riveted there by Melville's Captain Ahab, one of the key symbolic metaphors in *Moby Dick*. Fifty years later, Dylan's 2017 Nobel Prize Lecture acknowledged the intense drama and allegory that played out around the large gleaming coin hammered into the timber. The ship's crew, a collection of individuals with varied beliefs and diverse backgrounds who each respond to the same events in different ways, became an allegory for his own career: 'That theme and all that it implies', he concluded, 'would work its way into more than a few of my songs' (Dylan, 2017).

Dylan's reworking of Melville's plea for democracy as a moral reference point for his own generation demonstrated how a nineteenth-century novel could inspire a progressive 1960s message. This sense of social responsibility was shared by the transcendentalists, too, some of whom functioned as the 'movement artists' of their day. Emerson's (1844) essay 'The Poet' defined a writer as one who: 'stands among partial men for the complete man and apprises us not of his wealth, but of the common-wealth'. A typical Transcendental Club meeting at that time discussed: 'The Inspiration of the Prophet and Bard, the nature of Poetry and the causes of sterility of poetic inspiration in our Age and Country' (Gura and Myerson, 1982: 604). In 'Nature' Emerson affirmed the unique ability of language 'to pierce this rotten diction and fasten words again to visible things' and called for a new and distinctly American voice: 'Our logrolling, our stumps and their politics, our fisheries, our Negroes and Indians, our boasts and our repudiations, the wrath of rogues and the pusillanimity of honest men, the northern trade, the southern planting, the western clearing, Oregon and Texas, are yet unsung' (Emerson, 1844: 28).

Dylan's early 1960s songs and poems exemplify the social conscience found in so many of these transcendentalist texts. Just as Emerson's 'The Poet' outlined a writer's responsibility to interpret and document the truth, the title song and sleeve notes of *The Times They Are a-Changin'* (1964) recognised every journalist's moral obligation as a reliable witness to current events: 'Come writers and critics who prophesise with your pen / And keep your eyes wide the chance won't come again.' Elsewhere, Dylan freely acknowledged how the incisive lyrics and prose of twentieth-century movement artists inspired his own work. In '11 Outlined Epitaphs' (Dylan, 1964) and again in *Chronicles: Volume 1* (Dylan, 2004a), he explained Woody Guthrie's influence on his artistic and philosophical vision: 'I went through it from cover to cover like a hurricane, totally focused on every word and the book sang out to me like a radio . . . *Bound for Glory* is a hell of a book. It's huge' (Dylan, 2004a: 245).

Conversely, Dylan also criticised those who could not, or would not, use their words responsibly and wisely. In '11 Outlined Epitaphs' he passed judgement on poorly prepared interviewers. In 'Ballad of a Thin Man' he famously excoriated the incompetent 'Mr Jones', whose name threatened to become synonymous for uninformed journalists as a result. The implicit recognition of a writer's moral obligations was evident throughout his early 1960s protest music, which included eleven civil rights songs and fifteen anti-war songs. Other compositions highlighted the plight of the urban homeless, poor rural farmers and miners. Dylan also made numerous references to social justice in sleeve notes, poetry, interviews and other texts throughout this time. The intellectual fluency of this early work caused him to be hailed as an archetypal movement artist and the 'spokesman for a generation' although he obstinately refused that title. Indeed, Dylan's rejection of this role only emphasised his adherence to the second principle of transcendent thought: *individualism*.

Dylan's Second Horizon: The Individual

Dylan's representations of Jameson's second horizon, *class antagonism*, are complex and paradoxical. Although he came to prominence as the leading songwriter and performer in the early 1960s folk protest movement, Dylan's reluctance to engage with almost any form of collective action often frustrated others. Yet for anyone who looked closely enough, the roots of his obdurate individualism were plain to see, from even his earliest compositions. Here and throughout his career Dylan frequently used one-off case studies of suffering as exemplars for greater collective injustice, employed predominantly singular first-person pronouns in his lyrics, displayed widespread antipathy towards the idea of in-group or class solidarity, insisted on the right to self-determined creative reinvention and celebrated outsider archetypes in literature and history. This section explores the many parallels between Dylan's individualism and the transcendental notion of 'self-reliance'. It offers a nuanced perspective on the intricate relationship between the individual and the collective in North American politics and culture:

Dylan's songs grow out of solitude, not solidarity, and whatever revolutions they provoke are personal and spiritual, not social . . . From first to last, the one religion to which Dylan has remained true in his songs has been the Emersonian gospel of the inner light and self-reliance . . . It is what the critic Harold Bloom calls 'the American Religion' and it is in his embodiment and renewal of this tradition that I think Dylan's fascination finally lies. (Saluszinsky, 2001: 535)

He may have made his name as a movement artist, but Dylan's commitment to individual rights over class interests was noticeable from his earliest protest songs. Instead of articulating general claims on behalf of collective groups, as in R. Serge Denisoff's preferred format of 'magnetic' protest music, he consistently reduced wider issues down to intricate case studies of economic or social inequality. Examples include 'John Brown' (1962), 'The Lonesome Death of Hattie Carroll' (1963), 'Only a Pawn in Their Game' (1964) and 'Ballad of Hollis Brown' (1964). As James Dunlap (2006) observed, these compositions focussed on the protagonist's immediate feelings and their subjective lived experience rather than any call for cooperative political action on their behalf. Charles Hersch (1998: 139) writes persuasively about Dylan's ability to 'take social problems out of the realm of abstraction'. His personalised examples of injustice generated a sense of empathy in privileged upper middle-class college students who, as a result, were encouraged to identify with poor and disenfranchised minority groups for possibly the first time in their lives.

The consistent use of singular first-person pronouns in political compositions such as 'With God on Our Side' (1963), 'Masters of War' (1963), 'Talkin' World War III Blues' (1963) and 'Oxford Town' (1963) also encouraged Dylan's audience to understand global and national events from the individual's perspective. Plural first-person pronouns such as the collective 'we' rather than the singular 'I' are relatively rare and only appear in five of his early 1960s protest songs: 'Talkin' John Birch Paranoid Blues' (1962), 'The Death of Emmett Till' (1962), 'Oxford Town' (1963), 'Who Killed Davey Moore' (1963) and 'With God on Our Side' (1963). In fact, Dylan even *substituted* singular first-person pronouns for plural first-person pronouns when he appropriated the work of others at this time. His two versions of Woody Guthrie and Huddie Ledbetter's 'We Shall Be Free' (1944) offer examples of this technique. Guthrie's 'We' was replaced by Dylan's 'I' in both iterations: 'I Shall Be Free' (1963) and 'I Shall Be Free #10' (1964) (Curtis, 1987: 147).[3] The

---

[3] It is interesting to compare Dylan's and the Beatles' profligate use of first-person pronouns in their early material (Bradby, 2005; Cook and Mercer, 2000; Petrie et al., 2008; Whissell, 1996). Both drew

rhetorical and introspective political songs Dylan recorded from 1965 onwards, as discussed in Chapter 3, relied heavily on the singular first-person perspective, too. These include 'Maggie's Farm' from *Bringing It All Back Home* (1965); 'Tombstone Blues' from *Highway 61 Revisited* (1965); 'Dear Landlord' from *John Wesley Harding* (1967); and 'Señor (Tales of Yankee Power)' from *Street-Legal* (1978).

The transcendentalist's commitment to individualism also informed their own reluctance to engage with collective endeavours. Emerson, for example, found it impossible to maintain membership of his local Unitarian chapel and viewed 'Self Reliance' as a greater sign of moral strength than church attendance: 'Whoso would be a man must be a nonconformist' (Emerson, 1841: 41). Despite a lifelong commitment to abolitionism that included working in safe houses on the Underground Railroad, Thoreau never joined any society or other formally organised anti-slavery group, as genuine reform could only materialise on an individual basis. Both men also declined invitations to become members of George and Sophia Ripley's transcendentalist community at Brook Farm:

> As Emerson found in the essay form he took up after abandoning the Unitarian church the perfect vehicle for all he'd wanted to say but couldn't in his weekly sermons, so Dylan discovered that by fusing folk and rock that at last he could find and sing the words he'd been looking for. (Ford, 2003: 133)

Several events in Dylan's life story illustrate his habitual aversion to collective activity and his high tolerance for what social psychologists call 'outgroup derogation' and the 'black sheep effect' (Marques et al., 1988). *Chronicles: Volume 1* recounts how he arrived in New York City during the harsh winter of January/February 1961 almost entirely alone: 'I didn't know a single soul in this dark freezing metropolis' (Dylan 2004a: 9). A year later, having established himself on the Greenwich Village folk scene, Dylan began contributing to the editorial collective of *Broadside* magazine – then suddenly dropped out of their meetings (Sawyers, 2011; Shelton, 1986). Even his most infamous group endeavour, his 1965 decision to 'go electric' and tour as a rock artist, did not involve the creation of a 'group' in the conventional sense. Frequent changes to his backing band meant that Dylan collaborated live and on record with over forty different musicians in the four years between 1965 and 1969, including nine drummers and fourteen bass players.[4]

---

in the listener by creating a sense of immediacy and urgency, but Dylan did so to strengthen his political message whereas the Beatles had a more commercial agenda.

[4] See Appendix 3: Bob Dylan's 'Backing Band', 1965–9.

In fact, with the rare exception of his conversion to Christianity in the late 1970s, he appears not to have joined or publicly supported virtually *any* conventional collective social endeavour. Much like the protagonist in 'Changing of the Guards' (1978), Dylan has no need for anyone's 'organisation'. He even refused to stay 'on message' in front of the largest television audience in history. As over a billion people tuned in to the 1985 Live Aid famine relief concert, Dylan's controversial request to divert some of the funds raised drew opprobrium from the organisers: 'I hope that some of the money ... maybe they can just take a little bit of it, maybe ... one or two million, maybe ... and use it, say, to pay the mortgages on some of the farms and, the farmers here, owe to the banks' (Ullestad, 1992: 41)[5] (see Figure 5.1).

Figure 5.1 All alone in a crowd, recording 'We Are the World' at A&M Recording Studios, Hollywood, CA, 28 January 1985. Dylan's indiscretion on stage at the Live Aid concert in Philadelphia followed this uncomfortable experience. (© Henry Diltz / Pictorial Press Ltd / Alamy Stock Photo)

[5] Jack Nicholson's memorable introduction to Dylan's 1985 Live Aid performance also hinted at his transcendental inheritance: 'Some artists' work speaks for itself, and some artists' work speaks for its generation ... Ladies and gentlemen, the transcendent Bob Dylan!' (Scarza, 1985). While it is unlikely that Nicholson's term referred to the nineteenth-century intellectual and social reform movement discussed here, this phraseology acknowledged Dylan's longstanding avoidance of categorisation, and his stubbornly individualistic moral framework.

From the Greenwich Village folk scene to Live Aid, this reluctance to be contained or defined by almost any form of group solidarity seemed entirely congruent with the transcendentalist principle of self-reliance. Transcendentalists saw *individualism*, rather than in-group solidarity, as the only genuine measure of personal integrity. As Thoreau's (1854) famous analogy confirmed: 'If a man does not keep pace with his companions, perhaps it is because he hears a different drummer. Let him step to the music which he hears, however measured or far away.' Dylan justified his withdrawal from the folk protest movement by citing similar principles: 'I had very little in common with and know even less about a generation that I was supposed to be the voice of ... *Being true to yourself, that was the thing*' (Dylan, 2004a: 115, my italics). Of course, in prioritising his own goals ahead of the collective, Dylan acted counter to the interests of those who helped launch his career and tested the loyalty of his fan base. Prominent early supporters such as Irwin Silber and Pete Seeger struggled to disguise their annoyance and dismay at this betrayal. As Silber's 'An Open Letter to Bob Dylan' from the November 1964 edition of *Sing Out!* lamented: 'some of what has happened is troubling me. And not me alone ... Your new songs seem to be all *inner directed* ... you're a different Bob Dylan from the one we knew' (Gray, 2008: 615, my italics). Subsequently, Dylan's increasingly abstruse lyrics, lost amid the volume of his new 'electric' live sound, alienated his audience during his May 1966 British tour. Yet in all these circumstances, and despite the strongest possible opposition, Dylan persisted in following his own direction, remaking his identity on his own terms.

Throughout the second half of the 1960s Dylan's insistence on self-reliance and re-invention led to more accusations of inconsistency and betrayal as the United States bombing of Vietnam escalated. When his 1966 World Tour reached Australia, a country with troops actively engaged in the conflict, he still refused to condemn the war despite being pressed to comment numerous times (Marqusee, 2005):

> 'What do you think about the Vietnam War?'
> 'Nothing. It's Australia's war'.
> 'But Americans are there'.
> 'They're helping the Australians'. (Dylan in Jarosinski, 2006: 356)

In 1968 as the Tet Offensive in Vietnam and anti-war protests in Chicago intensified domestic debate over the conflict, Dylan consistently declined to fall in line on this issue. In an interview for *Sing Out!*, the magazine produced by former ally Irwin Silber, he disowned earlier anti-war protest songs and even claimed 'Masters of War' was only composed as a career move: 'there were thousands and thousands of people just wanting that song, so I wrote it up' (Heylin, 2010a: 118). Later in the same conversation, Dylan even implied that he might now, in fact, actually support America's intervention in Vietnam: 'anyway, how do you know that I'm not, as you say, for the war?' (Marqusee, 2005: 267).

For Dylan and the transcendentalists, such determined individualism became its own reward. Self-reliance and re-invention demonstrated an individual's strength of character, their inclination to reject conformity and their unwillingness to stand still, notwithstanding the inevitable contradictions and misunderstandings that followed:

> A foolish consistency is the hobgoblin of little minds . . . With consistency a great soul has simply nothing to do . . . Is it so bad then to be misunderstood? Pythagoras was misunderstood and Socrates and Jesus and Luther and Copernicus and Galileo and Newton and every pure and wise spirit that ever took flesh. To be great is to be misunderstood. (Emerson, 1841)

As noted earlier, Walt Whitman was one of the few transcendentalist writers cited directly or obliquely in Dylan's own compositions. 'I Contain Multitudes', from his most recent album of original material *Rough and Rowdy Ways* (2020), offered a direct quote from Whitman's (1860) famous argument against the virtue of consistency in 'Song of Myself': 'Do I contradict myself? Very well then, I contradict myself. I am large, I contain multitudes.' This seemed to confirm the transcendental ideal in Dylan's output and validate his lifelong contrarianism.

There are other parallels in creative practice between the two. Whitman consistently augmented and revised successive iterations of *Leaves of Grass* between its first publication in 1855 and his death in 1891. Dylan has substantially rearranged his own material in much the same way, as Betsy Bowden (2001) discovered when she analysed twenty-four concert performances of eleven songs. Notable examples include 'Tangled up in Blue', from *Blood on the Tracks* (1974), which was reworked six times between 1975 and 1987 (Heylin, 2010b). The live album *Bob Dylan at Budokan* (1978) included radical revisions of even his most celebrated compositions, including a bizarre pastiche reggae 'Knockin' on Heaven's Door'. Indeed, this compulsive need for self-renewal is conceivably the most consistent element of Dylan's performance aesthetic. That it accords with transcendentalist self-reliance was indicated in the title of *Empire Burlesque*'s 'Trust Yourself' (1985), which echoed Emerson's adage: 'Trust thyself: every heart vibrates to that iron string' (Ford, 2003; Saluszinsky, 1992, 2001). Dylan's memoir compared this need for stylistic reinvention to that of Ricky Nelson, who also crossed genres mid-career and alienated his fan base as a result, using Thoreau as a reference point: 'It was like he'd been born on Walden Pond where everything was hunky dory and I'd come out of the dark demonic woods, same forest, just a different way of looking at things' (Dylan, 2004a: 14). More recently, Dylan's long speech at the 2015 Grammy Awards reflected on his reputation for individualism and nonconformity:

> Critics have made a career out of accusing me of having a career of confounding expectations. Really? Because that's all I do. That's how I think about it. Confounding expectations.
> 'What do you do for a living, man?'
> 'Oh, I confound expectations'. (Dylan, 2015)

This instinctive and righteous resistance to the authority and desires of others also echoed the message of Thoreau's essay, popularly known as 'Civil Disobedience' (Thoreau, 1849), a profoundly impactful document among social justice leaders such as Mahatma Gandhi, Martin Luther King, Jnr and others. Thoreau's message was derived not from collective class interests, but from every individual's moral obligation to disobey unjust laws:

> Must the citizen ever for a moment, or in the least degree, resign his conscience to the legislator? Why has every man a conscience then? It is not desirable to cultivate a respect for the law, so much as for the right. The only obligation which I have a right to assume is to do at any time what I think right ... I cannot for an instant recognise that political organisation as my government which is the slave's government also. (Thoreau, 1849: 192)

Interestingly both of Dylan's two notably magnetic protest songs identified in Chapter 3, 'Let Me Die in My Footsteps' (1962) and 'Ye Playboys and Playgirls' (1962), were constructed around a similar ethical imperative: the primacy of an individual's conscience and their moral duty to disregard immoral or impractical civil defence regulations.

During his *A Plea for Captain John Brown* (1860), Thoreau even endorsed violent resistance in extreme circumstances, in this instance John Brown's attempt to initiate a slave revolt during his raid on Harper's Ferry. Thoreau was subsequently accused of a sentimental portrayal of Brown (Turner, 2005). Dylan, too, romanticised his depictions of controversial characters – although unlike Thoreau, or indeed John Lennon, he never endorsed political violence. Nonetheless, notable outlaw figures proved a regular source of inspiration as possibly the ultimate signifiers of self-reliance and robust individualism. Early portrayals included 'The Ballad of Donald White' (1962), an indigent recidivist criminal who committed double murder so he could be returned to prison; while the bells in 'Chimes of Freedom' (1964) tolled to commemorate underdogs, outcasts, rebels and assorted fugitives from justice. 'John Wesley Harding' (1967) memorialised a Texas gun-fighter who killed over forty men, and 'Joey' (1976) celebrated a New York Mafiosi with a long history of violent crime. 'George Jackson' (1972) lamented the death of the Black Guerrilla Family founder during a prison riot. Given Jackson's political history and the circumstances of his death this seems in some ways analogous to Thoreau's support for the anti-slavery insurrectionist John Brown.

Here and elsewhere, Dylan wrote compelling indictments against the United States criminal justice system. Some of his earliest compositions described the unjust conviction and unfair punishments visited on unfortunate citizens who transgressed *legal* but not *moral* boundaries. In 'Percy's Song' (1963) and 'Seven Curses' (1963) Dylan vehemently denounced a corrupt judiciary. 'Hurricane' (1976) was another prison song that told the story of wrongly convicted African-American boxer Rubin Carter. Episode 6 of Dylan's Theme Time Radio Hour, 'Jail', quoted Cassius' lines from William Shakespeare's *Julius Caesar* where he vows to commit suicide rather than face capture: 'Nor stony tower, nor walls of beaten brass, nor airless dungeon, nor strong links of iron, can be retentive to the strength of spirit' (Dylan, 2006b). Thoreau too was, of course, a noted antagonist against the prison system of his day. 'Civil Disobedience' (1849) reflected on a night spent in jail and the plight of his cellmate.

Dylan and the transcendentalists also shared a sense of empathy for the powerlessness and impoverished: 'I embrace the common, I explore and sit at the feet of the familiar, the low', Emerson (1837) declared in 'The American Scholar'. Thoreau (1854) identified poverty with purity and made romantic associations between a simple life of personal economy and basic self-reliance: 'none has been poorer in outward riches, none so rich in inward'. Yet neither identified with any form of class antagonism because they prioritised the moral rights of individuals above those of groups. Similarly, Dylan's criticisms of economic injustice rarely engaged in class discourse – instead they focused on individualised case studies of poverty such as 'Ballad of Hollis Brown' (1964) or 'I Am a Lonesome Hobo' and 'Drifter's Escape' from *John Wesley Harding* (1967).

Much as there is a 'Thoreau for everyone' (naturalist, vegetarian, anarchist or libertarian) Dylan's politics have been attached to a range of causes from liberal left to conservative Christian Zionist (Forland, 1992; Seybold, 1960). Yet while Eyerman and Jamison portrayed Dylan as the very definition of a progressive movement artist, his true colours remain difficult to identify. His radio programmes, books and songs all offer detailed but sharply contrasting perspectives on class politics and labour organisations. His longest and most sustained meditations on the political economy of late capitalism are probably in his two Theme Time Radio Hour shows: 'Rich Man, Poor Man' (Dylan, 2006c) and 'Work' (Dylan, 2009). Yet neither offers any reference to unions, collective bargaining, industrial action or any other form of class discourse. On the contrary, the tone of the songs chosen for both broadcasts – notably Tony Bennett's 'Rags to Riches' (1953) and Adriana Caselotti's 'Whistle While You Work' (1937) – celebrate neo-liberal individualism, the importance of a strong work ethic and the American Dream. 'Work' even offered Dylan's advice on how to perform well at a job interview: speak clearly, don't wear too much aftershave and be sure to put on a clean shirt. He also quoted Thomas Edison's aphorism, 'opportunity is missed by most people because it is dressed in overalls and looks like work', and closed with the advice: 'It's important to put your shoulder to the wheel and keep your nose to the grindstone'. 'Rich Man, Poor Man' briefly referenced Scandinavian welfare economics, but only as a set up for a sexist joke: 'In Sweden they have a system of higher taxes but welfare for everyone. They call it the Swedish Model. Well I could go for a Swedish model right about now'.

Dylan's memoir *Chronicles: Volume 1* included twelve references to union songs, union halls, union organisers, labour organisations or union rallies, most of which are linked to his involvement with the Greenwich Village folk protest scene in the early and mid-1960s. Yet it also revealed his deep admiration for conservative Republican Barry Goldwater, who Dylan cited as his 'favourite politician' from that era – a revelation almost entirely overlooked by fans and academics (Dylan, 2004a: 283). His novel *Tarantula* (1971), written in 1965–6, made four allusions to organised labour, although these are so conspicuously stylised they almost caricature the union movement: 'look buddy I'm a union man ... look yourself – you ever heard of woody guthrie [sic]? he was a union man too & he fought to organise unions like yers [sic]' (Dylan, 1971: 113). Only three of Dylan's songs from his 1960s protest period mention labour unions. The earliest is 'Talkin' New York Blues' (1962) which, as he acknowledged in his memoir, refers to the necessity of paying a union to obtain a cabaret performer's card in

Greenwich Village folk clubs. His infrequent instances of post-1960s political compositions, such as 'Political World' (1989), contain very few examples of class discourse. 'Cry a While' (2001) included the protagonists proud declaration of trade union loyalty – although the lyric, overall, seemed to draw on various lines from a number of much older blues recordings.

Dylan's ongoing scepticism towards labour organisations was revealed in the mid-1980s during interviews discussing his song 'Union Sundown' (1983): 'Unions in the early thirties were all communist organisations and now they're big business' (Jarosinski, 2006: 915). As the lyrics to 'Union Sundown' make clear, the title signifies much more than labour organisations. It also reflects the gradual decline of the manufacturing capacity in the north-eastern and upper Midwestern industrial regions, once known as the 'Union states' but now familiar as the 'rust belt':

> Well, my shoes, they come from Singapore
> My flashlight's from Taiwan
> My tablecloth's from Malaysia
> My belt buckle's from the Amazon
> You know, this shirt I wear comes from the Philippines
> And the car I drive is a Chevrolet
> It was put together down in Argentina
> By a guy makin' thirty cents a day
> Well, it's sundown on the union
> And what's made in the USA
> Sure was a good idea
> 'Til greed got in the way.
>
> (Bob Dylan, 'Union Sundown')

As Dylan explained at the time: 'Right now ... there's a big push on to make a big global country – one big country – where you can get all the materials from one place and assemble them someplace else and sell 'em in another place' (Jarosinski, 2006: 768). In this context, 'Union Sundown' offered an anti-globalist critique that presaged the 'America First' protectionism of Donald Trump by three decades. Later, while reflecting on individualism during a *Rolling Stone* interview in 2006, Dylan celebrated the virtue of self-reliance in a passage that compared Trump's tenacity to that of his transcendental literary forebears:

> Who's the last individual performer you can think of? I'm talking about artists with the willpower not to conform to anybody's reality but their own. Patsy Cline and Billy Lee Riley. Plato and Socrates. *Whitman and Emerson.* Slim Harpo and *Donald Trump.* It's a lost art form. I don't know who else

does it beside myself to tell you the truth. (Dylan in Jarosinski, 2006: 1385, my italics)

By privileging self-reliance over collective interests Dylan and the transcendentalists centred their understanding of justice in the rights of the *individual* rather than in membership of any group or class. Untouched by European Marxist thought, this was in every sense a distinctly North American worldview. Much as Walt Whitman (1860) celebrated the United States as 'essentially the greatest poem', Dylan's memoir accredited the source of this self-reliance: 'Being born and raised in America, the country of freedom and independence, I had always cherished the values and ideals of equality and liberty' (Dylan, 2004a: 115).

Dylan's Third Horizon: Nature

If both Dylan's and the transcendentalist movement's preferences for individual over class interests (Jameson's second horizon) were rooted in their North American ideological heritage, their responses to *changing modes of production* (Jameson's third horizon) were equally a product of this shared historical context. Both lived through significant shifts in the economy of the United States and both articulated anxieties about these developments in their romanticised view of nature. Here, each was looking at different ends of the same beast: capitalism. The transcendentalist movement arose as the consequences of North America's first industrial revolution became apparent to the citizens of New England, many of whom identified with the residual agrarian mode of production and expressed concerns over the emergent factory system. Dylan, conversely, came of age at the tail end of North American Fordist production, in a city entirely defined by its links with US Steel and surrounded by a landscape utterly ruined by mechanical exploitation. He rarely referenced or even alluded to transcendentalism yet his reliance on the immanent beauty and virtue of nature, plus his hostility towards industrial development, contain striking similarities in tone. This section examines the parallels in Dylan's and the transcendentalists' piety towards nature and their distaste for the machine age, then uses the work of Leo Marx (2000) and Eric Lott (1993) to draw some new conclusions about these common themes.

The natural world formed the foundation for Emerson and Thoreau's moral philosophy. Emerson's (1844) two volumes of *Essays* posited 'Nature' as a direct connection between the universal consciousness, the 'Over-Soul' (Emerson, 1841), and a presence of the Divine within every person via their own subjective sense of God. Only by observing and interacting with nature might we reveal universal truths. It constituted the primary means of guidance for the 'inner light' of the individual's conscience. Thoreau's broader metaphysical perspective invoked an immanent pantheistic spirit that connected all living things. In *Walden* (Thoreau, 1854) he built and inhabited a small hermitage in woodland owned by Emerson adjacent to their hometown of Concord, Massachusetts, in order to experience a period of self-immersion in nature. Here, humbled by the sublime beauty of his surroundings, Thoreau sought insights into individual self-reliance and the relationship between humankind and the environment.

Dylan enjoyed a similarly profound relationship with nature. His formative years in the remote Midwest were entirely defined by colossal forces of industrialisation focussed on the vast iron ore deposits around and beneath his hometown of Hibbing, Minnesota. David Pichaske (2010), Susan Clayton (2009) and Greil Marcus (2009) examined various aspects of Dylan's Iron Range upbringing – landscape, local politics and public education – to show how this environment shaped his worldview prior to his arrival in metropolitan New York City. For much of his early career Dylan dismissed questions about his background with short shrift: 'I've thought about it some, but Hibbing really has nothing to do with what I am today, with what I became. Really, nothing!' (Shelton, 2011). Two early songs, 'Girl from the North Country' (1963) and 'Long Time Gone' (1963), plus the sleeve notes '11 Outlined Epitaphs' (1964) revealed his ambivalent nostalgia for the Midwest's limitations and his desire to escape them.

Later, Dylan became more honest, more open and more self-reflective when questioned about his past. Here, he employed Thoreauvian tropes to explain his connection to this dramatic landscape:

> The earth there is unusual, filled with ore. So there is something happening there that is hard to define. There is a magnetic attraction there . . . A great spiritual quality . . . Very subtle, very strong and that's where I grew up . . . I got something different in my soul. Like a spirit. It's like being from the Smoky Mountains or the backwoods of Mississippi. It's going to make you a certain type of person if you stay twenty years in one place. (Dylan in Jarosinski, 2006: 540)

And:

> You're pretty much ruled by nature up there . . . You have to sort of fall in line with that, regardless of how you're feeling that day or what you might

want to do with your life or what you think about. (Dylan in Jarosinski, 2006: 768)

These words speak volumes about Dylan's relationship with the environment. During six decades of output as a songwriter, poet and author he consistently alluded to animals, plants and geographic or meteorological phenomena – all repeatedly invoked as metaphors for social justice and moral behaviour. Even Dylan's earliest lyrics are littered with copious references to nature, and they draw on it as a source of instinctive inner truth and personal integrity. As noted in Chapter 3, his first anti-war song, 'Let Me Die in My Footsteps' (1962) culminated in a romantic appeal to the North American countryside, in a manner strongly reminiscent of Thoreau's pastoral tone:

> Let me drink from the waters where the mountain streams flood
> Let the smell of the wildflowers flow free through my blood
> Let me sleep in your meadows with the green grassy leaves
> Let me walk down the highway with my brother in peace
> Go out in your country where the land meets the sun
> See the craters and the canyons where the waterfalls run
> Nevada, New Mexico, Arizona, Idaho
> Let every state in this union seep down deep in your soul.
>
> (Bob Dylan, 'Let Me Die in My Footsteps')

'Last Thoughts on Woody Guthrie', a poem recited during his 1963 concert at New York City Town Hall, celebrated the natural splendour of the North American landscape as a source of moral authority:

> You'll find God in the church of your choice
> You'll find Woody Guthrie in Brooklyn State Hospital
> And though it's only my opinion
> I may be right or wrong
> You'll find them both
> In the Grand Canyon
> At sundown.
>
> (Bob Dylan, 'Last Thoughts on Woody Guthrie')

Meteorological symbolism constitutes Dylan's most persistent motif. When used to invoke moral imperatives, this technique is strikingly Thoreauvian. Dylan frequently employed *the sun* as a visual metaphor with brightness as an image of hope and sunset a symbol of closure, much as in Thoreau's *Walden* where, 'The setting sun is reflected from the windows of the almshouse as brightly as from the rich man's abode' (Thoreau, 1854: 247). Similar tropes appear in the verses reproduced above from 'Let Me Die in My Footsteps' and 'Last Thoughts on Woody Guthrie'. Other examples include the light dancing across a river at sunrise in 'Tomorrow Is a Long Time' (1962), plus the twilight that greeted Medgar Evars' assassin in 'Only a Pawn in Their Game', the setting sun in 'North Country Blues' and the rays that played across the 'Paths of Victory' – all of which feature on *The Times They Are a-Changin'* (1964).

Extremes of weather appear to function as signifiers of ethical or social injustice – with storms, of course, providing many ominous moments. Dangerous oceans and towering waves threatened Donald White in 'Ballad of Donald White' (1962); a menacing gale battered 'The Walls of Redwing' prison (1963); winds assailed the tormented farmer Hollis Brown in 'Ballad of Hollis Brown' (1964); a pause in the weather presaged the arrival of a hurricane in 'When the Ship Comes In' (1964); storms howled over the border in 'Girl From the North Country' (1963); and driving rain and hail muffled the 'Chimes of Freedom' (1964). Unlike Lennon, Dylan has never been politically militant – but the 1970s domestic terrorist group the Weather Underground Organization famously took their name from a meteorological analogy in 'Subterranean Homesick Blues' (1965).

'Blowin' in the Wind' (1963) provided Dylan's most commercially successful iteration of this metaphor. This song proffered an environmental agenda in the form of mountain, sea and sky, grounding its ethical questions in the landscape. The lyrics proposed no material remedy for the moral dilemmas they posed. Instead, each verse closed with the same force of nature: the wind. Rather than appealing to his audience's collective humanity, Dylan directed their attention towards a subjective interaction with their surroundings, invoking an ecological piety that resembled Emerson's 'Nature' (1844) and Thoreau's *Walden* (1854):

> Men say they know many things;
> But lo! they have taken wings—
> The arts and sciences,
> And a thousand appliances;
> The wind that blows
> Is all that anybody knows.
>
> (Thoreau, 1854: 68)

'A Hard Rain's a-Gonna Fall' (1963) employed *topographical* symbolism in the form of mountains, valleys, forests, oceans and the fauna that inhabit them – accompanied by familiar weather-related similes describing thunder, waves and rain. In a hallucinatory jeremiad the protagonist recounted visions of a natural world destroyed by pollution, famine, violence and decay. This composition substantiated the misgivings about industrial technology Thoreau expressed during his bucolic retreat at *Walden*: 'We do not ride on the railroad; it rides upon us' (Thoreau, 1854: 92). Dylan closed with a profound appeal to moral justice and natural law that embodied Emerson's plea for a poet who could 'fasten words' to the world, offering new political and social insights:

> And I'll tell it and think it and speak it and breathe it
> And reflect it from the mountain so all souls can see it
> Then I'll stand on the ocean until I start sinkin'
> But I'll know my song well before I start singin'
> (Bob Dylan, 'A Hard Rain's a-Gonna Fall')

'Lay Down Your Weary Tune' (1964) a celebrated out-take from *The Times They Are a-Changin'*, contained another powerful set of natural images. This song effectively linked the environmental dystopia of 'A Hard Rain's a-Gonna Fall' with the psychedelic vision of 'Mr Tambourine Man' (Heylin, 2010a):

> The last of leaves fell from the trees
> And clung to a new love's breast
> The branches bare like a banjo played
> To the winds that listened best
> (Bob Dylan, 'Lay Down Your Weary Tune')

British music critic and Dylan authority Michael Gray made a detailed appraisal of this recording after it was finally issued on *Biograph* (1985). He hailed 'Lay Down Your Weary Tune' as a 'universal melody' and an underrated masterpiece. Gray also acknowledged the typically European bias of his interpretation, which inevitably pointed towards literary sources from outside North America: 'As an Englishman, I automatically link the pantheism of Dylan's 'Lay Down Your Weary Tune' with Wordsworth' (Gray, 2008: 404). In correcting this mistake, however, Gray suggested an even *less* appropriate inspiration: J. R. R. Tolkien, an English fantasy author not normally considered a significant influence on Dylan. Gray certainly grasped the sentiment behind 'Lay Down Your Weary Tune' even if he could not identify its origin. Ironically, his analysis concluded with a heartfelt affirmation of Dylan's lyricism that neatly (although inadvertently) epitomised its transcendental roots:

> Never before or since has Dylan created a pantheistic vision – a vision of the
> world, that is, in which nature appears not as a manifestation of God but as

> containing God within every aspect … the idea of God as an evenly
> distributed presence suggesting a moral gulf between divinity in nature
> and the reductive inadequacy of man. (Gray, 2008: 404)

The environment remains an important element of Dylan's aesthetic to
this day. The topic of his inaugural Theme Time Radio Hour was
'weather' and the first track aired was Muddy Waters 'Blow Wind
Blow' (Dylan, 2006d). The title song of *Tempest* (2012) described the
storm that sank the Titanic using Shakespeare's famous tragicomedy.
Every other composition on this album seems to reference natural phenomena, from the old oak tree in opening track 'Duchesne Whistle' to
the south-bound trade winds of the long finale 'Roll on John'. Images of
plants, animals, seasons, landscapes, mountains, fountains, oceans, lakes,
forests, winds, sunrise, moonlight and – ironically, given the terminology
of Jameson's analytical framework – the horizon appear throughout
Rough and Rowdy Ways (2020), too. Dylan's memoir was also redolent
with naturalistic imagery. Recollections of a childhood in Duluth
describe 'slate grey skies and the mysterious foghorns, violent storms
that always seemed to be coming straight at you and merciless howling
winds off the big black mysterious lake with treacherous ten-foot waves'
(Dylan, 2004a: 230). An early chapter includes this characteristically
Thoreauvian observation:

> In nature there's a remedy for everything and that's where I'd usually
> go hunting for it. I'd find myself on a houseboat, a floating mobile
> home, hoping to hear a voice – crawling at low speed – nosed up on
> a protective beach at night in the wilderness – moose, bear, deer
> around – the elusive timber wolf not so far off, calm summer evenings
> listening to the call of the loon. Think things out. (Dylan, 2004a: 147)

Oftentimes, Dylan's idealistic images of nature were offset by images
portraying its antithesis: the deleterious consequences of industrial progress. Leo Marx's (2000) *The Machine in the Garden: Technology and the
Pastoral Ideal in America* provides useful context for his anxiety over the ill-
effects of the machine age. Marx explains how transcendentalist concerns
over the implications of the industrial revolution were articulated in the
recurring image of a pastoral scene interrupted by vulgar technology.
A steam train thundering through a bucolic landscape is probably the
most famous example. This 'machine in the garden' trope was common
throughout the nineteenth century and employed in one form or another
by prominent transcendentalists Emerson, Thoreau and Nathaniel

Hawthorne, plus in other works by George Inness, Washington Irving and Mark Twain.

More recently, David Pichaske (2010) extended the reach of Marx's 'machine in the garden' analogy, mapping it from the first industrial revolution in agrarian New England to the exploitation of natural resources in Minnesota. He traced the retreat of mythically pristine 'Virgin Territory' ever westward during the late nineteenth century, until the closure of the frontier caused it to slough back inland from the Pacific coast towards 'the still sparsely populated Upper Midwest ... Bob Dylan's backyard' (Pichaske, 2010: 109).[6] Here, on the new Iron Frontier of the Mesabi Iron Range, vast ore deposits around and underneath the mining settlement of Hibbing became the primary source of the most important raw material in every phase of the United States' industrial growth (Walker, 1979). From the Progressive Era and the Roaring Twenties through to the peak of Fordism during the 1950s long boom, and via two war economies in between, The Oliver Iron Mining Company and its owners US Steel entirely underpinned the prosperity of a town that grew from 'the world's richest village' to the region's most populous city. Their profits directly funded one of the best public schools in North America, Hibbing High, where the doorknobs were cut glass and the flagpole covered in gold leaf – at least according to rumour (Baeten, 2017). This is also, of course, where an enthusiastic young student by the name of Robert Zimmerman attended B. J. Rolfzen's legendary tenth grade English classes.

Yet the unrelenting mechanical extraction and indiscriminate environmental destruction that brought such miraculous economic good fortune to Hibbing also completely consumed the area around it. Indeed, the city still abuts the world's largest iron ore surface mine, the Hull–Rust–Mahoning Open Pit, now recognised as a National Historic Landmark and promoted to tourists as 'The Grand Canyon of the North' (see Figure 5.2). The physical displacement of an entire landscape remade the horizon from one direction to another and saw whole communities moved

---

[6] Henry Nash Smith's *Virgin Land: American West as Symbol and Myth* (1950), the monograph generally recognised as the foundational text of American Studies, and Frederick Jackson Turner's *The Frontier in American History* (1921) are the basis for this assertion. It is an interesting coincidence that Turner first published this work as an influential essay, 'The Significance of the Frontier in American History', in 1893 – the same year that the Minnesota mining town of Hibbing was founded by Frank Hibbing.

Figure 5.2 Miner John Palumbo Jr overlooking Hull–Rust–Mahoning Open Pit
Iron Mine, 1941, the year of Dylan's birth. Behind and below, at the foot of the pit, is
a full-size steam train and steam shovel. (Courtesy of the Library of Congress.)

'lock, stock and barrel' as they were swallowed by the vast excavations.
Dylan's (1964) eulogy for North Hibbing in '11 Outlined Epitaphs'
described how his home town relocated two miles southwards to grant

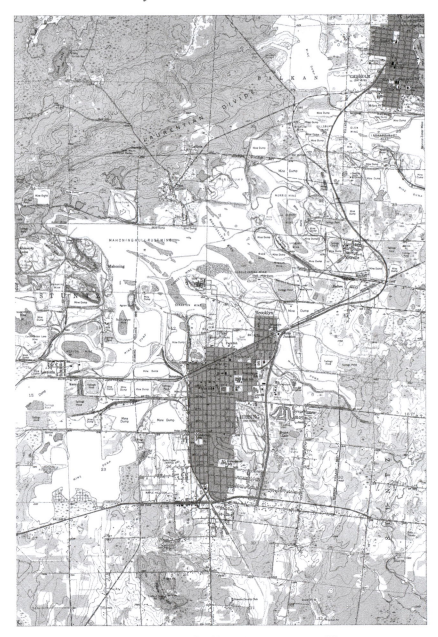

Figure 5.3 Topographical map of Hibbing, Minnesota, 1957. The town is surrounded on three sides (north, east, west) by iron ore mining operations. The white scar running diagonally through the centre of the image is Hull–Rust–Mahoning Open Pit Iron Mine, the largest of its type in the world, which has now entirely swallowed Hibbing's original location. The conspicuous bend in Route 169 shows the rerouting of this highway after the town's relocation in the 1920s. (Courtesy of the US Geological Survey.)

access to the iron ore that lay under its streets (see Figure 5.3).[7] Inevitably, this inexorable drive for industrial progress obliterated the natural history of the area, too. As regional newspaper *The Virginia Enterprise* noted when announcing the decision to fill Carson Lake, an important local recreational facility and beauty spot, with spoil: 'There are still fish in the lake, but like those found in Torch Lake in Michigan, pollution of the water from mining operations has caused them to go blind' (Baeten, 2017: 62).

· In this context, it is tempting to reimagine the toxic oceans and blackened tree boughs of 'A Hard Rain's a-Gonna Fall' as Dylan's eulogy for Carson Lake and the attractive woodland that once surrounded it. This song, however, is just one example of his displeasure at the consequences of industrial development. Here and elsewhere Dylan's idealistic visions of nature are repeatedly offset by foreboding and oppressive urban and industrial spaces. The natural world is a source of moral guidance in '11 Outlined Epitaphs' (Dylan, 1964), but it is we humans who pollute the oceans. The dust and dirt of the Midwest is clean and pure compared to the urban detritus of 'Hard Times in New York Town' (1962); a cityscape in 'Chimes of Freedom' (1964) is likened to the industrial image of a 'furnace'; urban vegetation in 'To Ramona' (1964) is like 'death'; the whole town of 'Tombstone Blues' (1965) is 'nervous'; and 'Desolation Row' (1965) is populated by an offbeat community of cultural icons and sideshow oddities. As Dylan acknowledged while reflecting on his body of work during a 1997 *New York Times* interview: 'Environment affects me a great deal ... My music, my songs, they have very little to do with *technology*' (Jarosinski, 2006: 1181, my italics).

In truth, with the possible exception of his 'going electric' in 1965, Dylan rarely extolled *any* form of mechanical or scientific progress.[8] Instead, the best-known artefacts and most useful inventions of Fordist industry tend only to generate a sense of unease in his work. Dylan's many disparaging references to cars and roads provide an interesting case study here. Automobile manufacturers were always significant consumers of US Steel, second only to the construction industry, and a substantial majority of their raw material was torn from the ground around Hibbing. Even today America's biggest car

[7] *No Direction Home,* the title of Robert Shelton's (1986) biography, of Martin Scorsese's (2005) documentary film and the refrain of Dylan's biggest hit 'Like a Rolling Stone' (1965) echoed Hibbing's fate as, literally, a town with 'no direction home'.

[8] In 1971, during an unpublished interview with his friend Tony Glover, Dylan even disparaged the recent series of Apollo moon landings: 'I couldn't get through the moon thing – it just didn't ring a bell.' 'Does it mean anything to you that man has walked on the moon?' 'No, it really doesn't' (Brinkley, 2020).

producer, General Motors, still claims to source up 90 per cent of its metal from US Steel (Terrarosa, 2018). As the first great creation of the Fordist consumer economy, cars became a universal symbol of individual freedom in the post-war long boom, and hit songs celebrating vehicles became an important element in North American popular music as a result. Robert Johnson's 'Terraplane Blues' (1937), Jackie Brenston's 'Rocket 88' (1951), Chuck Berry's 'Maybelline' (1955), Woody Guthrie's 'Riding in My Car' (1956), Beach Boys' 'Little Deuce Coupe' (1963), Jan and Dean's 'Drag City' (1963) and Wilson Pickett's 'Mustang Sally' (1966) are some better-known examples.

Indeed, Dylan was not shy of composing his own hard-travelling narratives. They feature in 'Standin' on the Highway' (1962), 'Down the Highway' (1963), 'Highway 61 Revisited' (1965) and 'Bob Dylan's 115th Dream' (1965). Unlike the artists listed above, however, Dylan seemed surprisingly reluctant to celebrate this technology in his lyrics. 'Bob Dylan's Blues' (1962) eschewed the idea of owning a fast car, while vehicles provided a source of danger and destruction in 'Percy's Song' (1963) and 'Motorpsycho Nightmare' (1964). In 'Talkin' World War III Blues' (1963) North America's most distinguished luxury motoring marque became a satirical device to accentuate the horrors of a post-apocalyptic landscape as Dylan traversed Manhattan's theatre district in a Cadillac. 'From a Buick 6' (1965) placed another high-end brand in ironic counterpoint against older items of machinery that included a steam shovel, the powered excavator responsible for stripping away much of the landscape around Hibbing, alongside images of decaying dumper trucks, broken pipelines and dirty junkyards. A similar depiction appeared later in the dismantled vehicles of 'Golden Loom', an out-take from the *Desire* (1976) album:

> I walk across the bridge in the dismal light
> Where all the cars are stripped between the gates of night
> (Bob Dylan, 'Golden Loom')

Dylan's monologue in the 'Cars' episode of Theme Time Radio Hour exemplified this trope. It synthesised the theme of industrial dystopia (the pollution and frustration of congested traffic) with his romantic view of nature (the dove, a universal symbol of peace and freedom) by invoking the moral law of the New Testament ('Oh, that I had wings like a dove! for then would I fly away and be at rest', Psalm 55:6):

> Taillights on the freeway tonight . . . they're backed up all the way to the big bridge. Oh! If I had wings like a dove. Oh! Would I fly away, fly right out above all that traffic out there. All them cars. Look at 'em all. So far off. So far so good. Over the hills, far away. Farewell! (Dylan, 2006a)

Table 5.4 *Cars, roads and industry in Dylan's lyrics, poetry and prose,*
1962–2004

Negative or dismissive remarks

'Bob Dylan's Blues' (1963)	The protagonist critiques sports cars
'I'd Hate to Be You on That Dreadful Day' (1964)	The subject cannot ride in their car
'Rainy Day Women #12 & 35' (1966)	The protagonist is stoned for driving a car
Melody Maker interview (1965)	'I have a little car, a Chevy. But it's a wreck. That's all I need, y'know'
Playboy Magazine interview (1966)	'My sympathy runs to the lame and crippled and beautiful things . . . I don't feel that for mechanical things like cars '
Chronicles: Vol. 1. (Dylan, 2004a: 79)	'[The pseudonym] Bob Allyn never would have worked, it sounded like a used-car salesman'

Malfunctioning vehicles, accidents

'Ballad for a Friend' (1962)	Dylan's friend is killed by a diesel truck leaving his family bereft
'Percy's Song' (1964)	Dylan's friend is in a crash in which four people die and he is held responsible
'This Wheel's on Fire' (1967)	The wheel explodes
'Shot of Love' (1981)	Dylan's car is not working properly
'Brownsville Girl' (1986)	The protagonist's car is broken down
'Honest with Me' (2001)	The protagonist crashed their car
Chronicles: Vol. 1. (Dylan, 2004a: 33)	'[Roy Orbison's voice] made you want to drive your car off a cliff'
Chronicles: Vol. 1. (Dylan, 2004a: 229–30)	'My father was from Duluth, born and raised there. When he was sixteen he'd seen a car smash into a telephone pole and burst into flames. He jumped off his bicycle, reached in and pulled the driver out, smothering the driver's body with his own, risking his life to save someone he didn't even know'

Abandoned vehicles, junkyards, economic wastelands, apocalyptic images

'Let Me Die in My Footsteps' (1962)	Dylan walks on a highway
'11 Outlined Epitaphs' (1963)	Images of a rusting Model T Ford
'Bob Dylan's Dream' (1963)	Dylan loses friends who have travelled different roads
'Talkin' World War III Blues' (1963)	Dylan dreams about driving a Cadillac during World War III
'A Hard Rain's a-Gonna Fall' (1963)	Dylan crawls on a road
'Chimes of Freedom' (1964)	The city as a furnace
'My Back Pages' (1964)	The roads are on fire
Hollywood Foto-Rhetoric: The Lost Manuscripts (1964)	Dylan has an accident in his sports car and runs to a phone booth but can't reach his wife or his best friend. He eventually abandons the vehicle in a panic and runs into the road, half blind

Table 5.4 (*cont.*)

'Black Crow Blues' (1964)	Dylan stands at the side of the road
'Mr Tambourine Man' (1964)	Streets are dead and empty
'Highway 61 Revisited' (1965)	Highway 61 is the site of the bleachers for people viewing the war
'Chimes of Freedom' (1965)	Fleeing refugees
'From a Buick Six' (1965)	A steam shovel and a dumper truck, machines that facilitated twentieth-century open cast mining and transformed the Minnesota Iron Range landscape
Tarantula (1971)	'Pearl Bailey stomps him against a Buick . . . / standing on a bullet holed volkswagen / my mind is blank . . . my eyes are two used car lots / he was so drunk that he fell in a barrel and a tractor being driven by some dogs ran over him and dumped him into a garage / you were on the street when that black car drove up and tossed some form in the river' (p. 8)
'When I Paint My Masterpiece' (1971)	The road is filled with rubble
'Shelter from the Storm' (1974)	The road is filled with mud
'Golden Loom' (1975)	A junkyard at night
'Señor (Tales of Yankee Power)' (1978)	Opens with the question of which way the protagonist is headed, down Lincoln County Road or towards Armageddon
'Cry a While' (2001)	The road is melting
Chronicles: Vol. 1. (Dylan, 2004a; 233)	'Dirt stock car racing on cool summer nights, mostly '49 or '50 Fords, bashed in cars, coffin contraptions, humpbacked cage . . . bumpin' and ramblin', slammin' and swivlin' on a half mile track, summersaulting [sic] off the rails . . . tracks littered with junkyard cars'
'Beyond Here Lies Nothin' (2009)	Broken down cars

'The road' as a signifier of poverty and oppression

'He Was a Friend of Mine' (1961)	A homeless man dies on the road
'Long Ago, Far Away' (1962)	Another beggar on a city street
'Standing on the Highway' (1962)	Dylan can't secure a ride at the roadside
'Quit Your Low Down Ways' (1962)	The protagonist is standing alone at the roadside
'Last Thoughts on Woody Guthrie' (1963)	A poor man walks on a road
'Blowin' in the Wind' (1963)	A man walks on a road
'Only a Hobo' (1963)	A homeless man on the road
'Paths of Victory' (1964)	The road is bumpy and hard

Table 5.4 (*cont.*)

'Guess I'm Doing Fine' (1964)	The road is unstable
'I Am a Lonesome Hobo' (1967)	A street beggar

Associations between cars and heartbreak

'Highway 51' (1962)	Dylan is buried on Highway 51
'Quit Your Low Down Ways' (1962)	The protagonist can't use a car and has to hitchhike
'Don't Think Twice, It's All Right' (1962)	The road is dark and lonely
'Down the Highway' (1963)	Dylan is walking on a deserted road
'One Too Many Mornings' (1964)	Dogs are barking on a street
'Motorpsycho Nightmare' (1964)	Dylan runs down a road
'Tombstone Blues' (1965)	Dylan is in the street
'It's All Over Now, Baby Blue' (1965)	The road is risky
'Visions of Johanna' (1966)	The road gives Mona Lisa the blues
'Leopard Skin Pill-Box Hat' (1966)	Dylan uses sex in a garage, presumably on or in a car, as a slur
'Broke Down Engine' (1993)	The car is broken down
Chronicles: Vol. 1. (Dylan, 2004a: 9, 20, 59, 121, 147, 241, 276, 292)	'Icy roads ...' '...happiness isn't on the road to anything' 'He shot at us in the dark down a gravel road' 'I had never intended to be on the road of heavy consequences and I didn't like it' 'The road had narrowed ...' '... same road full of the same contradictions' 'She took one turn in the road and I took another' 'The road out would be treacherous, and I didn't know where it would lead'

A catalogue of Dylan's various references to cars, roads and associated industrial or urban images reveals many other examples of this alienation. Table 5.4 displays these song titles and interview comments, organised according to five categories: negative or dismissive remarks; malfunctioning vehicles and accidents; abandoned vehicles and apocalyptic imagery; 'the road' as a signifier of poverty and oppression; cars and personal heartache. Here, Dylan's unease over the pernicious consequences of Fordist industrial development is laid bare.

This sense of foreboding around industrial and transport technology remains palpable even in Dylan's most recent non-musical output. His first fine art exhibition, *The Drawn Blank Series* (2008), featured 'Train Tracks' – a striking image of railway lines under an ominous skyline. This was followed by *The Beaten Path* (2016, 2017, 2019), a collection of landscape paintings whose title encapsulated their road-weary nostalgia. Here, the bleak image of 'Endless Highway' (see Figure 5.4) stood out alongside other depictions of tired-looking bridges, motels and vehicles. Between these came a striking set of sculptures: *Mood Swings, Iron Works* (2013) (see Figure 5.5). These large ornate metal gates, hand-welded by Dylan using vintage scrap items, confirmed his lifelong connection to America's industrial heritage: 'I've been around iron all my life ever since I was a kid. I was born and raised in iron ore country – where you could breathe it and smell it every day. And I've always worked with it in one form or another' (Dylan in Kelly, 2013: 11).

Dylan and the transcendentalists both straddled significant periods of economic and social change in Jameson's third horizon, evolving modes

Figure 5.4 'Endless Highway', *Bob Dylan: The Beaten Path* at Halcyon Gallery, London, 2016. (© WENN Rights Ltd / Alamy Stock Photo)

Figure 5.5 'Untitled VI' from *Bob Dylan: Mood Swings, Iron Works* at Halcyon Gallery, London, 2013. (© PA Images / Alamy Stock Photo)

of production, and the tensions generated by these underlying developments are apparent throughout their work. Emerson and Thoreau witnessed the frictions between agrarianism and emergent industrial capitalism: 'the last struggle of the liberal spirit of the eighteenth century in conflict with the rising forces of exploitation' (Matthiessen, 1941: ix). Leo Marx captured the menace of this transformation via the trope of a 'machine in the garden', or the sudden appearance of a train interrupting a rural idyll. More than a century later Dylan's reverence for nature and his distaste for industrial progress reflected the irresolvable dichotomy between environment and economy at the height of Fordist mass production. These contradictions came to a head in a series of economic crises during the 1970s that eventually resolved into technology-driven globalised capitalism and contemporary postmodern culture. In this respect, perhaps the most significant attribute Dylan shared with his transcendentalist forebears was their common role as cultural mediators between conflicting sensibilities at a time of increasing disharmony in the economic and social superstructure.

Eric Lott's (1993) history of blackface minstrelsy, *Love and Theft*, offers a helpful comparison in respect of the interactions between culture and the economy at this point. It drew heavily on Fredric Jameson's work to show how minstrelsy, the most prolific form of public entertainment in the mid-nineteenth century, embodied tensions between two antagonistic modes of production: southern feudalism and northern capitalism:

> every social formation resides not in a single mode of economic production but in a complex overlay of several modes at once, with residual modes now subordinated to the dominant one and emergent modes potentially disruptive of it ... To the extent that competing economic modes (and their networks of ideological self-representation) coexist at any given moment, so will clash and conflict occur in the realm of culture, dominant or not and even in the space of a single text. (Lott, 1993: 220)

The phenomenon of blackface minstrelsy represented the social dialectics of the mid-nineteenth century in a series of collisions between opposing interests: African American and European American, rural and metropolitan, agriculture and industry. The title of Lott's book encapsulated these themes. Dylan later appropriated it for one of his own albums, using speech marks on the sleeve artwork to recognise the quotation: '*Love and Theft*' (2001). It is possible to think of his reverence towards nature and his suspicion towards progress in the same binary terms as those used by Lott. In Dylan's life and work the natural world was decimated by industrial developments, his rural aesthetic moulded by urban tastes, in much the same way as – perhaps symbolically – the acoustic guitar of his early folk performances was drowned out by the electric amplifiers in his mid-1960s rock band. After all, the relationship between country and city, the natural world and human progress, is wholly determined by changing modes of production – not least because every industrial revolution attracts mass migration to urban areas.[9]

Lott showed how cultural developments in northern towns entirely redefined the image of southern states during the nineteenth century. Similarly, Thoreau's experience of 'life in the woods' at Walden Pond was shaped in many ways by the adjacent town of Concord and other nearby settlements. His circumstances would certainly have been different had these resources not been so readily accessible. Even the train that interrupted Thoreau's bucolic lifestyle only existed to connect Concord to larger destinations at either end of the newly constructed Boston to

---

[9] Fredric Jameson's *The Political Unconscious* is structured around his critique of Northrop Frye's analysis of Romanticism. Frye underestimated the economics of culture and mistook the environment as a 'natural' phenomenon, not something shaped by the dominant mode of production, a specific creation of '*social* and *historical*' circumstances (Jameson, 1981: 112, my italics).

Fitchburg route. Much of the iron ore extracted from around Hibbing ended up in the cars, trucks, bridges and skyscrapers of New York City – from where Greenwich Village's urban folk revival sculpted the romanticised images of nature heard in 'Lay Down Your Weary Tune', 'A Hard Rain's a-Gonna Fall' and 'Blowin' in the Wind'. These songs in turn contributed to a longstanding discourse around the complex and uneven relationship between agriculture and industry, nostalgia and progress, wood and steel, acoustic and electric – just as the engine of capitalism shifted gears into its current mode of globalised production. If, as Jacques Attali (1985) famously claimed, music really can presage fundamental economic developments, Dylan seemed unusually receptive to these possibilities.

Conclusion: Dylan's and Lennon's Distinctive Historicity

Fredric Jameson's framework reveals many differences as well as similarities between Dylan's and Lennon's approach to history. In the first horizon of *individual utterances or artefacts* Lennon drew on Victorian and Edwardian imperial tropes familiar from the English literature and popular culture of his formative years, whereas Dylan's perspective had more in common with nineteenth-century North American transcendentalism. In Jameson's second horizon, *class discourse*, Lennon identified with his Irish migrant heritage and British working-class culture to such an extent that he sympathised with revolutionaries such as the International Marxist Group, the IRA and Jerry Rubin of the Youth International Party – although he never fully accepted historical materialism and remained more convinced by the need for a subjective 'change from within'. As such, Vedic philosophy constituted the most consistent and significant influence on his worldview. In contrast, Dylan rejected class politics and embodied the transcendentalist principle of obdurate individualism, despite the significant personal and commercial challenges this entailed.

Jameson's third horizon, *the underlying mode of production*, elicited other levels of contrast. The perspective offered by this model, plus the additional context provided by Henry W. Sullivan, Leo Marx and Eric Lott, showed how underlying economic changes can manifest in cultural artefacts. The Beatles' commercial high-water mark, *Sgt. Pepper's Lonely Hearts Club Band*, was a sonic masterpiece that reinvented the norms of popular music production. This success established EMI Records as a global media company and provided an early example of postmodern multinational capitalism. Ironically, it transpired that Lennon's Victorian nostalgia helped position his band as global ambassadors for Swinging London during the final dissolution of the British Empire. At the same time, Dylan's aversion to technology fostered a recording aesthetic in which every LP he cut captured only the spontaneous performance of natural sounds, with almost no editing, overdubbing, remixing or studio effects (Negus, 2010). This culminated in the austere *John Wesley Harding*, taped in just twelve hours with an out of tune acoustic guitar and no overdubs. Here, Dylan's correlations with transcendentalist figures such as Emerson and Thoreau provide a useful point of comparison. While the latter voiced anxieties over the *birth* of industrial capitalism, Dylan articulated the tensions occasioned by its *decline*.

In this context both Lennon's postcolonial tropes and Dylan's romantic pastoralism attest to deeper concerns about the friction between residual and emergent structures of society. For Jameson, successive stages of capitalism determined the culture dominant in each epoch, and some element of that relationship is present in every artefact or text. Dylan's and Lennon's greatest achievements were rooted in their ability to recognise and articulate these era-defining social and economic changes – which is why their output was so distinctive at the time, and why it is still so relevant today.

CHAPTER 6

Dylan, Lennon and Spirituality

Introduction

Previous chapters examined the issues around collective action and shared history in Dylan's and Lennon's music. Chapter 3 looked at protest music's role in mobilising in-group solidarity, and Chapters 4 and 5 aligned their output with economic and social developments over the preceding two centuries. These themes have a wider context, of course. From a long-term perspective, this is what we call *prehistory*: that which occurred before the existence of written records in culture and society. Karl Marx alluded to prehistoric conditions in his references to 'primitive communism' – the mode of production among hunter-gatherer tribes. This chapter expands on this concept using evolutionary psychology, a form of inquiry that asks how modern human preferences and thought patterns were shaped by long-standing pressures on survival and reproduction. It offers a compelling explanation for tropes and behaviours common throughout human cultures and settles many time-worn debates about who we *think* we are, and who we *really* are.

While the discussion of Dylan's and Lennon's anti-war protest songs and their historical context employed a Marxist analysis associated with the New Left, the subject of spirituality is more closely aligned with that other significant strand of 1960s activism, the North American *counterculture*. Supernatural precepts were largely antithetical to the historical materialism propounded by New Left writers and campaigners; however, the counter-culture's emphasis on personal well-being encouraged a focus on concepts such as connectedness, mind-expansion and self-realisation. Jack Kerouac, Kathleen Kinkade, Ram Dass and other prominent individuals promulgated various combinations of Eastern spirituality, Western esotericism, indigenous practices, communal lifestyles and altered states of consciousness. This chapter explains the evolutionary origins of these practices and beliefs, and evaluates the wide range of supernatural tropes in Dylan's and

Lennon's output. It achieves this by using four key criteria from J. Anderson Thomson's and Clare Aukofer's (2011) work on the psychology of faith: mind–body dualism, agency attribution, evolved moral systems and teleology.[1] It also draws on Daniel Kahneman's (2011) model of 'fast and slow' thinking and Richard Thalbourne's 'Transliminality Scale' (Thalbourne and Delin, 1999). It concludes by suggesting new directions for research with reference to Robert J. Lifton's (1961) classic study of in-group thought reform.

Dylan's and Lennon's Spirituality

The terms 'spirituality' and 'religion' are often used interchangeably, but they are not entirely synonymous. Religion can be defined as the belief in and worship of a divine supernatural authority, accompanied by a system of practice that engenders and reinforces this faith (Durkheim et al., 2001). The word derives from the Latin *religio*, an obligation or bond. Spirituality denotes the subjective sense of interaction with a transcendent higher power. It can be a spontaneous overwhelming experience, as in St Paul's Damascene conversion, or an incremental process. William James (1929) characterised the latter as a 'volitional' spiritual awakening. An individual's sense of spirituality can be reinforced by group worship practices. Witnessing, rituals, services, festivals and feasts all bolster a religious community's collective spirituality, and most religious people naturally consider themselves spiritual by default.

In the Judeo–Christian tradition inherited by Dylan and Lennon, spirituality is usually expressed through a personal relationship with God. For Christians, this is via Jesus and the Holy Spirit. Together these elements constitute the Trinity: The Father, The Son, and The Holy Ghost. The concept of the Holy Spirit is sometimes likened to a divine wind.[2] This notion probably originated with the Israelite storm deity Yahweh, an *air god* who dwelt in the firmament above – rather than in water, or fire, or under the earth. Air gods such as Yahweh were born from the lack of knowledge, during the early Iron Age, about the physiology of the human respiratory system or the particulate constituents of our atmosphere. Hence, the etymology of 'spirituality' in the Latin *spiritus*, which

---

[1] Thomson's (2009b) popular *YouTube* lecture 'Why We Believe in God(s)' is an excellent introduction to this subject: https://youtu.be/1iMmvu9eMrg.

[2] Jesus used this metaphor, for example, in John 3:8: 'The wind blows where it wishes, and you hear its sound, but cannot tell where it comes from, and where it goes. So is everyone who is born of the Spirit.'

itself comes from *spirare*, to breathe (Ra, 2016). Following his conversion to evangelical Christianity in the late 1970s, Bob Dylan embraced this mode of spirituality: 'I'm not a believer in that born-again type thing. Jesus told Nicodemus, "A man must be born again". And Nicodemus said, "How can I go through my mother's womb?" and Jesus said, "You must be born of *the Spirit*". And that's where that comes from, that born-again thing' (Dylan in Jarosinski, 2006: 883, my italics).

In a non-religious context, spirituality also denotes a subjective sense of communication with a benevolent supernatural presence. This metaphysical connectedness often occurs outside the traditional codes of institutional practice. The popular trope 'spiritual but not religious' refers to self-defined individuals unaffiliated to the Abrahamic faiths or any other mainstream doctrines. John Lennon migrated from a Judeo–Christian concept of spirituality, the legacy of his Roman Catholic upbringing, to one founded in the Vedic tradition, and consistently espoused a 'spiritual but not religious' worldview in his lyrics and public statements during and after his Beatles career: 'I believe in God, but not as one thing, not as an old man in the sky. I believe that what people call God is something in all of us. I believe that what Jesus and Mohammed and Buddha and all the rest said was right. It's just that the translations have gone wrong' (Lennon in Wiener, 1991: 15).

Non-Christian spirituality can also incorporate panpsychism, pantheism and other iterations of universal consciousness. Indeed, Lennon repeated the metaphysical assertion that 'if there is a God, we're all it' (Wenner, 2000: 48) in songs and statements throughout his adult life:

> I don't and never did imagine God as one thing. But now I can see God as a power source – or as an energy. But you can't see any kind of energy . . . only track it on radar or things like that. You can be aware of your own energy and all the energy that's around you. All the energy is God. Your own energy and their energy, whether doing god-like things or ungodly things. It's all like one big jelly. We're all in the big jelly. (Lennon, 1967)

Being less reliant on conventional schools of thought, non-religious spirituality is often relatively fluid and can bring together loosely correlated concepts such as environmentalism, feminism, non-traditional medicine, neo-paganism and shamanism. Personal connectivity with a supernatural force can also align with other esoteric precepts. For example, an individual who identifies as spiritually enlightened is more likely to believe in the possibility of alien visitations, extrasensory perception, ghosts and other paranormal phenomena (Thalbourne and Delin, 1999). By definition, spiritual people also subscribe to *vitalism*: the notion that biologically active matter possesses a life force distinct from its observable chemical properties. Many cultures offer their own explanation for this organic energy: *qi* in China, *mana* in Polynesia, *orenda* for indigenous Iroquois, the ancient Germanic *Od*, the Sanskrit word *prana* or Aristotle's concept of *entelechy*. Prior to his evangelical Christianity, Dylan cited a pantheistic muse as the stimulus for his own vitalism in 'Something There Is About You' (1973): 'Suddenly I found you and the spirit in me sings / Don't have to look no further, you're the soul of many things.'

An individual's faith practices and their acceptance of numinous forces can determine their sense of self, their attitude towards others and their individual goals. Dylan's complex and fluctuating relationship with Judeo–Christian traditions, which varied from a transcendentalist piety towards nature to the totalising experience of biblical evangelism, helped define his worldview – just as Lennon's advocacy for 'spiritual but not religious' Vedic thought shaped his. Previous chapters showed how each held contrasting attitudes towards protest music and history, and how their perspectives were informed, in part, by different forms of spirituality. This chapter examines the psychological processes behind that faith, the common evolutionary factors underlying their beliefs. Each invoked various forms of 'the spirit' in their lyrics, texts, interviews and other creative output, and these impulses provided the inspiration for some of their most impactful and long-lasting compositions – from the oblique metaphors of 'I Dreamed I Saw St Augustine' (1967) and 'The Word' (1965), via interpretations of religious texts in 'All Along the Watchtower' (1967) and 'Tomorrow Never Knows' (1966), to the direct petition of a higher power in 'Every Grain of Sand' (1981) or 'Across the Universe' (1969).

The affinity between art and spirituality has been a popular area for academic research. Some view the composition of music as a uniquely imaginative means of self-expression and connectivity. Others identify psycho-spiritual elements in moments of creative inspiration or liken such fleeting experiences to the thought patterns of dream states.[3] It is a common trope among songwriters and performers, too. U2's Bono defined the connecting thread between any songwriter's sense of the numinous and their creative practice as 'the point where craft ends and spirit begins' (Calhoun, 2012: 158).

Scholarly inquiry into Dylan's and Lennon's output has certainly intensified over the last two decades and their spirituality has become an inviting

---

[3] See Cobb, 2016; Coleman, 1998; Ehrlich, 1997; Miller and Cook-Greuter, 2000; Sylvan, 2002; Wuthnow, 2001.

topic as writers jostle for space in a crowded field. Christopher Ricks (2011) examined Dylan's 'visions of sin' and Stephen H. Webb (2006) explored his evangelical conversion. Mark Flory (2012) cast him as 'postmodern prophet', Michael J. Gilmour (2011) as a religious luminary, Jeff Taylor and Chad Israelson (2017) as a 'Christian anarchist' and Seth Rogovoy (2010) as an esoteric poet. Turning to the Beatles, Matthew Schneider (2008) evaluated the band's prodigious mysticism, while Steve Turner (2006) portrayed them as gospel exemplars. Outside the confines of popular music, Rogan P. Taylor (1985) and Chris Rojek (2001) have compared the phenomenon of celebrity to long-standing religious traditions. This chapter builds on this work to produce a new form of interdisciplinary scholarship combining two approaches rarely employed in popular music or cultural studies: *ontological naturalism* and *evolutionary psychology*.

Ontological Naturalism and Evolutionary Psychology

Ontological naturalism claims that we inhabit a single plane of existence whose limits are constrained entirely by the material world and whose structure is governed solely by its natural laws. As these forces operate and interact exclusively in the observable universe, it regards the scientific method as the only reliable means of investigating reality. *Evolutionary psychology* is a naturalistic approach to psychology. It argues that the selection mechanisms which explain any species' material form also account for its rudimentary mindset. If the human brain and our experience of consciousness can ultimately be reduced to biochemistry, the evolutionary forces that determined our basic anatomy and physiology must also have shaped our underlying thought processes, too. 'In essence', argues J. Anderson Thomson, 'there is no such thing as a *non*-evolutionary psychology, psychoanalysis, or theory of behaviour' (Thomson, 2009a: 26). Thomson and Clare Aukofer's (2011) *Why We Believe in God(s): A Concise Guide to the Science of Faith* collated recent peer-reviewed research to show how evolutionary selection processes shaped human thinking in ways that propagated and reinforced spirituality and religion. They sought to explain, once and for all, 'why and how our minds manufacture and spread belief in god(s)' (Thomson and Aukofer, 2011: xvi).

This chapter deconstructs Dylan's and Lennon's spirituality by mapping their lyrics, prose, statements and activities against Thomson and Aukofer's criteria. Four cognitive mechanisms are discussed, beginning with the most significant: *mind–body dualism*. This is followed by *hyperactive agency detection*, *evolved moral systems* and *promiscuous teleology*.

These tools enable a new and robust evaluation of the faith tropes in Dylan's and Lennon's music. The results hint at innovative possibilities for ongoing research as this technique may be repurposed to explore the religiosity in any other artist's output. It might also reveal what is going on in the relationship between creativity and spirituality or explain some of the unusual supernatural beliefs sometimes associated with performing and writing music. For example, virtually all scientists and most citizens in Europe and North America accept the reality of human evolution, but there was a period in Dylan's and Lennon's lives when both publicly rejected this proposition. Dylan embraced young earth creationism with gusto at the end of the 1970s: 'This earth supposedly has a certain number of years which I think is 7,000 years, 7,000 or 6,000. We're in the last cycle of it now . . . I go strictly according to the Gospels' (Jarosinski, 2006: 748–9). Around the same time Lennon denied human evolution in one of his final interviews:

> Nor do I think we came from monkeys, by the way . . . That's another piece of garbage. What the hell's it based on? We couldn't have come from anything – fish, maybe, but not monkeys. I don't believe in the evolution of fish to monkeys to men. Why aren't monkeys changing into men now? It's absolute garbage. It's absolutely irrational garbage. (Lennon in Lennon et al., 1981: 95)

As these quotes demonstrate, just because Dylan and Lennon were both creative artists of great intensity with extraordinary sensitivity to change, this does not also mean that they were incapable of being spectacularly wrong in the most important existential and scientific matters. They may have written songs that changed the course of popular culture, but that did not make them immune to irrational ideas. This chapter examines Dylan's and Lennon's lyrics, quotes and other texts to uncover the evolutionary psychology behind these beliefs and practices.

Mind–Body Dualism: Consciousness and the Soul

Mind–body dualism holds that there is something more to the mind than simply a working brain. It is, by definition, antithetical to ontological naturalism because it suggests that our mental processes include non-material elements, phenomena that exist separately to our physical selves. This notion dates to the pre-Christian metaphysics of the Buddha and Plato, and was refined by Rene Descartes in the early modern era. As a worldview that cleaves the cognitive from the corporeal, dualism allows us to imagine the possibility of a soul. As such, it provides the philosophical basis for many forms of religious and non-religious spirituality and has a nuanced and prolonged relationship with a wide range of theological doctrines.

In separating the mental processes of the brain from the physiological mechanisms of the body, dualism also raises the conundrum of human consciousness. This is the 'mind' part of mind–body dualism, the great mystery of how and why we are self-aware, sometimes framed as one of the natural world's truly intractable enigmas. David Chalmers (1995) codified this as the 'hard problem of consciousness' by positing that qualia and other emotional human experiences can *never* be explained by our neurological capacities. Conversely, for Thomson and Aukofer (2011) subjective consciousness is simply the emergent property of complex cognitive systems. It arises from intricately interconnected synaptic networks, is fully accountable by the basic constituents of brain matter, and evolved in parallel with our physiological development. This why, they argue, we can observe the phenomenon at different levels in other species and can locate its neurological correlates using brain-imaging technology.

Natural philosophers and scientists began to make more forceful claims for the mechanistic explanations of consciousness around the turn of the twenty-first century. Dan Dennett (1993) argued that there is no meaningful evidence for the phenomenon of qualia posited by Chalmers and, as a consequence, there is also no 'hard problem' to solve. As Steven Pinker (2003) explained, the mind is simply the product of a working brain. V. S. Ramachandran (2005: 3) posited that given the vast permutations of connections between neurons and synapses our possible brain states may exceed the number of elementary particles in the known universe: 'all the richness of our mental life . . . is simply the activity of these little specks of jelly in your head, in your brain. There is nothing else'. Michael Graziano's (2013) Attention Schema Theory sought to prove consciousness as an inevitable emergent property of biological evolution. For Thomson and Aukofer (2011: 6), this discourse fundamentally re-ordered our perception of the profane and the divine, as it means that humans made God and not the other way around: 'We are risen apes, not fallen angels – and we now have the evidence to prove it.'

These developments have significant consequences for the study of human spirituality over the last decade. Yet Dylan and Lennon came of age in the 1960s, a time when such ideas were not well-represented in popular culture. Robert Ardrey's (1961) trailblazing monograph *African Genesis: A Personal Investigation into the Animal Origins and Nature of Man* was a popular bestseller on its release, but its hypothesis remained an outlier opinion for several decades to come. Ardrey does not feature in either songwriter's known reading, and his revolutionary paleo-anthropology is not referenced in any interviews. So long as the possibility of an evolutionary origin to consciousness remained relatively obscure, it was only natural that Dylan's and Lennon's instinctive cognitive bias for mind–body dualism should promote their unquestioning acceptance of this concept.

Moreover, as philosophical idealists the phenomenon of consciousness was ascribed with considerable privilege for Dylan and Lennon. Moments of distorted or heightened perception were interpreted as opportunities for transcendent communication, unexplained inspiration and visionary insight in the creative process of music-making. They and their contemporaries attributed extraordinary properties to the altered mental states generated by meditation, flights of the imagination, chemical stimulation or various forms of cognitive impairment (Partridge, 2017). Numerous songs from the late 1960s reference this trope, including Paul McCartney's 'The Fool on the Hill' (1967) and George Harrison's 'Within You Without You' (1967).[4] Indeed, it contributed to the rise of 'introspective' protest music identified by R. Serge Denisoff and discussed in Chapter 3. The phenomenon is not restricted to songwriters, of course. Michel Foucault argued that throughout history eccentric characters and idiosyncratic artists were considered gifted with a unique perspective that allowed them to critique or expose prevailing power structures: 'For the madness of men is a divine spectacle' (Foucault, 1965: 28). Many instances of spiritual wisdom, supernatural revelation or esoteric knowledge have based their truth claims on insights derived from altered consciousness, too. Texts such as the Old and New Testaments, the Quran, the Book of Mormon, Alistair Crowley's (1909) *Liber AL vel Legis: The Book of the Law* and L. Ron Hubbard's (1968) *Dianetics: The Modern Science of Mental Health* all draw on variants of automatic writing, fasting, meditation and trance. Other parallels exist between popular music performance and shamanism, for example, where participants exhibit a state of flow or experience elevated self-awareness (Bashwiner, 2018; St John, 2017).

---

[4] Consider also, Keith Richards and Mick Jagger's 'Paint It Black' (1966); Brian Wilson's 'God Only Knows' (1966) and 'Good Vibrations' (1966); Grace Slick's 'White Rabbit' (1967); Jimi Hendrix's 'Purple Haze' (1967); and Laura Nyro's 'Stoned Soul Picnic' (1968).

Dylan's Mind–Body Dualism

Many of Dylan's keenest literary influences were steeped in mind–body dualism. These include William Blake, Jack Kerouac, William S. Burroughs, Arthur Rimbaud, Allen Ginsberg and E. E. Cummings (Dylan, 2004a; Gray, 2008; Heylin, 2011; Long, 2002). Dylan has also spoken about the importance of remaining open to numinous and supernatural influences in his songwriting practice. He explained his role in the composition of his best-selling single 'Like a Rolling Stone' (1965) as merely a conduit for the mystical forces that delivered the composition: 'It's like a ghost is writing a song like that. It just gives you the song and it goes away, it goes away. You don't know what it means. Except the ghost picked me to write the song' (Dylan in Jarosinski, 2006: 1339).

Dylan's memoir *Chronicles: Volume 1* cited several works apparently gifted from the ether. Examples from *Oh Mercy* (1989) include 'What Good Am I?', where, 'The entire song came to me all at once. I don't know what could have brought it on' (Dylan, 2004a: 167); 'What Was It You Wanted?', when, 'The song almost wrote itself. It just descended upon my head' (Dylan, 2004a: 172); 'Shooting Star', where, 'I didn't write it so much as I inherited it' (Dylan, 2004a: 212); and 'Disease of Conceit', in which: 'The song came in ready form and not a thing was changed about it. The night we recorded it, there was a lightning storm outside – leaves slapping on the banana trees. Something was guiding the song. It was like Joan of Arc was out there' (Dylan, 2004a: 212–13).

The genres that most influenced Dylan's music, such as Mississippi Delta blues, were grounded in mind–body dualism, too. Overt religiosity allied with an equally sincere belief in demons and ghosts lie behind some of the most celebrated blues narratives, most notably Robert Johnson's story of selling his everlasting soul to the Devil at 'the crossroads'. 'Crossroad Blues' and 'Hellhound on My Trail' leaned heavily on this familiar trope. In 'Malted Milk', Johnson recalls a supernatural encounter in which his bedroom door opens and ghosts enter the room. A handwritten death letter subsequently found among his family paperwork, now inscribed on his gravestone, made an earnest claim for redemption: 'Jesus of Nazareth, King of Jerusalem. I know that me Redeemer liveth and that He will call me from the grave' (Pearson and McCulloch, 2010: 10).

When Dylan first heard Robert Johnson's *King of the Delta Blues Singers* (1961) he listened in awe. His recollection of the experience in *Chronicles: Volume 1* itself resembled a Johnson song: 'it felt like a ghost had come into the room, a fearsome apparition' (Dylan, 2004a: 285). Dylan makes six other references to hauntings in the memoir beginning with: 'On the same block was the Bull's Head, a cellar tavern where John Wilkes Booth, the American Brutus, used to drink. I'd been in there once and saw his ghost in the mirror – an ill spirit' (Dylan, 2004a: 25). This ongoing preoccupation is revealed elsewhere in his conspicuous use of spectral encounters and fascination with 'legend, myth, bible and ghosts' (Dylan in Jarosinski, 2006: 174). 'Tombstone Blues' (1965) features the ghost of Belle Starr. Joan Baez's character in *Renaldo and Clara* (1978), the Woman in White, was: 'the ghost of Death – Death's ghost … the ghost of Clara's former self' (Dylan in Jarosinski, 2006: 528). *Tarantula* (1971) contains nine different phantom characters or metaphors. 'Lenny Bruce' (1981) lived on in spirit after his death.

Dylan's early allusions to *religious* forms of mind–body dualism, usually via the existence of a non-material soul or the sense of a spiritual connection to God, were more nuanced and self-aware than his supernatural references – almost as if they were attenuated by the unusual circumstances of his own upbringing. Jewish communities on the Minnesotan Iron Range were modest in size and relatively isolated, and Dylan's family was one of perhaps forty observant kosher households in his hometown (Weber, 2014). He attended cheder at Hibbing's only synagogue and spent summers at the Zionist 'Camp Herzl' from 1954 to 1958 but later acknowledged: 'There weren't too many Jews in Hibbing, Minnesota … I've never felt Jewish. I don't really consider myself Jewish or non-Jewish. I don't have much of a Jewish background' (Jarosinski, 2006: 553). Indeed, Dylan received a mainstream education in a predominantly Catholic and Lutheran environment, and clearly became familiar with both the Old and the New Testament as a result. He has referenced both documents consistently in his lyrics, from his very first compositions to his most recent releases. 'What You Gonna Do?' (1962), one of his earliest recordings, alludes to the first miracle attributed to Jesus – the transformation of water into wine during the Wedding at Cana; 'Forever Young' (1974) begins with the Priestly Blessing from the Old Testament's Book of Numbers: 'May God bless and keep you always'; while his current album *Rough and Rowdy Ways* (2020) mentions the Holy Grail, the Lord's Prayer, and many other biblical tropes.

Of course, whenever such lyrics advance the possibility of a human soul they inevitably invoke mind–body dualism. 'In My Time of Dying' (1962), an early interpretation of a traditional deathbed blues, was inspired by Psalm 41:3 ('The Lord will strengthen him upon the bed of languishing, thou wilt make all his bed in his sickness'). As his spirit ascends to heaven, literally rising through the air, the protagonist cries out for Jesus as he passes into the firmament. By contrast 'I'd Hate to Be You on That Dreadful Day' (1964) described the unfortunate circumstances of a condemned soul being turned away from salvation at St Peter's gate. In 'II Outlined Epitaphs', the sleeve notes for *The Times They Are a-Changin'* (1964), Dylan walked alongside a spectre risen from the ground, a narrative that echoed St Paul's encounter in *I* Samuel 28:7–20: 'I see a ghostly figure coming up out of the earth'. An angelic cowboy rode through the 'Gates of Eden' (1964). Dr Filth's nurse asked the Lord to grant mercy on the souls of the deceased in 'Desolation Row' (1965). The protagonist of 'I Dreamed I Saw St Augustine' (1968) had a vision of long-dead fourth-century Christian theologian St Augustine of Hippo. After his evangelical conversion in November 1978, Dylan's lyrics and interviews suddenly presented theological mind–body dualism as a literal truth: 'We are all spirit, it's all we are; we're just walking, you know, dressed up in suits of skin ... and we're gonna leave that behind' (Dylan in Jarosinski, 2006: 892). Several bold statements emerged from the multi-layered doctrinal messages in his songs at that time. These include the moral basis for redemption in 'Solid Rock' (1980), the rebirth narrative in 'Saving Grace' (1980) and a depiction of the Great Tribulation in 'Ye Shall Be Changed' (1991).

After his trilogy of explicitly gospel albums – *Slow Train Coming* (1979), *Saved* (1980) and *Shot of Love* (1981) – Dylan moderated this overt religiosity. Nonetheless, other than *'Love and Theft'* (2001) every album of original material since then has contained at least one tacit faith song. Many allude to Judeo–Christian notions of mind–body dualism, and examples are found throughout Dylan's post-millennial releases *Modern Times* (2006), *Together through Life* (2009), *Tempest* (2012) and *Rough and Rowdy Ways* (2020). The first includes the human soul and the presence of angels in 'Beyond the Horizon', 'Thunder on the Mountain' and 'When the Deal Goes Down'. The last references the soul, purgatory, the afterlife and the Holy Spirit in 'I Contain Multitudes', 'Murder Most Foul', 'Black Rider' and 'I Crossed the Rubicon'. The concept of immortality is also found on two tracks, 'Mother of Muses' and 'Key West (Philosopher Pirate)'. However, Dylan's most overt statement of mind–body dualism remains 'Death Is Not the End' from *Down in the Groove* (1988). This song was released a full decade after his religious conversion, but only three years after his interview comments espousing young earth creationism. Its lyric referenced Robert Johnson's crossroads myth, then offered a biblical flood metaphor and combined Darwin's idea of the 'tree of life' with various overtly Christian tropes contrasting the darkness of evil with the light of salvation.

Lennon's Mind–Body Dualism

John Lennon shared a common backstory with Dylan in that he was raised in a culture where religious mind–body dualism was unquestioningly accepted. From the age of five, after the separation of his parents, Lennon fell under the care of his protective and matriarchal Mary 'Aunt Mimi' Smith. Mimi steered her young charge away from what she saw as the vulgar cultural influences shared by his Scouse-accented, working-class school friends: the local cinema, popular music on the BBC's *Light Programme* and juvenile comics. According to Lennon's contemporaries, the only literature of this type permitted in her home was *The Eagle*, a high-minded publication edited by a clergyman (Kenny, 2015). Mimi regarded the facilities at the local Anglican church, St Peter's in Woolton, as one of the few healthy means of socialisation available. Lennon duly joined the church youth club, attended confirmation classes and even sang in the choir at weddings (Carter, 2009). As he reflected later in life: 'People always got the image I was an anti-Christ or anti-religion. I'm not. I'm a most religious fellow. I was brought up a Christian' (Golson, 1981: 720). In this context, it is no coincidence that Lennon's famous introduction to his songwriting collaborator Paul McCartney came between two sets by his band, the Quarrymen, at St Peter's Church summer garden party in July 1957.

Cloistered in his adoptive home, half-jokingly called the 'House of Correction' by Mimi Smith, Lennon was ushered towards English literature and classical music. As with Dylan's literary influences, much of Lennon's childhood reading was saturated with intuitive mind–body dualism. Matthew Schneider (2008) traced the roots of his musical dreamscapes back to the romanticism of William Wordsworth, John Keats and William Blake. Other commonly cited literary influences featuring dualistic tropes included Edward Lear, Lewis Carroll, Arthur Conan Doyle, Edgar Allen Poe and, later, James Joyce.

Unsurprisingly, Christian and post-Christian notions of the soul and other forms of dualism are evident throughout Lennon's compositions and in numerous interviews, particularly whenever he discussed moments of inspiration: 'It's like being *possessed*; like a *psychic* or a *medium*. The thing *has* to go down' (Lennon et al., 1981: 163). Here, in one of several detailed reflections on the subject, Lennon outlined how an imaginative and open-minded approach to the numinous informed his creative practice:

> The most enjoyable thing for me . . . is the inspirational, in the spirit . . . my joy is when you're like possessed, like a *medium*. I'll be sitting around, it will come in the middle of the night, or the time when you don't want to do it. That's the exciting part. I'm lying around and then this thing comes as a whole piece, you know, words and music. I think, can I say I wrote it? I don't know who the hell wrote it. I'm just sitting here and the whole damn song comes out. So you're like *driven* and you find yourself over on the piano or guitar, and you put it down because it's been *given* to you, or whatever it is that you tune in to. (Taylor, 1985: 205–6)

Mind–body dualism was also a familiar concept for most of Lennon's important influences – from Elvis Presley and Little Richard to numerous artists on Motown, Stax and other R&B record labels. Soul music was, of course, constructed entirely around traditions of the gospel shout, praise songs, witnessing and other worship practices. The genre's very name itself implies a profound acceptance of dualistic principles. Many soul classics expanded on established spiritual tropes, including Ray Charles' 'Hallelujah I Love Her So' which was performed regularly by the Quarrymen and the Beatles and ultimately issued on the retrospective album *Anthology 1* (1995). Several early soul–pop crossover hits repurposed familiar gospel tunes as ecstatic courtship songs, a notable example being Charles' rewrite of 'It Must Be Jesus' as 'I Got a Woman'. Mind–body dualism was also incorporated into pre-existing romantic narratives in Little Richard's 'Ooh! My Soul'. Coincidentally, both of these tracks were recorded by the Beatles in 1963.

Unlike Dylan, the Beatles' earliest original songs were largely comprised of boy-meets-girl courtship themes. These more straightforward lyrics contain few references to mind–body dualism other than the universal heart-as-the-seat-of-emotions trope common among such compositions. Familiar examples include 'I Saw Her Standing There' (1963) and 'If I Fell' (1964). Lennon persisted with this metaphor throughout his career, using it in 'Oh My Love' (1971), 'Jealous Guy' (1971), 'Scared' (1974) and 'Woman' (1980). Dylan, like other songwriters from the period, relied heavily on the same figure of speech. It appears in over 100 lyrics, from one of his earliest published songs 'Long Ago, Far Away' (1962) to more recent releases such as 'Forgetful Heart' (2009).

As discussed in Chapter 4, Lennon's two collections of prose and poetry *In His Own Write* (1964) and *A Spaniard in the Works* (1965) allowed him the space to confront more contentious subject matters during his early

Beatles career. They incorporated a kind of free-flowing and indelicate satire towards public figures and religious institutions that was not possible in popular songs at the time: 'Aman came up to me the other dap and said – "Tell me bicar – tell me the deafinition of sin?" – and you know, I couldn't answer him!' (Lennon, 1965: 89). Yet these two volumes offered no overt mind–body dualism beyond the familiar heart-as-seat-of-emotions metaphors that appeared in nonsense poems, notably, 'Our Dad' and 'Bernice's Sheep': 'This night I lable down to sleep / With hefty heart arid much saddened' (Lennon, 1965: 72). Only after his 'introduction' to cannabis during his first meeting with Bob Dylan in late summer 1964, and his initiation to LSD at a London dinner party in the spring of 1965, did Lennon finally incorporate mind–body dualism in his lyrics – beginning with two contributions to *Revolver* (1966).

'Tomorrow Never Knows' was the first new material put to tape for the album but proved so adventurous that it was placed as the closing track of the LP (MacDonald, 1994). With a repetitive stumbling drum beat and hypnotic bass drone overlaid with tape loops, its lyrics exhorted listeners to detach their consciousness from their material form. They seemed designed to resemble, or even induce, the very definition of mind–body dualism. Lennon used the instructions in Timothy Leary et al.'s (1964) *The Psychedelic Experience: Manual Based on the Tibetan Book of the Dead* for inspiration by recording his voice reading the text aloud ('whenever in doubt, turn off your mind, relax, float downstream') then listening back to these words while under the influence of LSD in order to attain a state of: 'complete transcendence – beyond words, beyond space–time, beyond self ... only pure awareness and ecstatic freedom from all game (and biological) involvements' (Leary et al., 1964: 13–14). In its original format, the purpose of this exercise was to facilitate the reincarnation of Buddhist monks as their consciousness separated from their cadaver at the moment of death. As Lennon explained, he was quite sincere in his application of Leary's method: 'You have to *do* the things in the book. It's a book of instructions, and through doing them you have ... you go through a trip, and you go through an awareness; you have *an experience*' (Burger, 2016: 221). Later, in 1969, Leary visited Lennon and Ono at their week-long Montreal 'Bed-In for Peace' on at least two occasions. On 29 May they discussed the nature of consciousness then, on 1 June, Leary returned and sang on the recording of 'Give Peace a Chance' (Rein, 2012). The next month Lennon wrote 'Come Together' as a campaign song for Leary's putative candidacy in the upcoming California gubernatorial election (Courrier, 2009).

'She Said She Said' contained the second of Lennon's two dualistic references on *Revolver*. Like 'Tomorrow Never Knows', it was inspired by the experience of mind–body disassociation and the possibility that an LSD trip might resemble the brain state of death. In this instance, the lyric referred to a conversation with actor Henry Fonda while the Beatles were in Los Angeles, California, during the late summer of 1965. Thereafter, such tropes became a mainstay for Lennon's wishful pantheism. Allusions to dream states, altered states of consciousness, astral projection and panpsychism appear in several Beatles songs recorded between 1967–9, including 'Strawberry Fields Forever', 'Lucy in the Sky with Diamonds', 'Across the Universe', 'Yer Blues' and 'Because'. Even 'The Ballad of John and Yoko' (1969) includes a bold anti-materialist statement based on the existence of the human soul and an afterlife, citing Ono's variation on the familiar aphorism: 'you don't take anything with you when you go'.

Vedic metaphors for mind–body dualism were prevalent throughout Lennon's post-Beatles compositions. 'Mind Games' (1973) described a spiritual revolution in which massed armies of 'mind guerrillas' lean into the wheel of karma with their collective consciousness. This re-oriented the message of 'Imagine' from an individualised protest medita-tion into a psychic mass movement. Christian tropes continued to appear in Lennon's work, too, increasingly so in later songs. These included 'Out the Blue', also from the *Mind Games* album, which literally gives thanks to the Lord, plus *Double Fantasy*'s 'Cleanup Time' and 'Beautiful Boy' (1980) in which Lennon sings of gods, angels and prayers alongside neo-Pagan concepts such as oracles and spells.

Lennon emphasised his newfound respect for the religion of his child-hood during what became his last ever round of press interviews. These redressed the misconception that 'Imagine' was a non-spiritual or anti-Christian song. Here, any sympathy for atheism or naturalism was now conspicuously absent from this message:

> ['Imagine' means] imagining no religion, not imagining no God … imagine no denominations, imagining that we revere Jesus Christ, Muhammad, Krishna, Milarepa, equally. We don't have to worship either one that we don't have to, but imagine there's no Catholic / Protestant. No Jew / Christian. That we allow it all – freedom of religion for real. For real. (Burger, 2016: 432)

A heartfelt expression of mind–body dualism – that there is something more to the mind than simply the biological brain, that our sense of self can exist beyond this physical organ – forms a poignant image in one of

Lennon's final and finest love songs, 'Grow Old with Me' (1984). This employed another overtly Christian trope to express his and Yoko's desire for everlasting spiritual reunion, asking God that when they die their souls may be reunited in the afterlife.

Dylan's Hyperactive Agency Attribution

Hyperactive agency attribution is the second component of Thomson and Aukofer's (2011) evolutionary analysis of religious and spiritual belief. Agency attribution, they argue, confers a selection advantage because it facilitates the rapid identification of potential threats. Put simply, early hominins who ascribed some form of hostile agency to the sound of a twig snapping behind a nearby bush were more likely to survive and reproduce than those who took a casual approach to such phenomena: 'Humans are strongly biased to interpret unclear evidence as being caused consciously by an agent ... Better to jump at shadows than risk something or someone jumping at you' (Thomson and Aukofer, 2011: 24). By such means, modern humans inherited subconscious mechanisms attributing agency and significance to naturally occurring phenomena, a bias that is now a core constituent of faith systems. These notions probably began with the attempts of early subsistence farmers to increase crop yields by interacting with forces of nature. Over the ensuing millennia, religious doctrines arose that interpreted naturally occurring coincidences, such as rain after a period of drought or a destructive flood during a time of cultural permissiveness, as evidence of celestial guidance or divine intervention. Today, even naturalistic thinkers habitually use expressions that infer some form of agency in meteorological events. Common phrases include 'angry clouds', 'raging seas', 'brutal heat', 'punishing humidity' or 'gentle winds'.

In this context, Dylan's readiness to ascribe portentousness or causality to environmental events in his depictions of storms or landscapes, as outlined in Chapter 5, assumes a new significance. Alongside his copious religious references songs that call upon forces of nature as a metaphor for destiny, as a signifier of human vulnerability, or as an agent of environmental determinism are possibly his most consistent forms of imagery. They are present in Dylan's earliest compositions, his most recent releases and all points in between. Weather-related titles alone include 'A Hard Rain's a-Gonna Fall' (1963), 'Blowin' in the Wind' (1963), 'Idiot Wind' (1975), 'Shelter from the Storm' (1975), 'Buckets of Rain' (1975), 'Hurricane' (1976), 'High Water (For Charley Patton)' (2001), 'The

Levee's Gonna Break' (2006), 'Thunder on the Mountain' (2006), 'Tempest' (2012) among others. The natural images buried within Dylan's vast body of lyrics are almost too numerous to list. 'Make You Feel My Love', for example, is from *Time Out of Mind* (1997):

> The storms are raging on the rollin' sea
> And on the highway of regret
> The winds of change are blowing wild and free
> You ain't seen nothing like me yet
>
> (Bob Dylan, 'Make You Feel My Love')

This trope is also commonly found in his poetry and sleeve notes, and throughout the novel *Tarantula* (1971). It also forms a recurring motif in his memoir *Chronicles: Volume 1*, which closes with: 'It was a strange world that would unfold, a thunderhead of a world with jagged lightening edges' (Dylan, 2004a: 293). Here, and elsewhere, Dylan's texts invest natural forces with a diverse range of powers. On one page they offer an analogy for individual circumstances or emotions; on the next they become intercessory moral agents that determine human destiny.

The habit of ascribing causality to dreams, visions or supernatural guidance from random coincidences is the second variety of agency attribution common in Dylan's work. 'Talkin' World War III Blues' (1963), 'Bob Dylan's 115th Dream' (1965), 'Visions of Johanna' (1966) and 'I Dreamed I Saw St Augustine' (1968) are early examples. During his evangelical period these references drew almost exclusively on theological citations. In *Slow Train Coming* (1979), for example, 'Precious Angel' described Dylan's vision of a woman who strayed from Christianity, while 'Gonna Change My Way of Thinking' extolled his audience to seek daily direction from the real causal agent of life, the Lord, and emphasised the importance of regular prayer as a means of establishing conscious contact with Him in order to attain righteousness and justice. In 'Saving Grace' from *Saved* (1980), Dylan thanks God for His divine guidance in rescuing him from death.

Theory of mind is another psychological correlation to agency attribution commonly found in Dylan's output. This is the notion that humans can understand and anticipate the unspoken motives and thought processes of others. It contributes to religiosity by providing a mechanism that imbues the intervening agent with an identity or personality. Theory of mind is more commonly found among the interactions between characters in dramatic works, via their dialogue or the direction of their gaze, and functions as a tool for the exposition of motive or to encourage audiences to empathise with key roles. Some songwriters instinctively employ theory of mind to engender audience sympathy and understanding, but it appears infrequently in song lyrics. An unusually high proportion of Dylan's compositions feature character-driven narratives, however, and some are sufficiently complex to include lines where theory of mind explains a protagonist's motive or accounts for their behaviour. 'Desolation Row', for instance, constructed a densely populated landscape inhabited by thirty-six named individuals and groups. Theory of mind can be observed in the surreal interactions between the residents of this peculiar dystopia – not least in the image of the Phantom of the Opera spoon-feeding, then poisoning, Casanova. Two more songs on *Highway 61 Revisited* (1965) feature characters undone by their lack of ability to read the motives of others. 'Miss Lovely' in 'Like a Rolling Stone' was a young woman whose extreme self-absorption let to her own demise: 'it wasn't hatred, it was telling someone something they didn't know, telling them they were lucky' (Dylan in Polizzotti, 2006: 33). 'Ballad of a Thin Man' coruscated a socially inadequate and unfashionably conservative journalist in a room of apparent hipsters.

Intuition, or *feeling* as a way of *knowing*, is another correlate of agency detection. This style of perception is a consistent motif throughout Dylan's career, often via an emotional connection to nature in his meteorological images: 'In New Orleans you could almost see other dimensions ... Chronic melancholia hanging from the trees ... After a while you start to feel like a ghost from the tombs' (Dylan, 2004a: 181). This intuitive knowledge became more explicitly theological after Dylan's evangelical conversion in 1978: 'Jesus put his hand on me. It was a physical thing. I felt it. I felt it all over me. I felt my whole body tremble. The glory of the Lord knocked me down and picked me up' (Dylan in Jarosinski, 2006: 712). It is reasonable to assume that Dylan witnessed similar forms of feeling-as-knowing as a participant in the Vineyard Christian Fellowship – a group associated with faith healing, biblical prophecy, speaking in tongues and other elements of the 'signs and wonders' movement (Taylor and Israelson, 2017).

Dylan continued to call upon intuitive insight through the ensuing decades. In 1987, nine years after his first evangelical conversion, he experienced an epiphany in a bar in San Rafael, California. It came at a moment of exhaustion and writer's block while working with The Grateful Dead: 'It was like parts of my psyche were being communicated to by angels. There was a big fire in the fireplace and the wind was making it roar. The veil had lifted' (Dylan, 2004a: 146). Revitalised by this encounter, Dylan rededicated himself to his faith and, as he explained to a friend, 'rarely got out of bed without reading ten chapters of the Bible' (McCarron, 2017: 126). A decade later, in 1997, while in pain after a serious lung infection, Dylan reconfirmed his religious convictions (McCarron, 2017). This intuitive reliance on divine guidance continued into the new millennium. *Modern Times* (2006) repeatedly espoused faith-based ways of knowing. 'Thunder on the Mountain' described the intimate processes of spiritual renewal, the vitality of an open heart, the confidence and freedom in reliance on a higher power. 'When the Deal Goes Down' recounted a sense of being overwhelmed during a spiritual experience. 'Nettie Moore' reiterated his preference for instinct over investigation, his reliance on sacred texts and intuitive understanding rather than 'scientific' modes of enquiry:

> The world of research has gone berserk
> Too much paperwork
> Albert's in the graveyard, Frankie's raising hell
> I'm beginning to believe what the scriptures tell
> Today I'll stand in faith and raise
> The voice of praise
>
> (Bob Dylan, 'Nettie Moore')

Lennon's Hyperactive Agency Attribution

John Lennon's fourth solo album *Mind Games* (1973) included multiple affirmations for innate ways of knowing, most notably in the song 'Intuition'. Lennon presented this acute form of perception as the only reliable guide for action and direction *in all possible circumstances*. Here, insight repeatedly trumped evidence and real-life experiences served only to confirm traditional ways of knowing such as natural instinct, social mores and culturally inherited myths. This was only one of the numerous ways in which Lennon exhibited a lifelong predisposition for hyperactive agency detection in his songs, prose, interviews and private correspondence: 'Prayer is always answered ... so be precise and carefull [sic] when you wish/pray for someone/something ... We are all "magnets" ' (Lennon in Davies et al., 2012: 352). It was particularly evident in Lennon's predilection for *pattern seeking*: the tendency to abstract non-existent meaning from arbitrary information. Pattern seeking is a corollary to agency attribution that occurs when subjects impose imaginary structures on random data. At their most intense, such mind-states can generate convincing psychic and hallucinatory phenomena. Lennon clearly enjoyed an active imagination in his early childhood, when he sincerely believed he had a visionary 'gift', and this continued throughout his adult life:

> There was something wrong with me, I thought, because I seemed to see things other people didn't see ... I always was so psychic or intuitive or poetic or whatever you want to call it, that I was always seeing things in a hallucinatory way. It was scary as a child, because there was nobody to relate to ... the only contact I had was reading about an Oscar Wilde or a Dylan Thomas or a Vincent van Gogh – all those books that my auntie had that talked about their suffering because of their visions. (Lennon in Lennon et al., 1981: 133–4)

Pattern seeking often occurred during Lennon's explorations of 'trance' and 'alpha' brain states brought about by his use of drugs or meditation practices (Lennon et al., 1981: 134). Trance is a universal human behaviour often induced by fasting, hypnotism, meditation, narcotics, prayer or intense concentration. It is often associated with the phenomenon of flow, altered consciousness and other forms of disassociation. Alpha is a type of brainwave signifying a state of extreme relaxation. It was identified in 1924 by Dr Hans Berger who invented the neuroimaging technique of electroencephalography (EEG), which is still used today to diagnose epilepsy and sleep disorders. Lennon regarded such conditions as hyperperceptive cognitive states, somehow more 'real' or 'complete' than everyday waking consciousness, and actively sought out these experiences:

> Surrealism had a great effect on me, because then I realised that my imagery and my mind wasn't insanity; that if it was insane, I belong in an exclusive club that sees the world in those terms. Surrealism to me is reality. Psychic vision to me is reality. Even as a child. When I looked at myself in the mirror or when I was 12, 13, *I used to literally trance out into alpha*. I didn't know what it was called then. I found out years later there is a name for those conditions. But I would find myself seeing hallucinatory images of my face changing and becoming cosmic and complete. (Lennon in Lennon et al., 1981: 134, my italics).

Dylan, too, described his own vivid memories of childhood hallucinations. He surmised that these were inspired by the long winters in isolated Hibbing, the immense local iron ore deposits and the forsaken spirits of previous native inhabitants: 'I had some amazing projections when I was a kid ... You can have some amazing hallucinogenic experiences doing nothing but looking out your window' (Jarosinski, 2006: 535). They seemed to augur his future success. As he later confirmed in *Chronicles: Volume 1*, 'Mostly what I did growing up was bide my time' (Dylan, 2004a: 232). Pattern seeking can inspire belief in a wide range of supernatural phenomena, which is partly why Dylan's and Lennon's spiritual practices evolved in such different directions even though both were driven by the same cognitive biases. While Dylan's culminated in a Damascene conversion to evangelical Christianity, Lennon's were expressed via free-flowing public endorsements for a wide range of mystical pseudo-scientific practices and niche political factions. These included reincarnation rituals from Leary's psychedelic handbook, the Transcendental Meditation school of Maharishi Mahesh Yogi, the International Society for Krishna Consciousness, Arthur Janov's Primal Scream Therapy, collaborations with Tariq Ali's International Marxist Group and Michael X's Black House, the surrealist activism of Jerry Rubin's Youth International Party, and George Ohsawa's macrobiotic fad diet.

Much like Dylan, Lennon's predilection for pattern seeking seemed only to intensify as he grew older. He considered these visions highly auspicious and publicly acknowledged them to the end of his days. He and Ono underscored their 1979 open letter to the *New York Times* with the claim: 'We noticed that three angels were looking over our shoulders when we wrote this!' (Lennon in Davies et al., 2012: 358). While resident in New York, Lennon and Yoko Ono regularly employed prominent professional psychic John Green who they allegedly turned to for advice on financial decisions, sometimes even in advance of consulting lawyers and accountants (Giuliano, 2001; Green, 1983; Rosen, 2002). According to one biographer they even checked in with Green before calling the Federal Bureau of Investigation when an extortionist threatened to kidnap their son, Sean (Goldman, 1988: 599). Both were also practising astrologers who relied on horoscope and tarot readings for many of their most important artistic, personal and professional decisions. One of Lennon's best-known songs from that period, *Double Fantasy*'s 'Woman' (1980), declared his love for Ono using a common astrological trope: that the future is written, literally, in the stars above. Indeed, all the musicians and studio staff for the recording of *Double Fantasy* were selected by virtue of their zodiac signs and charts – and Lennon was not shy of announcing this in promotional interviews for the album (Sharp, 2011: 21). Some biographers claim that the summer before its release he even took an unaccompanied and almost entirely undocumented commercial flight to Cape Town in South Africa because Yoko advised him that it would bring astrological good fortune to travel around the globe in an easterly direction. Ironically he was, of course, assassinated only four months later (Goldman, 1988: 639; Rosen, 2002).

Lennon and Ono commonly employed numerology, another form of pattern seeking, as an important decision-making tool. Lennon wrote many songs featuring his lucky number – 'Revolution #9', 'One After 909', '#9 Dream' – and according to one insider slept with a large wooden figure nine on the wall above his bed (Rosen, 2002: 63). In 1969, when Lennon changed his middle name from Winston to Ono by deed poll, he did so in part because: 'It gives us nine "O's" between us, which is good luck' (Hopkins, 1987: 104). This number featured strongly in his personal history, too: Lennon's birthday was 9 October, his original childhood home was 9 Newcastle Road, Brain Epstein first saw the band play at Liverpool's Cavern Club on 9 November 1961 and John was introduced to Yoko at the Indica Gallery on 9 November 1966. His son Sean was also born on 9 October and again, in another historical irony, Lennon died in the early hours of 9 December by Greenwich Mean Time. Except for baby Sean's arrival – which, according to biographer Albert Goldman (1988: 560–3), was purposefully induced to match Lennon's own birthday, as was common practice in Japan at that time – all these events were entirely coincidental and any imagined connections merely the product of agency attribution and pattern seeking. That Lennon could be so committed to such a notion may seem eccentric in hindsight, but other prominent figures of that era, such as First Lady of the United States Nancy Reagan, also shared his enthusiasm for these and other pre-modern forms of augury.

Besides its auspicious title, '#9 Dream', from *Walls and Bridges* (1974), fulfilled several criteria of agent attribution. The idea came to Lennon in his sleep and is based on what was clearly a vivid dream, with its images of spirits dancing in the air and lyrics asking whether the experience was real or imagined. This composition was gifted to, or visited on, Lennon from an external source – at least in his interpretation. The finished product was clearly important to him. '#9 Dream' was written in a burst of creativity and Lennon, well known as a fast worker in the studio, toiled unusually diligently to construct a multi-layered soundscape on this production. Alternative titles such as 'Walls and Bridges' and 'So Long Ago' were considered, but, given the song's significance, Lennon chose a name that referenced his lucky number – as he had done with the song 'Revolution 9' on *The Beatles* (1968). Another similarity to 'Revolution 9' was that recording engineer Roy Cicala introduced each of Lennon's run throughs with a shout of 'take nine!' (Buskin, 2009). Even each line of the nonsens-ical 'ah-ba-wa-ka' mantra contained nine syllables. When released as the second single from Lennon's *Walls and Bridges* album, '#9 Dream' peaked auspiciously on the US Hot 100 pop chart – at number nine.[5]

Lennon and Ono's predilection for pattern seeking and agency attribution was also evident in their enthusiasm for esotericism, the occult, psychic phenomena and ancient artefacts – particularly Egyptian relics. As Ono confirmed: 'I love Egyptian art. I make sure to get all the Egyptian things, not for their value but for their magic power. Each piece has a certain magic power' (Lennon et al., 1981: 82). According to Frederic Seaman (1992), who became Lennon's personal assistant in February 1979, Lennon's reading material included Bika Reed's *Rebel in the Soul: An Ancient Egyptian Dialogue between a Man and His Destiny* (1979). This is a translation of *Berlin Papyrus 3024*, 'The Dispute of a Man with His Ba', a 4,000-year-old text discussing suicide which is analogous to the literature Lennon drew on for 'Tomorrow Never Knows', *The Tibetan Book of the Dead* (Freemantle, 1975). Other books in his collection included Margot Adler's (1979) *Drawing Down the Moon: Witches, Druids, Goddess Worshippers, and Other Pagans in America Today* and *Practical Occultism* by the co-founder of The Theosophical Society, Helena (Madame) Blavatsky (1967). Seaman also states that Lennon listened to over $1,000 worth of taped lectures by Zen Buddhist Alan Watts, an author and broadcaster who popularised Eastern philosophy in the United States during the 1950s. Watts perceived deep patterns of meaning in the universe and believed that human consciousness originated with the 'Big Bang'. His writings aligned neatly with the pantheism in Lennon's 'Child of Nature' (1968) and 'Across the Universe' (1969): 'Through our eyes, the universe is perceiving itself. Through our ears, the universe is listening to its harmonies. We are the witnesses through which the universe becomes conscious of its glory, of its magnificence' (Watts, in Jardine, 2016).

Dylan's Evolved Moral Systems

Moral inferential systems are a biological mechanism that have emerged over the vast span of evolutionary timescale by conferring survival advantage on any group of primates. Stephanie Preston and Frans de Waal (2002) found an elementary sense of justice in capuchin monkeys. Paul Bloom (2013) detected innate moral structures in infant humans from as

---

[5] This resembles the old Tommy Cooper joke in which he dreamed of a giant number seven floating over a racecourse, so the next day put seven pounds on the seventh horse in the seventh race – and it finished seventh.

young as six months. These systems are complex yet instantaneous, and hardwired to the extent that research scientists have now mapped the neural correlates of moral thinking (Verplaetse et al., 2009). Social psychologist Jonathan Haidt (2012) has established five ethical domains – caring, justice, loyalty, authority and cleanliness. These preferences probably evolved alongside our capacity for speech. Much as Noam Chomsky (1965) posited that an innate capacity for grammar leads to the development of different languages in different locations, generalised ethical systems exist in all societies yet their specific behaviour codes are defined by varying cultural norms (de Waal et al., 2009; King, 2017).

Evolved moral systems provide the impetus for all our spiritual urges and also, of course, inspire many other forms of pro-social behaviour. Dylan's and Lennon's anti-war protest music (discussed in Chapter 3), their awareness of historical injustices and their desire to promote social reform (discussed in Chapters 4 and 5), and their basic human empathy discussed in this section – all were driven by these same cognitive mechanisms. As Dylan suggested in 1965: 'We're all moralists, we all believe in the same things in the same places' (Jarosinski, 2006: 406). Many of his most adroit observations of exploitation and misfortune were rooted in 'other-oriented' qualities of affinity and compassion, and this rare capacity to articulate emotional and physical anguish encouraged Dylan's audience to identify with the difficulties experienced by characters in his songs.[6]

Some of Dylan's observations employed multiple layers of emotional juxtaposition to highlight, then amplify, the moral incongruities therein. In these compositions Dylan stirred empathy with detailed descriptions of misfortune, then turned his attention to a particularly ironic or cruel circumstance that only intensified the protagonist's suffering. In 'The Man on the Street' (1962), a sleeping vagrant prodded awake by a policeman's billy club turned out to be a corpse that rolled off the sidewalk and into the gutter. In 'The Lonesome Death of Hattie Carroll' (1964), Dylan's empathy for an innocent murder victim was juxtaposed against the wealth and privilege of her callous assailant, a youthful tobacco baron. His narrative captured the detail of the courtroom dress codes and rituals as if to emphasise the impartiality and rigour of the United States criminal justice system, then undercut the listener's expectations with the award of a six-month jail sentence. 'Only a Pawn in Their Game' (1963)

---

[6] Examples include accounts of racial injustice in 'The Death of Emmett Till' (1963) and 'Oxford Town' (1963); depictions of personal tragedy in 'He Was a Friend of Mine' (1962) and 'Percy's Song' (1964); and criticisms of economic inequality such as 'Only a Hobo' (1963) and 'The Ballad of Hollis Brown' (1963).

took a different but equally innovative approach, outlining the neuro-logical and physiological processes behind the assassination of civil rights activist Medgar Evers – the finger that pulled the trigger, the eyes that took aim, the spark at the firing pin, the nerves and signals in the killer's brain. In so doing he captured what Hannah Arendt (1963) called 'the banality of evil', depicting the detailed mechanics of an event whose consequences reverberated throughout history.

These songs and others demonstrate Dylan's ability to convey both the intimate subjective experience of hardship or oppression and, simultan-eously, its wider socio-political context. As Sybil Weinberger, a friend in the early 1960s, observed: 'When we walked down the street, he saw things that absolutely nobody else saw. He was so aware of his surroundings, in every situation' (Heylin, 2010a: 54). Such keen observation and communi-cation skills rely on evolved cognitive structures in both artist and audi-ence. Theory of mind allows listeners to understand the motives of Dylan's protagonists. Narrative empathy encourages his descriptions of hardship to stimulate their mirror neurons. These learning mechanisms are found in highly advanced mammals and enable social groups to comprehend behav-iours, convey information and connect on an emotional basis (Keen, 2006; Taylor, 2003). Mirror neurons are why empathy can invoke a physical reaction in others, be that tears in response to distress or squeals of delight at a happy event. We instinctively 'feel' the pain we see our fellows endure or the joy they express. As such Dylan's ability to invoke compassion triggered responses that evolved over a vast shared history of suffering and survival. From the violent public humiliation of Hattie Carroll to the blood of Medgar Evers, pooling silently on a concrete porch, where a stain still holds to this day.

Lennon's Evolved Moral Systems

Lennon's evolved moral systems were expressed in contrasting ways at different stages of his life. Perceived as a belligerent troublemaker with a self-described 'chip on his shoulder' during the band's formative period (Blaney, 2005; Burger, 2016; Kenny, 2015), his early reputation as the irreverent Beatle who cared the least about causing offence became an important element of his identity in the group. This was evident in his willingness to speak truth to power, even during the band's important breakthrough performances and interviews. Examples from 1963 alone include his acerbic 'I'm not going to vote for Ted' response to Edward Heath's criticism of their regional accents (Riley,

2011: 221), his irreverent 'just rattle your jewellery' comment at the Royal Variety Performance, and his banter with Eric Morecambe and Ernie Wise on Anglia Television's *Two of a Kind*:

ERIC: Hey-hey! What's it like being famous?
JOHN: Well, it's not like in your day, you know.
ERIC: Ha! That was an insult, that is!

(Smeaton and Wonfor, 1995)

This brash overconfidence also led to cultural insensitivities such as the distasteful remarks and straight-arm Nazi salutes discussed in Chapter 4. Other tactless public displays included mimicking neuromuscular disorders by grimacing with his tongue thrust into his cheek while awkwardly clapping his extended fingers together in an exaggerated manner. These actions were captured several times on film in unrehearsed moments and even onstage during major concerts – from the Beatles' debut in the United States in February 1964 at Washington Coliseum, to their final world tour in July 1966 at Tokyo's Budokan arena (McGeorge, 2015; Smeaton and Wonfor, 1995). Lennon's grotesque gestures are easily found on *YouTube* and would guarantee immediate censure if repeated onstage today – as happened when Republican presidential candidate Donald Trump mocked *New York Times* reporter Serge F. Kovaleski by imitating his chronic joint condition. Just as Lennon's hand-drawn school magazine *The Daily Howl* and the surreal verse of *In His Own Write* (1964) and *A Spaniard in the Works* (1965) provided the means to engage in class discourse, they also allowed him to continue in a dehumanising preoccupation with disability and otherness: ' "Ye musna' call me Spastic whilst ma friends are here Jesus ma bonnie wee dwarf" . . . She looked down at him through a mass of naturally curly warts' (Lennon, 1965: 15). While such forms of address were common in private conversations during this period, it was unusual for a celebrity to express themselves in print using these terms.

Two songs from the early 1960s, 'You Can't Do That' (1964) and 'Run for Your Life' (1965), plumbed the unpleasant depths of Lennon's male sexual jealousy. In a depressingly familiar domestic abuse narrative, the latter appropriated a lyric from Elvis Presley's 'Baby Let's Play House' (1955) threatening serious physical violence against his young partner if he ever saw her with another man. Lennon reshaped Presley's clumsy co-dependency into a prolonged and unequivocally malicious threat. Later, he admitted that 'Getting Better' (1967) described his abuse of his first wife, Cynthia Lennon:

> It is a diary form of writing. All that 'I used to be cruel to my woman, I beat
> her and kept her apart from the things that she loved' was me. I used to be
> cruel to my woman, and physically . . . any woman. I was a hitter. I couldn't
> express myself and I hit . . . I am a violent man who has learned not to be
> violent and regrets his violence. I will have to be a lot older before I can face
> in public how I treated women as a youngster. (Lennon in Lennon et al.,
> 1981: 154).

Evolutionary psychologists suggest this damaging misbehaviour has deep roots as a maladapted primeval mating strategy (Buss, 2006; Gladden and Cleator, 2018), although what seems more relevant in the era of #MeToo is the 'wilful forgetting' and 'special dispensation' awarded to cultural high achievers. Author Claire Dederer (2017) recently asked whether it can *ever* be appropriate to separate a work from its creator: 'What do we do with the art of monstrous men?'.

Yoko Ono's moral grounding appears to have acted as a brake on Lennon's violence against women. Their relationship marked his sharp turn away from previous attitudes and behaviours – what others have called a 'journey into feminism' (Raiola, 2016). Lennon's new progressive stance on gender politics not only demanded equality across society as a whole, but also challenged the hypocrisy of sexism within the New Left and counterculture. 'Power to the People' urged Lennon's comrades to consider how they treat their partners at home. 'Woman is the N—r of the World' offered a searing critique of patriarchy via the calculated use of an exceptionally offensive racial slur. Melvin J. Lasky (1998) described this as a misguided attempt to change the focus, or reverse the direction, of the insult. Lennon summarised his motivation as an attempt to historicise the true extent of women's oppression as the slave of the enslaved: 'I really believe that women have the worst, whatever it is. However badly or how poor people are, it's the woman who takes it when they get home from work' (Raiola, 2016). These declarations of contrition continued throughout the remainder of Lennon's career, which later included a public apology to Yoko in the hit single 'Woman' (1980).

Like every other song on *Sometime in New York City* (1972) 'Woman is the N—r of the World' signalled Lennon's passion for social justice. In Chapter 3, I showed how he articulated this via unusually 'magnetic' compositions employing simple, rhythmical lyrics to generate a sense of in-group solidarity – notably in 'Give Peace a Chance' (1969), 'Power to the People' (1971) and 'Happy Christmas (War Is Over)' (1971). Evolutionary psychology offers several explanatory mechanisms for the appeal of such compositions. Mirror neurons are also the brain circuits partly responsible for our enthusiastic participation in chants and songs at political demonstrations or football matches. Collective entrainment is the phenomenon of beat perception as manifest in handclapping, swaying, head nodding and other rhythmical actions at such events (Phillips-Silver et al., 2010). This technique also appeared, to great effect, in Lennon's 'Instant Karma! (We All Shine On)' (1970).

Lennon was introduced to the concept of *karma* by the founder of Transcendental Meditation, Maharishi Mahesh Yogi, and the founder of the International Society for Krishna Consciousness (ISKCON), A. C. Bhaktivedanta Swami Prabhupāda (Goldberg, 2010; Lennon and Prabhupāda, 1981). A spiritual axiom originating in the Vedic tradition, karma is a natural law of cause and effect whereby the righteousness of any individual's thoughts and deeds contributes to their future well-being: 'As a man himself sows, so he himself reaps' (The Mahabharata, xii. 291.22). By such means, it offers the inviting prospect of universal moral justice. The definition and interpretation of this notion varies among its adherents, but many see karma as comparable to thermodynamics, gravity, electromagnetism or any other observable phenomena (Bhagwan, 2015). Evolutionary psychologists, of course, explain karma in more prosaic terms: a blend of agency attribution and teleology that flatters our evolved sense of fairness.

Karma has three interacting elements: causality, ethics and time – the belief that good and bad acts have real-world outcomes over the period of one or several lifetimes. In 'Instant Karma! (We All Shine On)' Lennon's notion of immediate, rather than lifelong or reincarnated karma, provided an innovative twist on this concept. The song's production embodied its message. Written in an hour, then recorded and released over the following ten days, the rapid distribution of this single was a significant achievement for any performing artist at that time. Lennon's sense of urgency also reflected the increasing pace of change in early postmodern culture and revealed his enthrallment with new 'instant' consumer products, such as the freeze-dried coffee granules, dehydrated mashed potato flakes, and ready-meal TV dinners he encountered while on tour with the Beatles in North America. 'I'm fascinated by commercials and promotion as an art form', he explained, 'so the idea of instant karma was like the idea of instant coffee: presenting something in a new form' (Lennon in Lennon et al., 1981: 182). In this sense, as Ian MacDonald (1994) noted, 'Instant Karma! (We All Shine On)' constituted one of Lennon's most timely declarations about the growing expectations of the Baby Boomer 'Now Generation'.

'Instant Karma! (We All Shine On)' also thrust Lennon's hurried demand for immediacy directly into a spiritual discourse where the quality of *forbearance* was, and still is, a valued signifier of emotional regulation and strategic thinking. Patience is a virtue in the Talmud; the New Testament; the Quran; the hadith Sahih Bukhar; the Buddhist Dhammapada; and the Hindu Sandilya Upanishad. Lennon inverted this metaphysics, hypothesising that delayed future rewards might be brought into the here and now simply by wishing it so. Here, he drew on the revolutionary first-century teachings of Christ: 'Jesus said: "The Kingdom of Heaven is within you", and he meant just that. "The Kingdom of Heaven is at hand". Not in some far distant time, or after death, but now' (Lennon in Davies et al., 2012: 121). This spiritual impetus was initiated by Lennon's abrupt and impatient admonition in the first verse for the listener to pull themselves together – for mortality faces us all and life will surely be over before we're ready for it to end. The lyric seemed designed to induce a sense of existential urgency, to emphasise our inevitable transience and to acknowledge the mystery of mind–body dualism and vitalism. The chorus and the 'We All Shine On' subtitle explained such phenomena using an astrological analogy that compared the human life force to the 'light' of celestial bodies such as the stars, the sun and the moon – although strictly speaking the moon emits no light of its own, of course. It then claimed that human consciousness aligns with the interplanetary gravity acting on our solar system – in a poetic but entirely incorrect interpretation of Newtonian physics.

Nonetheless, 'Instant Karma! (We All Shine On)' effectively synchronised the first three concepts in Thomson and Aukofer's (2011) explanation for spirituality:

- mind–body dualism in the form of an autonomous, independent human soul
- agency attribution, usually from a transcendent interventionist power
- evolved moral systems aligning our ethical preferences to natural forces.

It also posed the ultimate existential question – 'Why are we here?' – the fourth component in the evolutionary psychology of belief systems: *promiscuous teleology*.

Dylan's Promiscuous Teleology

Promiscuous teleology is defined by Thomson and Aukofer (2011) as an overwhelming desire for ultimate purpose. A corollary to mind–body dualism, agency attribution and moral systems, it manifests as an innate cognitive bias that ascribes meaning to random events or naturally occurring coincidences. This longing for determination is innate, difficult to overcome and overrides the indifferent mechanistic reality of the natural world. Dylan and Lennon both exhibited promiscuous teleology in their creative output, which varied in form and intensity alongside their fluctuating spiritual and religious commitments. This section turns to the teleological tropes that evolved in Dylan's work under the influence of Abrahamic religions, and in Lennon's via his immersion in Vedic philosophy.

Most individuals experience teleological thinking on some level. It is antithetical to ontological naturalism yet, paradoxically, even a staunch rationalist may casually remark that sometimes things happen 'for a reason'. Dual-process and dual-system thinking models provide a useful framework to explain our ongoing predisposition to such conspicuously unscientific ideas. Daniel Kahneman (2011) describes our initial response to most events and interactions as 'System 1' thinking: immediate, intuitive, emotional – and often inaccurate. By comparison our logical 'System 2' thinking is more calculated and discerning, but because of the complexities involved, this process is also more demanding. As a result, System 2 thinking often engages too slowly to countermand erroneous System 1 responses. When reinforced by such factors as confirmation bias, these mechanisms explain our predilection for teleological precepts (Evans and Stanovich, 2013; Risen, 2016).

Thomson and Aukofer's (2011) notion of *minimally counterintuitive worlds* corresponds with Kahneman's two-tier cognitive model and provides a helpful tool to map the gradual progression of Dylan's and Lennon's teleological thinking. Thomson and Aukofer suggest that humans absorb implausible concepts such as spiritual and religious beliefs on an incremental basis via a series of minimally counterintuitive propositions. As a result they come to accept, using piecemeal System 1 thinking, everyday supernatural tropes whose wider connotations lie beyond the boundary of System 2 rationality. Contemporary examples include superstitions over numbers and touching or knocking on wood for reassurance. The latter is a universal means of ameliorating anxiety founded in the folklore of sacred trees and forests. It represents a bite-sized version of a supernatural phenomenon that, in its totality, most people would find indigestible (Keinan, 2002).

A notional version of Michael Thalbourne's 'Transliminality Scale' (Thalbourne and Delin, 1999) can be helpful in evaluating Dylan's and

Lennon's vulnerability to these minimally counterintuitive concepts. Thalbourne mapped an individual's receptivity to the illogical conclusions and explanations encouraged by an over-reliance on System 1 intuition. High levels of transliminality suggest susceptibility to mysticism and magical thinking. They can also indicate artistic personality types. Previous chapters have documented Dylan's and Lennon's transliminal creativity. This includes songs written via trance or dream states and others that extol intuition and pattern seeking or appeal to intercessory natural forces.

Here, Thalbourne's scale provides a tool to trace Dylan's journey from self-proclaimed non-believer to eschatological Christian by the gradual appearance, then increasing prominence, of minimally counterintuitive phenomena in his press conferences and lyrics. Dylan's earliest recorded conversations are low in transliminality. They betray the impatient scepticism of an ambitious, headstrong young artist. Sometimes when frustrated by an obtuse line of inquiry his instinctive cynicism became palpable. In the comment below, Dylan articulated his exasperation in a disturbingly nihilistic statement of unvarnished existential truth, clearly intended to unsettle his interviewer:

> Each of us really knows nothing. But we all think we know things. And we really know nothing. I'm saying that you're going to die, and you're gonna go off the earth, you're gonna be dead. Man, it could be, you know, twenty years, it could be tomorrow ... we're just gonna be gone. The world's going to go on without us. (Dylan in Jarosinski, 2006: 152)

Keen to distance himself from religion during these early interviews Dylan even openly espoused atheism, an unusual position for a public figure in the United States at that time: 'I don't think religion can show anybody how to live. I don't have any religion' (Dylan in Jarosinski, 2006: 154). This underlying doubt guided his early creative practice: 'I live among the sceptics ... Living among the sceptics? That's the only world there is' (Dylan in Jarosinski, 2006: 321). As he sang on 'Long Time Gone' (1963): 'I ain't no prophet / An' I ain't no prophet's son.'

Yet this youthful cynicism was also offset by artful allusions to Judeo–Christian teleology. From his earliest songs Dylan habitually cited biblical tropes as a moral reference point to anchor his free-floating scepticism. Many allusions to scripture recounted a social injustice mended, a divine intervention to ameliorate suffering, or a gesture towards the possibilities of eventual salvation. 'Masters of War' (1963) and 'With God on Our Side' (1963) referenced the betrayal of Christ. 'The Times They Are a-Changin'

(1964) paraphrased Matthew 19:30: 'many who are first will be last, and many who are last will be first'. 'Gates of Eden' (1965) and 'Highway 61 Revisited' (1965) used place names and narratives. Songs with extended metaphors incorporated the darker elements of biblical teleology, particularly those with a foreboding or menacing atmosphere. 'When the Ship Comes In' (1964) drew on Moses and the Israelites' escape from Egypt. 'A Hard Rain's a-Gonna Fall' (1963) and 'It's Alright Ma (I'm Only Bleeding)' (1965) offered lengthy apocalypse ballads and jeremiads (Beebee, 1991; Campbell, 1975; Sutton, 2009). Conversely, 'Paths of Victory' (1962), 'Chimes of Freedom' (1964) and 'I Shall Be Released' (1967) implied a more positive sense of purpose in their appeal to a higher order and sense of human destiny. These citations confirmed Dylan's obvious familiarity with the imagery, tropes and prophecies of the New and the Old Testament – which was clear from his very first compositions. Michael J. Gilmour (2011: 13) described this as his 'Christianised imagination'. Indeed, in 1963, the same year that he took the unusual step of coming out as an atheist, Dylan also conceded that his ethical framework was moulded by an appeal to biblical values: 'I'm trying to be like the medium at a séance. There's mystery, magic, truth and the Bible in great folk music. I can't hope to touch that but I'm going to try' (Dylan in Jarosinski, 2006: 399).

As his knowledge of scripture gradually blossomed into a broad-based pantheism, Dylan's output exhibited a greater variety of transliminal and minimally counterintuitive signifiers. By the mid-1970s his views seemed to align with Lennon's open-minded Vedic universalism:

> I can see God in a daisy. I can see God at night in the wind and rain. I see *Creation* just about everywhere. The highest form of song is prayer. King David's, Solomon's, the wailing of a coyote, the rumble of the earth. It must be wonderful to be God. There's so much going on out there that you can't get to it all. It would take longer than forever. (Dylan in Jarosinski, 2006: 522)

Much as happened with their protest music in the mid-1960s, Dylan's and Lennon's religious imaginations coincided then separated once more. While Lennon explored different schools of Eastern spirituality, Dylan's easy familiarity with biblical precepts and texts hardened into an increasingly tangible Christian faith.

Key tropes in New Testament teleology started to recur in his work during the mid-1970s as Dylan apparently became preoccupied with themes of sacrifice and betrayal. Michael Gray noted how he seemed to identify ever more closely with the story of Jesus at this time. On 'Tough

Mama' (*Planet Waves*, 1974) Dylan sang of taking sacrificial lambs to the marketplace, while *Blood on the Tracks* (1975) offered 'parallel after parallel between Dylan and Christ' (Gray, 2008: 81). 'Idiot Wind' referred to an unfortunate soldier stranded on a cross, and 'Shelter from the Storm' contained a clear reference to Jesus's crucifixion:

> I came in from the wilderness . . .
> She walked up to me so gracefully
> And took my crown of thorns . . .
> In the little hilltop village
> They gambled for my clothes.
>
> (Bob Dylan, 'Shelter from the Storm')

Desire's 'Oh, Sister' (1976) referred to God as the Father, implored the subject of the song to follow His guidance, alluded to Christ's resurrection, and reimagined the experience of being saved and reborn. In *Street-Legal*'s 'Señor (Tales of Yankee Power)' (1978) the protagonist's emphasis of the words 'way' and 'truth' in adjacent lines hinted at Christ's prophetic self-definition: 'I am the way, the truth and the life' (John 14.6). The final verse referenced the cleansing of the temple in Jerusalem, where Jesus overthrew the market tables of the merchants and money changers.

Gray saw these New Testament references as harbingers of Dylan's conversion experience in November 1978, when he joined the evangelical Vineyard Christian Fellowship. His work was 'consistently characterised by a yearning for salvation' to the extent that it formed 'the central theme of his entire output' (Gray, 2008: 80). Indeed, this event may have astonished his audience, but it certainly did not come without notice in Dylan's earlier lyrics. Thomson and Aukofer's notion of minimally counterintuitive worlds and Thalbourne's 'Transliminality Scale' corroborate Gray's thesis here. Both support the assertion that Dylan's conversion represented the culmination of many years of incremental spiritual growth. During the 1960s, he relied on biblical imagery as a moral compass then, during the 1970s, the Gospels gradually lent a new sense of perspective to his personal life. Having absorbed, piecemeal, a long series of counterintuitive ideas, Dylan came to identify with Christ in a more profound way. Eventually he accepted, wholesale, suggestions that would once have been entirely unpalatable. Far from suddenly abandoning his broad-based and inclusive pantheism, he arrived at the position of resolute and uncompromising eschatology simply by following an incrementally narrow teleological path.

Hal Lyndsay's apocalyptic best-seller *The Late, Great Planet Earth* (1970) was an important influence on Dylan's evolving worldview during this period (Gilmour, 2011; Rogovoy, 2010). A prominent Christian Zionist, Lyndsay used biblical prophecy from the Old Testament (Ezekiel, Daniel, Isaiah and Zechariah) and the New Testament (the Gospels, Paul's Letters and the Book of Revelation) to argue that the establishment of the state of Israel in 1948 was a harbinger of the Messiah's imminent return and the resultant Great Tribulation. The Vineyard Christian Fellowship provided a logical solution for any reader half-convinced by Lindsay's millenarian vision. This charismatic church encouraged a literal interpretation of scripture that fell somewhere between dynamic evangelical Protestantism and more radical revivalist Pentecostalism. Here, Dylan's gradual absorption of minimally counterintuitive ideas finally coalesced into a radical, and entirely untenable, teleological evangelism that offered a path to God's grace via the Holy Spirit and the second coming of Jesus Christ (Strout, 2016).[7]

American psychologist William James' (1929) famous *The Varieties of Religious Experience: A Study in Human Nature* provides a useful tool to understand the process of this rebirth. James defined dramatic and sudden spiritual experiences such as the conversion of Paul the Apostle as an overwhelming and involuntary instance of ego-deflation and surrender. That may be the generally accepted account of what happened to Dylan at the Vineyard Christian Fellowship, all of which is confirmed by presuppositions about the worship practices of charismatic churches, but it is probably an inaccurate description of this particular event. James also hypothesised a more gentle and incremental awakening, a 'volitional' spiritual experience where piecemeal shifts in perspective encourage an individual to gradually rethink their worldview. This depiction aligns neatly with the suggestion that Dylan's religious growth progressed over a longer period via a series of minimally counterintuitive transliminal steps.

His transformation, of course, shocked Dylan's audience. Lennon certainly did not see it coming: 'I must say I was surprised when old Bobby boy did go that way. I was very surprised' (Lennon et al., 1981: 101). The controversy over his 'going electric' in 1965, particularly the adverse crowd

---

[7] Since then Dylan's faith could perhaps be summarised as that of a Christian with deep roots in the Torah. He visited the Wailing Wall in 1983, the year *Infidels* featured a full-throated defence of Israel in 'Neighbourhood Bully', yet his much-anticipated 1987 Jerusalem concert drew heavily on evangelical songs. In common with many Christian Zionists he has also maintained links with orthodox Jewish organisations, including the Haredi Sh'or Yoshuv and the Hasidic Chabad Lubavitch.

reactions at concert performances, offers a useful parallel here. After all, Dylan's first love was rock and roll so 'going electric' simply marked a return to his preferred genre style. It was a gesture of *authenticity* and *artistic integrity* not a betrayal of his folk roots. His spiritual experience a decade later is perhaps best understood in similar terms. Indeed, for some observers, it was not unexpected. As Eric Clapton commented: 'I always saw him as religious' (Webb, 2006: 37). Assistant Pastor Larry Myers, who counselled Dylan during his visits to the Vineyard Christian Fellowship and witnessed his conversion, certainly expressed little surprise at the outcome of their sessions together. This, according to Myers, was *not* an emotional moment of ego-deflation and surrender. To the contrary, Dylan's faith arrived quietly and privately, after a long period of reflection and deliberation:

> It was a quite intelligent conversation with a man who was seriously intent on understanding the Bible. There was no attempt to convince, manipulate or pressure this man into anything. But in my view God spoke through His Word, the Bible, to *a man who had been seeking for many years*. (Grossman and Wooding, 1999, my italics)

However incremental it may have been, one outcome of Dylan's spiritual awakening did nonetheless register as a seismic transliminal event: his heartfelt espousal of a biblical Judgment Day. This became a matter of cosmological import requiring committed and prompt action on his part: 'God's got his own purpose and time for everything. He knew when I would respond to His call' (Dylan in Jarosinski, 2006: 712). This new worldview entirely repurposed Dylan's old enthusiasm for social justice and reoriented his dynamic protest rhetoric. The heavy determinism of 'Gotta Serve Somebody' (1979), 'Gonna Change My Way of Thinking' (1979), 'When He Returns' (1979), 'Are You Ready?' (1980) and 'Every Grain of Sand' (1981) constituted a considered and sustained response, demonstrating his command of orthodox teleology:

> Am I ready, hope I'm ready.
> When the destruction cometh swiftly
> And there's no time to say a fare-thee-well
> Have you decided whether you want to be
> In heaven or in hell?
>
> Are you ready for the judgment?
> Are you ready for that terrible swift sword?
> Are you ready for Armageddon?
> Are you ready for the day of the Lord?
>
> (Bob Dylan, 'Are You Ready')

In some ways these sentiments reformulated the premonitions of Dylan's early 1960s protest songs 'A Hard Rain's a-Gonna Fall' (1962) and 'Talkin' World War III Blues' (1963). Now, however, his media interviews took a similar direction too, driven by the imperative to disseminate an urgent eschatology: 'I believe that ever since Adam and Eve got thrown out of the garden that the whole nature of the planet has been heading in one direction – towards apocalypse. It's all there in the *Book of Revelations*'(Dylan in Jarosinski, 2006: 799). And:

> The world is scheduled to go for 7,000 years. Six thousand years of this, where man has his way, and 1,000 years when God has his way . . . The last thousand years is called the Messianic Age. Messiah will rule. He is, was, and will be about God, doing God's business. Draught, famine, war, murder, theft, earthquake, and all other evil things will be no more. (Dylan in Jarosinski, 2006: 883)

The threat of doomsday brought a new creative momentum to Dylan's songwriting. In musicological terms these compositions are still, today, as robust as any of his better-known material. 'In the Garden' (1980), from *Saved*, contains an unusually adventurous chord progression by Dylan's standards that included a rare augmented chord and two whole-tone key changes in each verse. In 2017, Dylan nominated this as one of two songs from his career that failed to receive appropriate acclaim from his audience (Flanagan, 2017).[8] This is also possibly why he played it at so many concerts from 1979 to 2002, approximately 329 times (Dylan, 2018). 'Groom's Still Waiting at the Altar' (1981), a bluesy out-take from *Shot of Love*, featured an energetic vocal performance hailed as an unexpected highlight on the *Biograph* retrospective (Brackett and Hoard, 2004). Similarly, the lilting melody of 'Every Grain of Sand' (1981) is now recognised as a bona fide classic and it has inspired cover versions by Giant Sand, Emmylou Harris, Barb Jungr and The Blind Boys of Alabama (Gray, 2008).

As someone who had previously worked as quickly as possible to capture the feel of a song even at the expense of audio or technical fidelity, Dylan also began taking great care to ensure his faith music sounded as accomplished as possible. The studio team on his trilogy of Christian albums, led by Barry Beckett and Jerry Wexler, engineered unexpectedly meticulous recordings that remained unmatched until Dylan's *Oh Mercy* (1989)

---

[8] Dylan's second under-rated composition was the eleven-minute epic 'Brownsville Girl' from *Knocked Out Loaded* (1986).

collaboration with Daniel Lanois. Yet despite these positive developments his audience did not reciprocate. Fans inevitably became alienated and disengaged as his tolerance for transliminal ideas accelerated during the late 1970s. On *Shot of Love* (1981) and *Infidels* (1983) Dylan realigned with the expectations of his followers and attenuated his overt eschatology. However, a message of Christian teleology has not yet fallen from his work. As he sang on 'God Knows' from *Under the Red Sky* (1990): 'God knows there's a purpose . . . God knows there's a heaven.' This yearning for salvation also appeared in 'Trying to Get to Heaven' (1993), 'When the Deal Goes Down' (2006) and elsewhere. As noted earlier in this chapter, it continued in his later releases – *Together Through Life* (2009), *Tempest* (2012) and *Rough and Rowdy Ways* (2020).

Lennon's Promiscuous Teleology

Initially a sceptic who criticised organised religion, Lennon's purpose-driven thinking progressed via a series of minimally counterintuitive ideas through much the same psychological stages as Dylan. After discovering Vedic philosophy he absorbed increasingly transliminal concepts over time, before arriving at a uniquely inward-looking esotericism. Lennon's teleology was obscured by its origins in Eastern religions, the plasticity of his maverick imagined utopias, and his self-centred personality – but it remained evident in his songs, statements and behaviours.

Although Lennon's worldview was not grounded in Christian theology, he definitely shared Dylan's predilection for best-selling pseudohistorical studies of the Old and New Testament. Hugh J. Schonfield's (1965) publishing phenomenon *The Passover Plot* inspired Lennon in the mid-1960s just as much as Hal Lindsay's *The Late, Great Planet Earth* influenced Dylan a decade later. This book was almost certainly the source for Lennon's unguarded remarks comparing the Beatles to Jesus in Maureen Cleave's March 1966 *Evening Standard* interview. The judgement that Christ's disciples were 'thick and ordinary' followers who adulterated and undermined His message strongly resembled Schonfield's text. Here, the apostles were described as 'untutored' and 'of limited intelligence, simple Galileans for the most part' who were 'more concerned with the material rewards expected when the Kingdom of Jesus was established, and squabbled among themselves as to which of them should have the highest positions' (Schonfield, 1965: 99). Indeed, it is possible that this volume constituted the bulk of what Cleave described as his 'extensive' reading on religion in her piece (Schneider, 2003). The backlash that ensued when the interview was republished in North American magazine *Datebook*, including a firecracker thrown onstage in Memphis that led some to assume Lennon had been shot, contributed greatly to the Beatles' decision to abandon live performance after their 1966 United States tour. Retreating into the studio environment they constructed some of the most unprecedented and sonically adventurous work in the pop canon, including *Sgt. Pepper's Lonely Hearts Club Band* (1967) and *Magical Mystery Tour* (1967). In that respect, although its content is now widely discredited, *The Passover Plot* remains, in some ways, arguably one of the most consequential publications in the history of popular music.

Lennon was, of course, subject to the same teleological biases as Dylan; he merely articulated them in a less orthodox manner. Dylan readily incorporated Biblical tropes in his lyrics, whereas Lennon asked his audience to envisage a life without religion and a death with no heaven in 'Imagine' (1971). Yet this song still proffered its own subtle New Age teleology. The chorus of 'Imagine' is another appeal to Lennon's enduring goal of universal love, a firm resolution that the people of the world should live together as one. These sentiments match those in his Beatles compositions – 'The Word' (1965) and 'All You Need Is Love' (1967) – and in his solo songs 'Instant Karma! (We All Shine On)' (1970) and 'Watching the Wheels' (1980). Their inclusive and pluralistic spirituality remained the most important recurring theme in Lennon's output, and aligns broadly to the pantheistic worldview expressed by Dylan prior to his 1978 evangelical conversion.

This was most effectively articulated in 'Across the Universe' (1969), which carried the influence of Maharishi Mahesh Yogi's philosophy of Transcendental Meditation, a practice Lennon began in late August 1967 (Anon., 2014). The song's distinctive refrain, which translates as 'All Glory to Guru Dev', was taken from the Sanskrit mantra recited by the Maharishi when invoking his own spiritual mentor. Lennon also used this phrase to close his handwritten correspondence to fans while in Rishikesh: 'God bless. Jai guru dev. With love, John Lennon' (Davies et al., 2012: 123). The metaphysical formula of 'Across the Universe' is oddly analogous to twentieth-century cosmological teleology, or the life of star systems as we understand them today. The remarkable parallels between Eastern mysticism and modern physics was popularised by authors Fritjof Capra (1975) and Gary Zukav (1979) and acknowledged by prominent scientists Werner Heisenberg, Neils Bohr and Victor N. Mansfield (Kaiser, 2011). They date back to a peer-reviewed journal paper by Margaret Burbidge et al. (1957) titled 'Synthesis of the Elements in Stars' that first described how almost all the known chemical elements were forged from helium in the core of active suns then ejected into the universe by supernovae. While Lennon envisaged words, thoughts, images and sounds tumbling across space, science broadcaster and writer Carl Sagan coined his own memorable phrase to explain how the material constituents of everything we know, including consciousness itself, were created by a remarkably similar process: 'All of the rocky and metallic material we stand on, the iron in our blood, the calcium in our teeth, the carbon in our genes were produced billions of years ago in the interior of a red giant star. We are made of star-stuff' (Sagan, 1995: 233).

Lennon's Vedic spirituality was not only less dogmatic than Dylan's New Testament eschatology, it was also a less structured experience. Dylan's Christian Zionism seemed to provide more socialisation, theological direction and reinforcement – as did his subsequent links with orthodox Jewish communities Sh'or Yoshuv and the Chabad Lubavitch. By comparison Lennon's familiarity with any form of structured religious life was probably restricted to his involvement with the Maharishi Mahesh Yogi during 1967–8, as well as the brief period when he and Ono accommodated the International Society for Krishna Consciousness (ISKCON) founder A. C. Bhaktivedanta Swami Prabhupāda and a small cohort of Hari Krishna devotees at Tittenhurst Park in late 1969 (Lennon and Prabhupāda, 1981; Turner, 2006). In the absence of further guidance, Lennon's spiritual journey followed an autodidactic, self-absorbed path along which his expanding transliminality threshold can be mapped against the increasingly inward-looking supernatural and Vedic inferences in his songs and statements.

Lennon's equivocal positions on Christianity illustrate the unstructured nature of these ideas. *In His Own Write* (1964) and *A Spaniard in the Works* (1965) coruscated the church, whereas *Rubber Soul*'s 'The Word' paraphrased the positive message in the Gospel of John. Yet only two years after improvising his notorious 'we're more popular than Jesus' invective against organised religion, Lennon handwrote several letters to fans extolling the virtues of Christian and Vedic faith systems from Maharishi Mahesh Yogi's ashram at Rishikesh:

> when Jesus was fasting etc [sic] in the desert 40 days & nights he would have been doing some form of meditation – not just sitting in the sand and praying – although meditating is a form of prayer. I hope what I have said makes sense to you – I sure [sic] it will to a true Christian – *which I try to be with all sincerity* – it does not prevent me from acknowledging Buddha –

Mohammed – and all the great men of God. God Bless You – jai guru dev. (Lennon in Davies et al., 2012: 122)

Much like Dylan, Lennon also became overwhelmed by a profound identification with the figure of Jesus. Dylan's response was to revere Christ as 'the way, the truth and the life' whatever the personal cost (Jarosinski, 2006: 706). Lennon's narcissistic self-absorption caused him to redirect his unique interpretation of biblical teleology inwardly, to a point of messianic delusion. In May 1968, following the Beatles' return from Rishikesh, he called a meeting of bemused band members and business partners at Apple's Savile Row office to announce that he, John Lennon, was the Second Coming: ' "I've got something very important to tell you", Lennon says. "I am Jesus Christ. I have come back again. This is my thing" ... "Right", responds Ringo Starr. "Meeting adjourned. Let's go have some lunch" ' (Bramwell, 2004: 260–1). Lennon immediately lost weight, wore a beard and began to dress in white. The double-breasted jacket from his March 1969 Gibraltar wedding photographs, the Ted Lapidus haute couture suit featured on the *Abbey Road* (1969) album sleeve and similar outfits worn for *The David Frost Show* and the Toronto Live Peace Festival all further enhanced Lennon's Christ-like image. 'The Ballad of John and Yoko' (1969), recorded and released immediately after the Amsterdam Bed-In for Peace, again compared his fate to Jesus by arguing that his treatment at the hands of the media equated to a modern-age crucifixion. During the Montreal Bed-In that followed he, once more, defined himself as a Christian communist using distinctly self-referential terms: 'I'm one of Christ's biggest fans. And if I can turn the focus of the Beatles on to Christ's message, then that's what we're here to do' (Lennon in Wynne-Jones, 2008). Furthermore: 'If I could do what Christ did, be as Christ was, that's what being a Christian is all about. I try to live as Christ lived. It's tough I can tell you' (Lennon in Coleman, 1984: 112).

After leaving the Beatles, Lennon appeared to announce a break in his faith via the song 'God' (1970), which contained a protracted declaration of his outright disbelief in the Bible or in Jesus Christ. Yoko later cited this as an accurate representation of his views (Barker, 2011: 117). Yet Steve Turner and others claim that less than two years later Lennon wrote a sincere letter to television evangelist Oral Roberts asking for guidance in how to find happiness and freedom from drugs (Harrell, 1985: 310; Turner, 2006: 188–9). Biographer Geoffrey Giuliano (2001: 143–4) has also described a profound Christian conversion experience that Lennon underwent in the spring of 1977, which lasted for approximately four months. An unpublished demo tape of 'You Saved My Soul' (1980), a song from the last ever Dakota Buildings home recording session, does indeed recount an incident that occurred while Lennon was alone in a hotel in Tokyo watching a television evangelist (Cormany, 2009). This account tallies with Giuliano's assertion, which reveals he was on a journey to Hong Kong and Japan without Yoko Ono at that time. Lennon's reaction to Dylan's Christian conversion was equally uncertain. In public he responded with good grace: 'If Dylan is into Jesus because of needing to belong, whatever, perhaps the next step will be to see the good of the experience as well as the other side' (Lennon et al., 1981: 103). In private, however, he was extremely critical, recording at least twelve versions of his coruscating Dylan parody 'Serve Yourself' in his final year at the Dakota Building (Doggett, 2009).

At the end of his life, Lennon defined his religion as 'Pagan – Zen Pagan to be precise' in private correspondence (Lennon in Davies et al., 2012: 351). Yet *Double Fantasy* (1980) still featured noticeably Christian tropes. 'Beautiful Boy', for example, encouraged his son Sean to pray before bedtime much as he had done with Aunt Mimi as a child. Lennon continued to draw grand parallels between his own life and that of Jesus, particularly their shared experience as persecuted messiah archetypes: 'Do we have to divide the fish and the loaves for the multitudes again? Do we have to get crucified again? Do we have to do the walking on water again?' (Lennon et al., 1981: 72). That Lennon's teleology was so self-centred is ultimately quite poignant, as this propensity for likening himself to Jesus was also a motive cited by his murderer Mark David Chapman (Jones, 1992).

It is worth noting that although he was an outspoken atheist during his Marxist revolutionary period (1970–2) Lennon was still not free of evolved teleological biases at that time. 'Imagine' (1971) outlined Lennon's most coherent vision of the international socialism first codified by Karl Marx and Friedrich Engels (1848) in *The Communist Manifesto*, a work that relied on its own theorisation of historical progress and the inevitable collapse of capitalism. Lennon acknowledged these ideas as an important inspiration for the song but could not explain how they might transpire, other than via a 'nice' characteristically 'British' form of socialism, 'not the way some daft Russian might do it, or the Chinese might do it' (Lennon in Blaney, 2005: 83). In the end, Lennon's faith in supernatural powers proved far more robust than his appetite for revolution, as he and Yoko Ono wrote in a letter to the *New York Times* in 1979: 'Wishing is more effective than waving flags. It works. It's like magic. Magic is simple. Magic is real . . . all people who come to us are angels in disguise, carrying messages and gifts to us from the Universe. Magic is logical. Try it some time' (Lennon in Davies et al., 2012: 358).

Lennon's most overt statement of Vedic teleology appeared on his final LP *Double Fantasy* (1980). The notion of *Samsāra*, or the wheel of life, a key constituent of the karmic cycle, was the central metaphor of his posthumous hit single 'Watching the Wheels'. Lennon also referenced this concept in the slew of promotional interviews he conducted to prior to the album's release:

> The whole universe is a wheel, right? Wheels go round and round . . . nothing is real, if you break the word down. As the Hindus or Buddhists say, it's an illusion, meaning all matter is floating atoms, right? It's Rashomon. We all see it, but the agreed-upon illusion is what we live in. And the hardest thing is facing yourself. It's easier to shout 'Revolution' and 'Power to the people' than it is to look at yourself and try to find out what's real inside you and what isn't. (Lennon in Cott and Doudna, 1982: 191)

Conclusion

Music and spirituality share similar attributes as airborne, intangible, affective phenomena. They are also closely aligned in religious practices and traditions. The Old and the New Testament both cite the other-worldly energy of music as a parallel to the power of the Holy Spirit: 'Through music God plays his power, and the power is vested in the music' (Cobussen, 2008: 16). Examples include David's exorcism of Saul (1 Samuel, 16:23), the siege of Jericho (Joshua, 6:1–27), Paul's guidance on the use of 'songs from the Spirit' (Colossians, 3:16; Ephesians, 5:19) and Psalms 49, 71, 101, 105 and 150. Non-biblical claims for the supernatural power of organised sound include the Music of the Spheres (James, 1995), indigenous shamanic percussion instruments (Winkelman, 2005), sacred Hindu mantras (Beck, 2006), and the musical language of the Quran (Rasmussen, 2010). Jacques Attali extended the valence between music and religion into historical power structures, citing faith and harmony as vital to the maintenance of social relationships: 'When the rites and music are clear and complete, heaven and earth fulfil their normal functions' (Attali, 1985: 60).

Today, while the concept of spirituality remains contested, music is no longer an ontological mystery. Sound travels through the atmosphere as a series of molecular agitations. The frequency and resonance of these vibrations, when artfully organised, generates affect (Parker, 2010). Thomson and Aukofer's (2011) evolutionary psychology of faith aims to unpick our belief mechanisms in much the same way. The four cognitive biases considered in this chapter – dualism, agency attribution, moral systems and teleology – are certainly demonstrable in both Dylan's and Lennon's compositions. Indeed, faith tropes are common across several genres of popular music and mind–body dualism frequently functions as an analogy for artistic inspiration, usually in the form of a song gifted by an external agent or somehow drawn from the ether. Creativity and spirituality are often studied together in formal research,[9] and in that context a more systematic evolutionary analysis of religiosity in songwriters could produce interesting results. George Harrison is an obvious candidate, but other influential artists with overtly spiritual worldviews include Johnny Cash, Selena Gomez, Prince, Cat Stevens, Stormzy and Kanye West.

Dylan's and Lennon's beliefs also led to their immersion in various new religious movements, political campaigns and therapy cults: Dylan with the Vineyard Christian Fellowship and his subsequent interest in orthodox Jewish communities such as the Sh'or Yoshuv and Chabad Lubavitch; Lennon via Transcendental Meditation, ISKCON, primal therapy, the International Marxist Group, the Youth International Party and others. Interdisciplinary scholarship exploring popular music and in-group thinking could produce valuable outcomes here. Robert J. Lifton's (1961) classic work on thought reform might prove a useful framework. His eight criteria map well against statements made by Dylan and Lennon in support of their activism and beliefs.[10] Here Lennon fulfils Lifton's fifth category, 'sacred science', while promulgating macrobiotic diets:

INTERVIEWER: What does your diet include?
LENNON: We're mostly macrobiotic, but sometimes I bring the family out for a pizza.
ONO: Intuition tells you what to eat [mostly] foods indigenous to the area.
INTERVIEWER: And you both smoke up a storm.
LENNON: Macrobiotic people don't believe in the 'big C' ... don't believe that smoking is bad for you. Of course, if we die, we're wrong.

(Lennon in Lennon et al., 1981: 94)

After all, there is a rich history of interdisciplinary scholarship between psychology and the arts. Inspired by Freud's *The Interpretation of Dreams* (1899), Ernest Jones (1949) psychoanalysed Shakespearean characters and, in so doing, established an entirely new school of literary studies. Thomson

---

[9] See Ehrlich, 1997; Lewis-Giggetts, 2017; Reed, 2003; Till, 2010.
[10] These are: milieu control, mystical manipulation, demand for purity, confession, sacred science, loaded language, doctrine over person and dispensation of existence.

(2009a) cites Freud's *The Future of an Illusion* (1927) as an important early attempt to initiate an objective analysis of faith mechanisms, and Lifton (1975) was also influenced by Freud in his work on in-group thinking. Today, evolutionary psychology enjoys an equally broad methodological base and several peer-reviewed journals are accelerating the growth and influence of this subject area.[11] The Natural History of Song Project in The Music Lab at Harvard University's Department of Psychology (www .themusiclab.org) hosts an excellent repository of interdisciplinary research. Other areas of convergence include literary Darwinism and psychobiography. Denis Dutton (2009) showed how the cross-cultural aesthetics of visual art emerged as a product of human evolution, and Joseph Carroll (2011) argued that our understanding of human nature offers a powerful new framework for the analysis of literature. More recently, Scott Wilson (2015) and Andrew McCarron (2017) revived the music psychobiography pioneered by Henry W. Sullivan's (1995) work on the Beatles and Lacan:

> psychobiography attempts to demythologise lives that are challenging to interpret, especially ones that are knotty with contradictions, shifting centers of meaning, moral ambiguities, and apocryphal narratives ... psychobiography differs from biography in terms of focus. It attempts to capture the unique psychological 'fingerprint' of a person by trying to make sense of an idiosyncratic, hard-to-pin-down part of him or her that contributes significantly to identity and behaviour. (McCarron, 2017: xi)

Supernatural beliefs may have inspired some of Dylan's and Lennon's most impactful songs, but today the cognitive mechanisms underpinning their subjective experience of faith can be explained from a material basis. This chapter investigated the spiritual tropes in their lyrics using new and powerful explanatory tools that could not have been anticipated by even the most far-sighted creative artists of the 1960s. The outcomes point towards further opportunities for interdisciplinary research in the evolutionary psychology of music that may, over time, contribute to a more complete understanding of popular culture and human behaviour.

---

[11] These include *Psychomusicology: Music, Mind and Brain; Evolution, Mind and Behaviour; the Journal of Cultural and Evolutionary Psychology;* and *Evolution and Human Behaviour.*

CHAPTER 7

Conclusion

Dylan's and Lennon's legacies endured into the twenty-first century, where they remain two of popular music's most influential songwriters. In the decades following Lennon's murder his Beatles songs and solo output continued to be broadcast and purchased in large numbers, featured in high-profile media synchronisations and heard at globally important cultural events. 'Imagine', for example, received a worldwide television audience at ceremonial events for the 2006 Winter Olympics, plus the 2012 and 2020 Summer Olympics. It has also been performed immediately before midnight at the celebrations in Times Square, New York City, every New Year's Eve since 2005–6. Two separate all-star 'lockdown' versions were recorded and distributed via social media during the worldwide COVID-19 pandemic of spring 2020, one led by *Wonder Woman* actress Gal Gadot and the other by Free and Bad Company singer Paul Rogers.[1] Dylan continues to receive significant international recognition too. His thirty-eight Grammy Award nominations include successive Best Traditional Pop Vocal Album in 2015, 2016 and 2017. In 2015 he accepted the National Academy of Recording Arts and Sciences 'MusiCares' Person of the Year Award, he gained the distinction of being the first popular music lyricist to receive a Nobel Prize for Literature in 2016 and in 2020 his critically acclaimed *Rough and Rowdy Ways* topped the album charts in territories around the world. Both Dylan and Lennon remain iconic figures and attractive candidates for the comparative analysis of Eloise Knapp Hay's dual biography. In 2009 Dylan acknowledged the depth of their relationship when he made a private visit to

---

[1] Sadly, during summer 2014, Lennon's international renown was used to demonstrate the global reach of militant Islamic fundamentalists from the UK when British citizen Mohammed Emwazi attracted attention from the worldwide media as a member of Islamic State of Iraq and the Levant (ISIL) following the circulation of gruesome beheading videos online. After Emwazi's captives gave him the nickname 'Jailer John' he became better known as 'Jihadi John', one of four British ISIL militants ('the Beatles') who guarded, tortured and executed Western hostages in Raqqa, Syria (Chulov, 2018; Simpson et al., 2014).

Lennon's childhood home in Liverpool, which subsequently inspired 'Roll on John' on *Tempest*.

This book constitutes the first thematic and theorised evaluation of Dylan's and Lennon's cultural correlations. Their peace songs were classified using an enhanced version of R. Serge Denisoff's criteria for magnetic, rhetorical and introspective protest music. Denisoff's categories explain how and why each voiced their opposition to militarism and revealed the opposing trajectories traced by their anti-war messages. Here, they formed a neat mirror image. Dylan moved from overtly magnetic to increasingly enigmatic rhetorical and introspective compositions early in his career. Lennon produced introspective peace songs at the height of his success with the Beatles then moved on to fully magnetic protest activities in collaboration with Yoko Ono. Just as Dylan publicly abandoned the 'spokesperson for a generation' role, Lennon enthusiastically embodied it. In Eyerman and Jamison's (1998) terminology, one replaced the other as an archetypal exemplary movement artist.

From a twenty-first century perspective it is easy to forget the Victorian age was still in living memory for some during the 1960s. Yet a comparative analysis of Dylan's and Lennon's historicism illustrates just how deeply nineteenth-century traditions influenced their worldviews. Conspicuous references to events and individuals from the past in their lyrics and other texts were grouped by Fredric Jameson's (1981) three-tiered scheme of individual artefacts, collective interests, and underlying economic changes. Obvious parallels exist between Dylan and the North American transcendentalists in their affinity for literature, obdurate individualism and piety towards nature; Lennon readily attested to his Irish migrant ancestry, his northern working-class heritage and the cultural legacy of British colonialism. Jameson's framework also highlights how Dylan's and Lennon's output intersected with important socio-economic developments during their own times, which straddled the fault lines between residual and emergent modes of production in the late 1960s and early 1970s. Dylan's appreciation for the natural world aligned with his sensitivities towards the deleterious consequences of Fordist industrialism. Lennon's heritage, inevitably interwoven with Britain's imperial backstory, coincided with his band's rise as international cultural ambassadors during a period of extensive decolonisation.

Dylan's and Lennon's spiritual beliefs were then compared from a wider *pre*-historical perspective: J. Anderson Thomson and Clare Aukofer's (2011) analysis of the evolutionary psychology underlying faith. Several millennia of natural selection have endowed humans with persuasive cognitive preferences for mind–body dualism, hyperactive agency attribution, moral intuition and teleology. These innate biases render humans highly susceptible to supernatural phenomena. Dylan and Lennon were not immune to such predispositions, which are visible in song lyrics and interview statements throughout their careers and particularly conspicuous during their periods of involvement with new religious movements. Music and spirituality are closely aligned psychological experiences and the similarities in our affective response to each only enhances this relationship. For the individual, music-making offers an important means of self-expression and the possibility of connection to others. Collective participation in this activity facilitates in-group cohesion and, as a result, is universally associated with worship practices around the world. Evolutionary psychology has a great deal to offer in our understanding of both music and spirituality, and brings many opportunities for further interdisciplinary scholarship in these fields.

The three themes of *protest, history* and *spirituality* intersect with each other in interesting ways, too. In *protest* and *history*, for example, Dylan's and Lennon's contrasting attitudes towards class discourse and collective action were evident in their different approach to the anti-war movement artist role, which stemmed from their ideological roots on either side of the Atlantic Ocean. Dylan's reluctance to engage in mass mobilisations for peace resembled the obdurate individualism of North American transcendentalists. When he did write social justice songs, these were often from the perspective of an individualised case study. In contrast, Lennon's Irish family heritage and his northern English upbringing fuelled a commitment to class politics and collective protest that moved beyond his peace campaigns to include organisations such as the International Marxist Group and even, at one point, support for the IRA. Many of these activities involved campaigns that began as part of Britain's post-imperial legacy, such as Biafra and Northern Ireland. Ironically, Lennon's militant espousal for these causes was ultimately tempered by his exploration of Vedic traditions that also reached London as part of ongoing cultural and historical links between the United Kingdom and its former colonies.

Dylan's and Lennon's abandonment of class-based 'magnetic' protest music came a decade apart, but it also stands as another example of economically driven cultural change – the broad shift from Fordism to multinational capitalism, and from modernity to postmodernity, at the end of the post-war long boom. Here, Dylan's movement from magnetic to introspective anti-war songs in the mid-1960s, and Lennon's eventual retreat from the role of movement artist in the early 1970s, foreshadowed a general decline in explicitly political compositions. Deena Weinstein (2006) lauded the 'Golden Age' of protest music during the 1960s, but lamented the years that followed when such songs were ignored, misinterpreted or conspicuous by their absence. Brian Ashbee (1999) coined the memorable phrase 'art bollocks' to describe the aesthetic in ambiguity of visual art during this period.

In some ways Dylan's epistemological leap from the magnetic activism of 'Ye Playboys and Playgirls' to the abstract introspection of 'Highway 61 Revisited' was an early example of the unintelligibility that Weinstein and Ashbee found so exasperating. Meanwhile Lennon's progress in the opposite direction, from introspective 'mood songs' to purposefully magnetic campaign compositions, provided a memorable soundtrack for large-scale anti-war mobilisations. As a result 'Give Peace a Chance' became the most popular protest anthem during the 'Golden Age' of anti-war protest music. However, Lennon's most successful and enduring political song over the decades that followed was, by some distance, 'Imagine'. This subversive composition argued for the abolition of religion, borders and private property via a concise expression of idealism that distilled its message into *one word* and propagated radical politics through the benign manifestation of *thought itself*. An act of contemplation is almost by definition the least belligerent revolutionary proposition possible, and 'Imagine' was so comprehensively decoupled from any genuine militancy that mainstream artists could perform it without alienating their audiences – in much the same way as 'Blowin' in the Wind' became Dylan's most covered protest song a decade earlier.

Chapters 4, 5 and 6, on *history* and *spirituality*, examined Dylan's and Lennon's knowledge of reality (their ontology) and their explanations for that understanding (their epistemology) using two related concepts: historical materialism and scientific naturalism. While each artist recognised that economic and social realities shape culture, neither could be described as a historical materialist. Instead, as committed idealists, they viewed systems of thought as the prime mover in human history – meaning that, in philosophical terms, both were more Hegelian than Marxian. Again, a comparative analysis demonstrates how Dylan's and Lennon's beliefs were shaped by their geographical and historical circumstances. Dylan's upbringing amid a small, isolated Midwestern Jewish community resulted in an unusual familiarity with the New Testament, while his romantic appreciation of nature shared many characteristics with transcendentalist responses to the industrial revolution. These influences may also have contributed to his incremental evangelical conversion in the late 1970s.

Lennon's family history included several ironic coincidences, such as his grandfather's apparent career as a minstrel in the United States, his – and his father's – embodiment of the 'foundling-turned-seaman' literary trope and his mother's experience of an IRA gas attack.

The incongruity between the widespread acceptance of human evolution and Lennon's denial of that fact, alongside the imperial nostalgia that saturated his Beatles songs, gives rise to one final historical irony. Around the time Lennon began to refute the notion that we 'came from monkeys', likely under the influence of Hindu creationism, the first evidence for the so-called 'missing link' was located in Ethiopia's Great Rift Valley – the fossilised part-skeleton of a three-million-year-old australopithecine female. The anthropologists who unearthed this find disregarded the standard specimen-numbering conventions because 'A.L. 288' seemed inappropriate to the international importance of their discovery. So 'Lucy', inspired by Lennon's 'Lucy in the Sky with Diamonds' as it played on a cassette tape copy of *Sgt. Pepper's Lonely Hearts Club Band*, soon became the world's most famous early hominid. The Beatles connection may have helped publicise Lucy's discovery, but the choice of this name over the indigenous (Amharic) language suggestion[2] from the Ethiopian Ministry of Culture somehow encapsulates the postcolonial legacy running through much of Lennon's output (Johanson and Wong, 2009; Lennon et al., 1981).

That Dylan's and Lennon's relevance endured for so long is clear from the sheer weight of scholarship on their output. Their music was firmly rooted in the nineteenth century, yet it also anticipated the postmodern turn at the end of the twentieth century. Both remained relevant through the ensuing decades precisely because they articulated the economic and cultural tensions in their own time so well. Today, the lives and works of the post-war generation are themselves passing into history. We peer into an uncertain future of financial insecurity and a climate emergency, revolutionary activism and reactionary populism, a plastic waste crisis and a pandemic virus. No one can be sure how or even *whether* these situations will resolve, but we can certainly expect new generations to raise their voice and new movement artists to mobilise for their cause. How they relate to the individuals and issues discussed in this book remains to be seen. Yet if truly great songs are those that capture the mood of their moment there will always be a reason to listen to Dylan and Lennon – and always a reason to write about them.

---

[2] 'Dinkinesh', meaning 'you are marvellous'.

Detailed Chronology

The timeline below shows the key events, concerts, recordings and releases in the life of Bob Dylan and John Lennon. It is draw from Badman, 2001; Burrows, 2013; Goldman, 1988; Gooden, 2014b; Gray, 2008; Heylin, 1995, 1996; Jarosinski, 2006; Lewisohn, 1996; MacDonald, 1994; and Miles, 2001. Recording dates are cited according to official Beatles and John Lennon releases on Parlophone/Apple, and official Dylan releases on Columbia. Songs with no official release are cited according to date of home recording (Lennon) or date of recording for Witmark Publishing/ Broadside Records (Dylan). Dates of release are cited by month and year of release in the United Kingdom and United States, except where these do not coincide, in which case the relevant territory is indicated in parentheses.

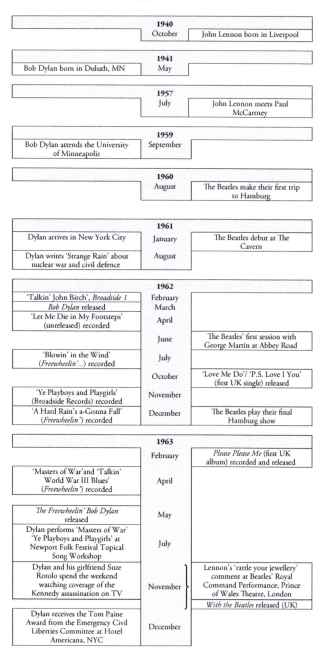

1940		
	October	John Lennon born in Liverpool

	1941	
Bob Dylan born in Duluth, MN	May	

	1957	
	July	John Lennon meets Paul McCartney

	1959	
Bob Dylan attends the University of Minneapolis	September	

	1960	
	August	The Beatles make their first trip to Hamburg

	1961	
Dylan arrives in New York City	January	The Beatles debut at The Cavern
Dylan writes 'Strange Rain' about nuclear war and civil defence	August	

	1962	
'Talkin' John Birch', *Broadside 1*	February	
Bob Dylan released	March	
'Let Me Die in My Footsteps' (unreleased) recorded	April	
	June	The Beatles' first session with George Martin at Abbey Road
'Blowin' in the Wind' (*Freewheelin'…*) recorded	July	
	October	'Love Me Do'/ 'P.S. Love I You' (first UK single) released
'Ye Playboys and Playgirls' (Broadside Records) recorded	November	
'A Hard Rain's a-Gonna Fall' (*Freewheelin'*) recorded	December	The Beatles play their final Hamburg show

	1963	
	February	*Please Please Me* (first UK album) recorded and released
'Masters of War' and 'Talkin' World War III Blues' (*Freewheelin'*) recorded	April	
The Freewheelin' Bob Dylan released	May	
Dylan performs 'Masters of War' 'Ye Playboys and Playgirls' at Newport Folk Festival Topical Song Workshop	July	
Dylan and his girlfriend Suze Rotolo spend the weekend watching coverage of the Kennedy assassination on TV	November	Lennon's 'rattle your jewellery' comment at Beatles' Royal Command Performance, Prince of Wales Theatre, London
		With the Beatles released (UK)
Dylan receives the Tom Paine Award from the Emergency Civil Liberties Committee at Hotel Americana, NYC	December	

Fig. A1

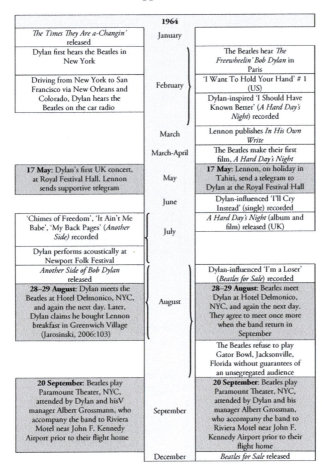

1964		
The Times They Are a-Changin' released	January	
Dylan first hears the Beatles in New York		The Beatles hear *The Freewheelin' Bob Dylan* in Paris
Driving from New York to San Francisco via New Orleans and Colorado, Dylan hears the Beatles on the car radio	February	'I Want To Hold Your Hand' # 1 (US)
		Dylan-inspired 'I Should Have Known Better' (*A Hard Day's Night*) recorded
	March	Lennon publishes *In His Own Write*
	March-April	The Beatles make their first film, *A Hard Day's Night*
17 May: Dylan's first UK concert, at Royal Festival Hall. Lennon sends supportive telegram	May	**17 May**: Lennon, on holiday in Tahiti, send a telegram to Dylan at the Royal Festival Hall
	June	Dylan-influenced 'I'll Cry Instead' (single) recorded
'Chimes of Freedom', 'It Ain't Me Babe', 'My Back Pages' (*Another Side)* recorded	July	*A Hard Day's Night* (album and film) released (UK)
Dylan performs acoustically at Newport Folk Festival		
Another Side of Bob Dylan released		Dylan-influenced 'I'm a Loser' (*Beatles for Sale*) recorded
28–29 August: Dylan meets the Beatles at Hotel Delmonico, NYC, and again the next day. Later, Dylan claims he bought Lennon breakfast in Greenwich Village (Jarosinski, 2006:103)	August	**28–29 August**: Beatles meet Dylan at Hotel Delmonico, NYC, and again the next day. They agree to meet once more when the band return in September
		The Beatles refuse to play Gator Bowl, Jacksonville, Florida without guarantees of an unsegregated audience
20 September: Beatles play Paramount Theater, NYC, attended by Dylan and hisV manager Albert Grossmann, who accompany the band to Riviera Motel near John F. Kennedy Airport prior to their flight home	September	**20 September**: Beatles play Paramount Theater, NYC, attended by Dylan and his manager Albert Grossman, who accompany the band to Riviera Motel near John F. Kennedy Airport prior to their flight home
	December	*Beatles for Sale* released

Fig. A1 (Cont.)

	1965	
Beatles-influenced 'If You Gotta Go, Go Now' (unreleased) recorded	January	
	February	Dylan-influenced 'You've Got to Hide Your Love Away' (*Help!*) recorded
Bringing It All Back Home released. Dylan refers to the growing controversy over Vietnam in the album's sleeve notes	March	
Dont Look Back [sic] filmed in England	April–May	The Beatles film *Help!* in London and on location
9 May: Dylan plays Royal Albert Hall and is visited by The Beatles at the Savoy Hotel, London. This encounter is described in Marianne Faithfull's memoir (1994)	May	**9 May**: The Beatles see Dylan perform at the Royal Albert Hall then visit Dylan at the Savoy Hotel, London. Lennon defends Dylan's decision to stay at the Savoy
	June	Lennon's *A Spaniard in the Works* published
Dylan performs with the Paul Butterfield Blues Band at the Newport Folk Festival	July	*Help!* (film) released
'Tombstone Blues' and 'Highway 61 Revisited' (*Highway 61*) recorded		*Help!* (album) released
15–16 August: Dylan visits the Beatles at the Warwick Hotel, NYC	August	**15–16 August**: Beatles play Shea Stadium and are visited by Dylan at the Warwick Hotel, NYC, after the show and again the following day
Highway 61 Revisited released		The Beatles meet Elvis Presley in Bel Air, LA
		Beatles awarded MBE at Buckingham Palace
Beatles-influenced 'Can You Please Crawl Out Your Window' (single) recorded	November	Dylan-influenced 'Norwegian Wood (This Bird Has Flown)' (*Rubber Soul*) recorded
		'The Word' (*Rubber Soul*) recorded
	December	*Rubber Soul* released

	1966	
'4th Time Around' (*Blonde on Blonde*) recorded	February	
	March	Lennon's 'more popular than Jesus' comment published in the *Evening Standard*, London
	April	'Tomorrow Never Knows' (*Revolver*) recorded
Blonde on Blonde released		
26–29 May: Dylan performs two concerts at the Royal Albert Hall. He meets Lennon at his hotel and visits his house in Weybridge, Surrey. The next morning their limousine conversation is filmed for *Eat the Document*	May	**26–29 May**: Lennon and Harrison attend Dylan's Royal Albert Hall concert. Lennon visits Dylan at The May Fair Hotel, London. Dylan has dinner at Lennon's house in Weybridge, Surrey. They are filmed in Dylan's limousine the next morning
	June	*Yesterday and Today* ('butcher cover') released (US)
Dylan injured in motorcycle accident, retires from touring	July	Lennon's 'more popular than Jesus' comment published in *Datebook*, US
		Lennon apologises after controversy spreads in the US
		Revolver released
	August	The Beatles final concert Candlestick Park, San Francisco
	September–October	*How I Won the War* filmed in Almería, Spain. Lennon plays Private Gripweed
	November	Lennon meets Yoko Ono at the Indica Gallery, London

Fig. A1 (Cont.)

	1967	
	June	*Sgt. Pepper's Lonely Hearts Club Band* released
		'All You Need Is Love' (single) recorded and broadcast on BBC's *Our World* global television programme
	August	The Beatles attend Maharishi Mahesh Yogi's lecture at the Hilton Hotel, London, and travel to his seminar in Bangor. Manager, Brian Epstein, dies
	October	*How I Won the War* released
John Wesley Harding released	December	*Magical Mystery Tour* (film and double EP) released

	1968	
	February	The Beatles travel to Rishikesh, India
	April	Lennon and Harrison return from India.
	May	Lennon and McCartney announce the creation of Apple Corps
		Lennon informs the other Beatles he thinks he is Jesus
		Unfinished Music No. 1: Two Virgins recorded
	July	*You Are Here* art exhibition, Robert Fraser Gallery, London
	August	'Yer Blues' (*The Beatles*) recorded
'Let Me Die in My Footsteps' and 'John Brown' released (as 'Blind Boy Grunt') on *Broadside Ballads Vol. 1*	September	'Happiness Is a Warm Gun' (*The Beatles*) recorded
	October	*The Beatles* (*The White Album*) released
George Harrison visits Dylan's home in Bearsville, New York, for Thanksgiving and they co-write three songs	November	*Unfinished Music No. 1: Two Virgins* released
	December	Lennon and Ono sit on stage in a bag at The Alchemical Wedding, a happening at Royal Albert Hall, London

Fig. A1 (Cont.)

	1969	
	January	*Let It Be,* Twickenham Studios
	March	Amsterdam Hilton Bed-In for Peace
Nashville Skyline released	April	Lennon and Ono's Bagism press conference, Vienna, Austria
		'The Ballad of John and Yoko' (single) recorded
		Lennon and Ono send acorns to world leaders
	May	*Unfinished Music No. 2: Life With the Lions* released
		Bahamas Sheraton Oceanus Hotel one-night Bed-In
		Montreal Queen Elizabeth Hotel seven-day Bed-In
		'The Ballad of John and Yoko' (single) released
	June	'Give Peace a Chance' (single) recorded
		Lennon and Ono attend Peace Seminar at Ottowa University
	July	'Give Peace a Chance' (single) released
		'Come Together' (*Abbey Road*) recorded
29–30 August: Lennon and Ono travel to the Isle of Wight where they visit Dylan in rehearsal at Forelands Farm **31 August:** Dylan performs at the Isle of Wight Festival **1 September:** Dylan visits Lennon at Tittenhurst Park, Berkshire	August– September	**29–30 August:** Lennon and Ono travel to Isle of Wight Festival and jam with Dylan in rehearsal at Forelands Farm. **31 August:** Dylan performs **1 September:** Dylan declines to play on 'Cold Turkey' in Lennon's home studio
	September	*Live Peace in Toronto* concert
		Lennon tells the Beatles he is leaving the band
		'Cold Turkey' recorded
		Hari Krishna (ISKCON) founder Srila Prabhupāda arrives at Lennon's Tittenhurst Park
	October	'Give Peace a Chance' sung at the Moratorium to End the War in Vietnam, Washington
		'Cold Turkey' released
	November	Lennon and Ono's *Wedding Album* released (UK)
		Lennon returns his MBE to Buckingham Palace
	December	'*WAR IS OVER! If You Want It*' Peace billboards in eleven cities
		Live Peace in Toronto released

Fig. A1 (Cont.)

	1970	
	February	'Instant Karma (We All Shine On)' (single) released
		Mosport Peace Festival (Toronto) cancelled
George Harrison visits Dylan's NYC apartment	April	Lennon visits Arthur Janov's Primal Institute in LA
Harrison records with Dylan at Columbia Studio B, NYC. Dylan sings 'Yesterday'	May	*Let It Be* (album and film) released
	September–October	'God' and 'Working Class Hero' (*John Lennon / Plastic Ono Band*) recorded
New Morning released	October	'Power to the People' (single) recorded
	December	*John Lennon / Plastic Ono Band* released

	1971	
	February	'I Don't Wanna Be a Soldier Mama I Don't Want to Die' (*Imagine*) recorded
	March	'Power to the People' (single) released
	May–June	'Imagine' (*Imagine*) recorded
Harrison and Dylan appear at Concert for Bangladesh, Madison Square Garden, NYC	August	Lennon refuses to appear at the Concert for Bangladesh
		Lennon and Ono move to St Regis Hotel, NYC
	September	*Imagine* released
9 October: Dylan attends the opening of Ono's *This Is Not Here*, Everson Museum of Art, Syracuse, NY contributes *Nashville Skyline* (minus sleeve)	October	**9 October**: Ono's *This Is Not Here* at Everson Museum of Art, Syracuse, NY. Dylan is among those celebrities who attend and donate artefacts
		'Happy Xmas (War Is Over)' recorded
Dylan records with Allen Ginsberg and Friends at the Record Plant in NYC	October–November	Lennon suggests Apple pay for Allen Ginsberg's recording at the Record Plant in NYC
Dylan, Lennon, Ono tour Greenwich Village		Dylan, Lennon, Ono tour Greenwich Village
Tarantula belatedly published by Macmillan	November	Lennon and Ono move to Bank Street, Greenwich Village, NYC
		Lennon and Ono sign Rock Liberation Front demand for A. J. Weberman's apology to Dylan
		'Happy Xmas (War Is Over)' released (US)
Dylan declines Jerry Rubin's invitation to appear at the John Sinclair Freedom Rally	December	Lennon and Ono appear at the John Sinclair Freedom Rally, Crisler Arena, Ann Arbor, MI

Fig. A1 (Cont.)

	1972	
Dylan visits Lennon in the Record Plant studio as he produces David Peel & The Lower East Side's 'The Ballad of Bob Dylan'	January	Dylan visits Lennon in the Record Plant studio, NYC, as he produces David Peel & The Lower East Side
	April	'Woman is the N----r of the World' (*Some Time*) released
Dylan writes a short letter to support Lennon and Ono's case against deportation	May	Dylan's letter in support of Lennon and Ono presented at their deportation hearing
	June	*Some Time in New York City*, 'The Luck of the Irish', 'Sunday Bloody Sunday', released
	August	*One to One* benefit concert at Madison Square Garden
	November	'Happy Xmas (War Is Over)' released (UK)

	1973	
	April	Lennon and Ono proclaim a conceptual country, Nutopia
	June	Lennon and Ono attend Watergate hearings, Washington, DC
Pat Garrett & Billy the Kid (album) released	July	
	July–August	'Mind Games' and 'Bring on the Lucy (Freda People)' (*Mind Games*) recorded
	November	*Mind Games* released

	1974	
31 January: Dylan's first concert tour since 1966 with the Band *Planet Waves* released	January	**31 January**: Lennon and Ono see Bob Dylan and the Band perform at Madison Square Garden
	July–August	'Scared' (*Walls and Bridges*) recorded
	October	*Walls and Bridges* released

	1975	
Blood on the Tracks, featuring 'Tangled up in Blue' released	January	
	July	Lennon considers naming his son (Sean) 'Dylan Ono Lennon'

	1978	
Dylan has a vision of Christ while in a Tucson hotel room	November	Lennon records 'News of the Day (From Reuters)' parody

Fig. A1 (Cont.)

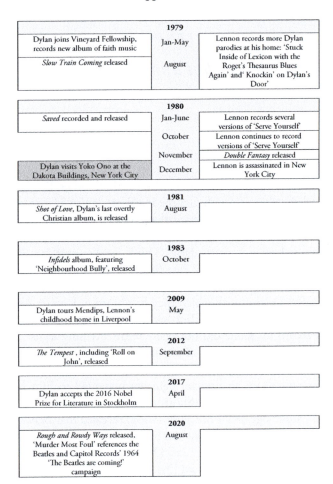

1979		
Dylan joins Vineyard Fellowship, records new album of faith music	Jan–May	Lennon records more Dylan parodies at his home: 'Stuck Inside of Lexicon with the Roget's Thesaurus Blues Again' and' Knockin' on Dylan's Door'
Slow Train Coming released	August	

1980		
Saved recorded and released	Jan–June	Lennon records several versions of 'Serve Yourself'
	October	Lennon continues to record versions of 'Serve Yourself'
	November	*Double Fantasy* released
Dylan visits Yoko Ono at the Dakota Buildings, New York City	December	Lennon is assassinated in New York City

1981		
Shot of Love, Dylan's last overtly Christian album, is released	August	

1983		
Infidels album, featuring 'Neighbourhood Bully', released	October	

2009		
Dylan tours Mendips, Lennon's childhood home in Liverpool	May	

2012		
The Tempest, including 'Roll on John', released	September	

2017		
Dylan accepts the 2016 Nobel Prize for Literature in Stockholm	April	

2020		
Rough and Rowdy Ways released, 'Murder Most Foul' references the Beatles and Capitol Records' 1964 'The Beatles are coming!' campaign	August	

Fig. A1 (Cont.)

APPENDIX 2

Bob Dylan and the Beatles

Bob Dylan had numerous interactions with the three 'other' Beatles. His most significant relationship was with George Harrison. It was Harrison, not John Lennon, who enjoyed the most personal and professional contact with Dylan. Harrison also, like Lennon, made key contributions to Beatles albums that betrayed this influence – particularly 'Think for Yourself' on *Rubber Soul* (1965) and 'Long Long Long' on *The Beatles* (aka *The White Album*, 1968). In *The Beatles Anthology* (1995) both remembered the dramatic impact of *The Freewheelin' Bob Dylan* (1963), which they first heard in January 1964 while in Paris (Roylance, 2000: 112–14): 'Paul had heard of him before but until we played that record his name did not really mean anything to us' (Lennon in Harry, 2000: 217). The memoir of Lennon's friend Pete Shotton described a visit to Harrison's house, 'Kinfauns' in Esher, where: '[George] showed me his proudest possession: an original painting presented to him by his (and John's) current idol, Bob Dylan' (Shotton and Schaffner, 1983: 105).

Harrison's autobiography *I Me Mine* (2004) revealed that *Blonde on Blonde* (1966) was the only Western pop record he carried on the Beatles' 1968 visit to Rishikesh, India. Later that same year, Dylan and Harrison co-wrote at least three songs when the guitarist visited Dylan during the Thanksgiving holiday. Harrison's memoir describes the genesis of 'I'd Have You Anytime' (1970) in meticulous detail: 'I was saying to Bob "Come on, write some words". He wrote the bridge . . . Beautiful! – and that was that. You can see the handwriting reproduced here with his kind permission' (Harrison, 2004: 164). Dylan's longhand lyrics, reprinted alongside Harrison's account, clearly show the lined notepaper he had saved from their co-writing session. Harrison chose this song to introduce his debut release *All Things Must Pass* (1970), even though the slow seventy beats per minute tempo and wistful vocals combined to generate an unusually downbeat opening track. He subsequently cited the fact that 'Bob had helped write it' (White, 2000) as a measure of confidence in the decision to place 'I'd Have You Anytime' so prominently on the album. *All Things Must Pass* also included a cover version of Dylan's 'If Not for You' and a lilting song about his shyness, 'Behind That Locked Door'. 'When Everybody Comes to Town', a joint composition, and 'I Don't Want to Do It', an unpublished and unreleased Dylan original, were also considered.

The Bob Dylan album that followed his Thanksgiving 1968 collaboration with Harrison, *Nashville Skyline* (1969), contained an unusually complex song, 'I Threw It All Away', whose chord structure and guitar playing strongly resembled Harrison's style. In May 1970, before the release of *Self Portrait* (1970), the two recorded together once more, this time for a full day in Columbia Studio B, New York. Although the session was reported in *Rolling Stone* magazine (Anon., 1970) collaborations such as 'Time Passes Slowly' and 'Working on a Guru' were not released until *Bootleg Series Vol. 10: Another Self Portrait (1969–1971)* (2013). Recollections from other musicians present in the studio confirm Dylan and Harrison's easy relationship and mutual approbation:

> George would say, 'Let's do "Rainy Day Women" ' . . . Usually when someone asks Bob to do a request, he's caustic to them. That wasn't the case there. They were very courteous to each other. (Drummer Russ Kunkel, in Browne, 2012: 151)

Harrison sportingly accompanied Dylan as he began to improvise a version of the McCartney composition 'Yesterday', and even contributed a guitar solo to this recording despite being in bitter dispute with McCartney over the dissolution of the Beatles during this time (Browne, 2012).

From June 1966 to January 1974 Dylan largely withdrew from live music performance and played a total of only five concerts. Indeed, it was George Harrison who facilitated two of these rare onstage appearances. Prior to the 1969 Isle of Wight Festival, he met Dylan at Portsmouth and visited him and the Band during their rehearsals on the island at Forelands Farm, Bembridge. Previously unpublished photographs from this occasion, showing Dylan and Harrison playing tennis, eventually appeared in *Rolling Stone* magazine (Hiatt, 2011). Following the Isle of Wight performance, Harrison escorted Dylan to Lennon's Tittenhurst Park residence. Lennon was in the middle of recording what eventually became the Plastic Ono Band single 'Cold Turkey' (1969), but an anticipated collaboration failed to materialise. Dylan actually hinted at such a possibility during his press conference before the Isle of Wight appearance: 'George Harrison has come to visit me. The Beatles have asked me to work with them. I love the Beatles and I think it would be a good idea to do a jam session' (Jarosinski, 2006: 429). Two years later, Harrison also persuaded Dylan to perform at his 1971 Concert for Bangladesh in Madison Square Garden. Reflecting on the event shortly afterwards, in an unpublished interview with friend Tony Glover, Dylan praised Harrison's quiet integrity and purposefulness:

> I mean, just the fact that he did it – incredible . . . Really in his own right. He just pulled it together in some kind of cohesive sense, and he rides it, right on top of it, and he's right there, all the time. Really, he was the only guy who did any talking – I didn't say shit. He put on a suit, got up there, and said, 'Quiet now, here's Ravi and pay attention' . . . Lennon couldn't have done it. (Brinkley, 2020)

As he acknowledged in 1977, Dylan has long admired Harrison's musicality, too: 'I've always liked the way George Harrison plays guitar – restrained and good' (Cott, 2007: 213). Indeed, they enjoyed a long history of live and recorded collaborations. One less well-known public appearance occurred at the Los Angeles Palomino Club in February 1987. Together they performed classics such as 'Blue Suede Shoes', 'Peggy Sue', 'Dizzy Miss Lizzy', 'Honey, Don't' and 'Matchbox' in an event captured on video and now available on *YouTube* (Subirats Miranda, 2013). Harrison, who clearly relished the moment, enthusiastically sang Dylan's 'Watching the River Flow'. One year later, as the Beatles were inducted into the Rock and Roll Hall of Fame, Dylan was among those who joined Harrison and Ringo Starr on stage to perform 'I Saw Her Standing There' – although this occasion was marked by the absence of Paul McCartney. Dylan and Harrison subsequently teamed up with Roy Orbison, Jeff Lynne and Tom Petty for *The Traveling Wilburys Volume 1* (1988) and its follow-up *Volume 3* (1990). In 1990 Harrison also played lead guitar on the title track of Dylan's *Under the Red Sky*. Two years later he performed 'Absolutely, Sweet Marie' during *The 30th Anniversary Concert Celebration* (1992) at Madison Square Garden in New York City, then introduced Dylan to the stage and accompanied him on 'My Back Pages'. Harrison frequently expressed his open admiration for Dylan: 'Bob was always the gaffer as far as I was concerned. With all due respect to John, I don't think there's anyone in the business who's ever even come close' (Giuliano, 1989: 52). Tom Petty confirmed the depth of this fandom when he recalled Harrison's habit of surreptitiously recording Dylan: 'George quoted Bob like people quote Scripture. Bob really adored George, too. George used to hang over the balcony videoing Bob while Bob wasn't aware of it. Bob would be sitting at the piano playing, and George would tape it and listen to it all night' (Hiatt, 2011).

Ringo Starr was a strong Dylan fan and remains the only other ex-Beatle to have recorded and performed with him. Starr also attended Dylan's Isle of Wight appearance and subsequently worked with producer Peter Drake (responsible for the distinctive steel guitar playing on 'Lay Lady Lay') in

Nashville on his country-influenced album *Beaucoups of Blues* (1970). The following year he accompanied Harrison and Dylan on tambourine at the Concert for Bangladesh (1971) and was backed by the Band on the album *Ringo* (1973). Dylan's guitarist Robbie Robertson played on Starr's next release *Goodnight Vienna* (1974), and Starr was present at the concluding Los Angeles show of Dylan's tour with the Band that year: 'It was bloody fantastic, the best concert I've ever been to' (Lepidus, 2010). He subsequently appeared during the finale of the Band's November 1976 concert, filmed for the movie *The Last Waltz* (Scorsese, 1978). Two months later, Starr performed alongside other guests in the Houston Astrodome at Dylan's *Rolling Thunder Revue* benefit for Rubin Carter. Later, Starr appeared on Dylan's 'Heart of Mine' (1981) single and both contributed to Artists United Against Apartheid's 'Sun City' (1985). Dylan made a guest appearance on Starr's 'I Wish I Knew Now What I Knew Then' (1987) and also, a year later, at the Beatles' 1988 Rock and Roll Hall of Fame induction. In 1989, Starr played drums for two set-closing songs at a Dylan show at Les Arènes de Frejus on the French Riviera, and in 1997 was introduced from the stage as 'one of the great drummers of this kind of music' during a Dylan show at the El Rey Theatre in Los Angeles (Lepidus, 2010). In a 2010 interview for *ABC News*, Starr praised Dylan's *Modern Times* (2006): 'You just got to love Bob. My all-time favourite lately is "When the Deal Goes Down", and it's just a beautiful love song' (Lepidus, 2010).

Paul McCartney has engaged in writing and production collaborations with artists such as Tony Bennett, George Michael, Yusuf Islam, Elvis Costello and Michael Jackson – yet unlike Harrison and Starr he has conspicuously avoided working with Dylan, either in the studio or onstage, despite many opportunities. McCartney was the only Beatle *not* to attend Dylan's 1969 Isle of Wight performance, apparently due to the imminent arrival of his and Linda McCartney's first child together. He was also the only Beatle not present at their 1988 Rock and Roll Hall of Fame induction – where Dylan performed alongside Harrison and Starr. McCartney boycotted this event due to litigation filed by Yoko Ono, Harrison and Starr four years earlier (Sounes, 2011b: 415). 'It's sad that there are other people who aren't here tonight', commented The Beach Boys' Mike Love, also inducted that evening: 'People like Paul McCartney who couldn't be here because he's in a lawsuit with Ringo and Yoko' (Greene, 2012).

Ian Inglis claims McCartney's lack of interest in Dylan centres on personality issues, citing a biographer who claims the former Beatle was unable to maintain intimate friendships and associated only with close employees. McCartney's insistence on creative control, he argued, also fostered his reluctance to perform with other artists of a similar status: he prefers working with subordinates instead. This is an interesting but harsh observation given McCartney's collaborators include Michael Jackson, Stevie Wonder and Johnny Cash: 'By insisting on complete control at all times, not just over the creative process, but the administrative, organisational and logistical aspects of his professional activities, McCartney's opportunity for genuine alliances and continuing reciprocities in musical production seems to have been eliminated' (Inglis, 1996b: 71).

McCartney, like his other former band members, remains an unequivocal Dylan enthusiast. Perhaps dubiously, he once claimed to have owned the folk singer's debut album: 'We loved him and had done since his first album which I'd had in Liverpool' (McCartney and Miles, 1997: 187). This is questionable due to the small number of copies of *Bob Dylan* (1962) distributed outside the United States at that time, and because its successor *Freewheelin'* is generally accepted as the first Dylan album the Beatles heard while performing in Paris in 1964. Interestingly, Dylan's early remarks about the band also suggest a natural antipathy toward McCartney's writing style. His first disparaging comment towards the Beatles, for example, came in an interview on the 1966 tour when he criticised McCartney's work: 'They play songs like "Michelle" and "Yesterday". A lot of smoothness there . . . It's such a cop-out . . . go into the Library of Congress you can find a lot better than that' (Shelton, 1986: 344). Ironically, Dylan's own version of 'Yesterday' from his 1970 New York City recording session with Harrison is now available on *YouTube* as a studio out-take (Clegg, 2015).

Later, Dylan commented on the gulf in recording styles between the sparse *John Wesley Harding* (1967) and the stylised *Sgt. Pepper's Lonely Hearts Club Band* (1967), a project driven by McCartney: 'The Beatles had just released *Sgt. Pepper*, which I didn't like at all . . . Talk about indulgence. I thought that was a very indulgent album' (Jarosinski, 2006: 655). McCartney replied to this criticism by parodying Dylan in 'Rocky Racoon' from *The Beatles* (The White Album) (1968). In one early take the protagonist hails from 'a small town in Minnesota' (Inglis, 1996b: 100). However, such exchanges do not represent the sum of Dylan's comments about McCartney or the Beatles as a whole. A cursory analysis of Dylan's published interviews reveals his consistent praise for the band, their songwriting, their consistency and their influence on popular culture (Jarosinski, 2006: 119, 126, 232, 363).

As Dylan and McCartney both reached their early seventies, each seemed more self-reflective and more mutually appreciative. Dylan contributed a balanced and perceptive summary of McCartney's legacy to *Rolling Stone*'s 40th anniversary issue:

Lennon, to this day, it's hard to find a singer better than Lennon was, or than McCartney was and still is. I'm in awe of McCartney. He's about the only one that I'm in awe of. He can do it all. And he's never let up. He's got the gift for melody, he's got the gift for rhythm, he can play any instrument. He can scream and shout as good as anyone, and he can sing a ballad as good as anyone. And his melodies are effortless, that's what you have to be in awe of . . . he's just so damn effortless. I just wish he'd quit (laughs). Everything that comes out of his mouth is just framed in melody. (Dylan in Wenner, 2007)

The following year McCartney reciprocated, suggesting that he *would* like to record with Dylan. Their position as two surviving 1960s icons presented a unique opportunity for collaboration: 'Bob Dylan would be lovely . . . because I admire him' (Vinnicombe, 2008). A year later Dylan acknowledged this, although less enthusiastically: 'That'd be exciting to do something with Paul! But, y'know, your paths have to cross for something like that to make sense' (Brinkley, 2009: 46). In response, McCartney retracted his previously expressed desire to work with Dylan as 'a totally unfounded . . . rumour' that originated as 'a newspaper thing' and was now 'a family joke' among his daughters: 'He just said some very complimentary things about me in some interviews . . . but we're not the kind of people who would ring each other up' (Blanchard, 2009). Any Dylan/McCartney partnership remains impossible to rule out until one of the protagonists either permanently retires or dies, although it is unlikely to ever happen:

> There were big rumours a couple of years ago about me and Bob Dylan writing together, and I've still got that at the back of my mind. I would like to do it. But I'm spoiled for collaborators, 'cos I had John. And I've gotta be very unrealistic to think I'll find a better collaborator than him. (McCartney, in Baggs, 2013)

This would certainly be one of popular music's more keenly anticipated alliances. Dylan's abrasive aesthetic might balance McCartney's more saccharine tastes, much as Lennon and McCartney's dissimilar mode of songwriting complemented each other. Ian MacDonald (1994) catalogued the significant differences between Lennon and McCartney's divergent styles. Lennon's melodies, he observed, reflected his sardonic temperament and sedentary lifestyle in their reluctance to climb up and down the stave. Sometimes they were reduced to repetitive phrases that simply oscillated between two notes of adjacent pitch, as in 'I Am the Walrus' (1967) or one-note passages such as in the verse sections of 'Help!' (1965) and 'I'm Only Sleeping' (1966).

> Basically a realist, [Lennon] instinctively kept his melodies close to the rhythms and cadences of speech, colouring his lyrics with bluesy tone and harmony rather than creating lines that made striking shapes of their own. McCartney's lines, by contrast, display his extrovert energy and optimism, ranging freely across the stave in scalar steps and wide intervals, often encompassing more than an octave. His is the expression of a natural melodist ... whereas Lennon's lines tend to be allusive, moody affairs ... McCartney's method is, in terms of intervals, 'vertical' (melodic, consonant), and Lennon's 'horizontal' (harmonic, dissonant). (MacDonald, 1994: 11)

In this context Dylan's attitude, rationale and songwriting techniques compare favourably with Lennon's approach as a potential foil for McCartney, and any prospective Dylan/McCartney collaboration could promise the same interesting synthesis. Dylan, too, appears to prefer simpler tunes, sometimes reducing them to a contiguous or even entirely monotonal 'horizontal' melody – as in 'Subterranean Homesick Blues' (1965) – that could compliment McCartney's more upbeat 'vertical' constructions. Michael Gray remarked upon the obvious correspondence between Dylan's and Lennon's innate cynicism: 'as the most acerbic Beatle, John was the one regarded as most similar to Dylan' (Gray, 2008: 41). Howard Sounes also recognised their stylistic parallels:

> Like Dylan, Lennon had the knack of writing couplets ... that seem to contain an essential truth. Paul was rarely such a philosopher. He glides along the surface of life in his songs, as he did to some extent on ... 'When I'm Sixty-Four'. Although this is one of Paul's best songs, and one that deals with a profound subject, old age, Paul sidestepped the darker issues involved – ill-health, loneliness, regret and fear of death – to create ... an attractive song with a facile lyric. (Sounes, 2011b: 161)

While McCartney's cultivated aesthetic differentiates him from the indelicate, unaffected approach shared by Dylan and Lennon, it also confirms the supposition that the latter two provide more complementary biographical subjects. Martin Amis recollected that 'there was something over-cute and chirpy about Paul' and considered that preferring McCartney over Lennon was akin to preferring Cliff Richard over Elvis Presley (Amis, 1993: 183). Despite an energetic late-career revival that included world tours almost every year from 2002 to 2019 and high-profile concerts at Queen Elizabeth II's Diamond Jubilee Concert, the 2012 Summer Olympics and 12-12-12: The Concert for Sandy Relief, it remains difficult to imagine how McCartney might ever attain the more visceral form of appeal shared by Dylan and Lennon.

Bob Dylan's 'Backing Band', 1965–1969

Bringing It All Back Home (1965)

John Boone: bass guitar
Al Gorgoni: guitar
Bobby Gregg: drums
Paul Griffin: piano, keyboards
John P. Hammond: guitar
Bruce Langhorne: guitar
Bill Lee: bass guitar
Joseph Macho, Jr: bass guitar
Frank Owens: piano
Kenny Rankin: guitar
John B. Sebastian: bass guitar

Highway 61 Revisited (1965)

Mike Bloomfield: electric guitar
Charlie McCoy: guitar
Paul Griffin: piano
Al Kooper: organ
Frank Owens: piano
Harvey Brooks: bass
Russ Savakus: bass
Joe Macho, Jr: bass
Bobby Gregg: drums
Sam Lay: drums

Newport Folk Festival (1965)

Mike Bloomfield: guitar
Al Kooper: organ
Jerome Arnold: bassist
Sam Lay: drums
Barry Goldberg: piano

US and World Tour (1965–1966)

Rick Danko: bass, background vocal
Levon Helm: drums
Garth Hudson: organ
Mickey Jones: drums
Sandy Konikoff: drums
Al Kooper: organ
Richard Manuel: piano
Robbie Robertson: guitar

Blonde on Blonde (1966)

Bill Aikins: keyboards
Wayne Butler: trombone
Kenneth Buttrey: drums
Rick Danko: bass
Bill Lee: bass
Bobby Gregg: drums
Paul Griffin: piano
Jerry Kennedy: guitar
Al Kooper: organ, guitar
Charlie McCoy: bass, guitar, trumpet
Wayne Moss: guitar, vocals
Hargus 'Pig' Robbins: piano, keyboards
Robbie Robertson: guitar, vocals
Henry Strzelecki: bass
Joe South: bass, guitar

John Wesley Harding (1967)

Kenneth A. Buttrey: drums
Pete Drake: pedal steel guitar
Charlie McCoy: bass

The Basement Tapes (1975)

Rick Danko: bass guitar, mandolin, vocals
Levon Helm: drums, mandolin, vocals
Garth Hudson: organ, clavinet, accordion, tenor saxophone, piano
Richard Manuel: piano, drums, vocals
Robbie Robertson: guitar, acoustic guitar, drums, vocals

Nashville Skyline (1969)

Norman Blake: guitar
Kenneth A. Buttrey: drums
Johnny Cash: vocals
Fred Carter, Jr: guitar
Charlie Daniels: bass, guitar
Pete Drake: pedal steel
Marshall Grant: bass
W. S. Holland: drums
Charlie McCoy: guitar, harmonica
Bob Wilson: organ, piano
Bob Wootton: guitar

References

Abram, W. A. (2014) *A History of Blackburn: Town and Parish*. Morrisville, NC: Lulu Press.

Abramson, P. R. and Inglehart, R. (1986) Generational replacement and value change in six West European societies. *American Journal of Political Science* *30*: 1–25.

Adler, M. (1979) *Drawing Down the Moon: Witches, Druids, Goddess-Worshippers and Other Pagans in America Today*. New York, NY: Viking Press.

Allert, T. (2009) *The Hitler Salute: On the Meaning of a Gesture*. New York, NY: Henry Holt and Company.

Amis, M. (1993) *Visiting Mrs. Nabokov & Other Excursions*. London: Jonathan Cape.

Anon. (1970) Bob Dylan's secret recording session with George Harrison and friends. *Rolling Stone*, 28 May. www.rollingstone.com/music/news/bob-dylans-secret-recording-session-with-george-harrison-and-friends-19700528 #ixzz2soyBuMjQ.

Anon. (2008) Mind Games (Early Take) *YouTube: piggies1*.

Anon. (2009) Dylan unnoticed on Beatles tour. *BBC News*, 12 May. http://news .bbc.co.uk/1/hi/8046278.stm.

Anon. (2011) John Lennon – swastika on the wall (RARE). *YouTube: Metrazol Electricity.*, 17 September. https://youtu.be/QoSsjNmzplE.

Anon. (2014) How the Beatles learned Transcendental Meditation – and what they thought about it. *Transcendental Meditation News & More*, 10 December. http://tmhome.com/experiences/interview-lennon-and-harrison-on-medita tion/.

Anon. (2015) John Lennon larking about Hitler salute / The Beatles. *YouTube: Fry Pan Music*, 9 November. https://youtu.be/hXe7M-y7hdg.

Anon. (2018) The Beatles – Commonwealth (Rare Track) – Get Back Sessions, 1969. *YouTube: The Beatles Archeology & Other Subjects*, 7 May. https://youtu.be /Zy9U5RdQzTc.

Ardrey, R. (1961) *African Genesis: A Personal Investigation into the Animal Origins and Nature of Man*. New York, NY: Atheneum Books.

Arendt, H. (1963) *Eichmann in Jerusalem: A Report on the Banality of Evil*. New York, NY: Viking Press.

Armstrong, K. (2004) *A Short History of Myth*. London: Cannongate Books.

Aronowitz, A. (1994) Eyewitness: Dylan turns The Beatles on to dope. *Q Magazine*, 92. www.rocksbackpages.com/Library/Article/eyewitness-dylan-turns-the-beatles-on-to-dope.

Ashbee, B. (1999) A beginner's guide to art bollocks and how to be a critic. *Art Review*. https://web.archive.org/web/20150131083911/ http://www.ipod.org.uk/reality/art_bollocks.asp.

Attali, J. (1985) *Noise: The Political Economy of Music*. Minneapolis, MN: University of Minnesota Press.

Badman, K. (2001) *The Beatles Diary Volume 2: After the Break-Up 1970–2001*. London: Omnibus Press.

Badman, K. (2009) *The Beatles: Off the Record*. London: Omnibus Press.

Baeten, J. (2017) Contested landscapes of displacement: Oliver Iron and Minnesota's Hibbing district. *Change Over Time 7*(1): 52–73.

Baggs, M. (2013) Paul McCartney 'paranoid' of asking Thom Yorke to record duet: Beatles icon also talks Dylan and Lennon. *Gigwise*, 3 October. www.gigwise.com/news/84720/.

Baird, J. (2007) *Imagine This: Growing up with My Brother John Lennon*. London: Hodder & Stoughton.

Baker, G. A. (1996) *The Beatles Down Under: The 1964 Australian and New Zealand Tour*. Lane End, UK: The Magnum Imprint.

Bari, M. A. (2008) *Mass Media Is the Message: Yoko Ono and John Lennon's 1969 Year of Peace*. PhD Thesis, University of Maryland, College Park, MD.

Barker, D. (2011) *The Good Atheist: Living a Purpose-Filled Life without God*. Berkeley, CA: Ulysses Press.

Barthes, R. (1981) *The Grain of the Voice: Interviews 1962–1980*. Evanston, IL: Northwestern University Press.

Bashwiner, D. (2018) The neuroscience of musical creativity. In R. E. Jung and O. Vartanian (eds.), *The Cambridge Handbook of the Neuroscience of Creativity* (pp. 495–516). Cambridge, UK: Cambridge University Press.

Bayton, M. (1998) *Frock Rock: Women Performing Popular Music*. Oxford: Oxford University Press.

Beauchamp, S. and Shephard, A. (2012) Bob Dylan and John Lennon's weird, one-sided relationship, *The Atlantic*, 24 September. www.theatlantic.com/entertainment/archive/2012/09/bob-dylan-and-john-lennons-weird-one-sided-relationship/262680/.

Beck, G. L. (2006) *Sacred Sound: Experiencing Music in World Religions*. Waterloo, Ontario: Wilfrid Laurier University Press.

Beebee, T. O. (1991) Ballad of the apocalypse: Another look at Bob Dylan's 'Hard Rain'. *Text and Performance Quarterly, 11*(1): 18–34.

Bennahum, D. (1991) *The Beatles – after the Break-up: In Their Own Words*. London: Omnibus Press.

Best, P. and Doncaster, P. (1985) *Beatle!: The Pete Best Story*. London: Plexus Books.

Bhagwan, D. (2015) *The Science of Karma*. Simandhar City, India: Dada Bhagwan Foundation.

Blanchard, T. (2009) Paul McCartney's meat-free Monday mission. *The Telegraph*, 25 June. www.telegraph.co.uk/news/earth/5621148/Paul-McCartneys-Meat-Free-Monday-mission.html.

Blaney, J. (2005) *John Lennon: Listen to This Book*. Guildford, UK: Paper Jukebox.

Blaney, J. (2007) *Lennon and McCartney: Together Alone: A Critical Discography of Their Solo Work*. London: Jawbone Press.

Blavatsky, H. P. (1967) *Practical Occultism*. Wheaton, IL: Theosophical Publishing House.

Bloom, P. (2013) *Just Babies: The Origins of Good and Evil*. New York, NY: Random House.

Born, G. and Hesmondhalgh, D. (2000) Introduction: On difference, representation, and appropriation in music. In G. Born and D. Hesmondhalgh (eds.), *Western Music and Its Others: Difference, Representation, and Appropriation in Music* (pp. 1–58). Berkeley, CA: University of California Press.

Boucher, D. (2004a) *Dylan and Cohen: Poets of Rock and Roll*. London: Continuum.

Boucher, D. (2004b) Images and distorted facts: Politics, poetry and protest in the songs of Bob Dylan. In D. Boucher and G. Browning (eds.), *The Political Art of Bob Dylan* (pp. 135–69). Basingstoke, UK: Palgrave Macmillan.

Boucher, D. and Browning, G. (eds.) (2004) *The Political Art of Bob Dylan*. Basingstoke, UK: Palgrave Macmillan.

Bowden, B. (2001) *Performed Literature: Words and Music by Bob Dylan*. Basingstoke, UK: Palgrave Macmillan.

Boyd, K. (2002) *Manliness and the Boys' Story Paper in Britain: A Cultural History, 1855–1940*. Basingstoke, UK: Palgrave Macmillan.

Brackett, N. and Hoard, C. D. (2004) *The New Rolling Stone Album Guide*. New York, NY: Simon & Schuster.

Bradby, B. (2005) 'She told me what to say': The Beatles and girl-group discourse. *Popular Music and Society* 28(3):359–90.

Bramwell, T. (2004) *Magical Mystery Tours: My Life with The Beatles*. London: Robson.

Breschard, J. and Snyder-Scumpy, P. (1974) Sometime in LA – Lennon plays it as it lays. *Crawdaddy Magazine,* March.

Brinkley, D. (2009) Bob Dylan's late-era, old-style American individualism. *Rolling Stone*, 14 May. www.rollingstone.com/music/news/bob-dylans-america -20090514.

Brinkley, D. (2020) Inside Bob Dylan's lost interviews and unseen letters. *Rolling Stone*, 21 October. www.rollingstone.com/music/music-features/bob-dylan-lost -letters-interviews-tony-glover-1074916/.

Browne, D. (2001) *Dream Brother: The Lives and Music of Jeff and Tim Buckley*. London: Fourth Estate.

Browne, D. (2012) *Fire and Rain: The Beatles, Simon and Garfunkel, James Taylor, CSNY, and the Lost Story of 1970*. Cambridge, MA: Da Capo Press.

Bullock, A. (1993) *Hitler and Stalin: Parallel Lives*. London: Fontana Press.

Burbidge, E. M., Burbidge, G. R., Fowler, W. A. and Hoyle, F. (1957) Synthesis of the elements in stars. *Reviews of Modern Physics* 29(4): 547–60.

Burger, J. (2016) *Lennon on Lennon: Conversations with John Lennon*. Chicago, IL: Chicago Review Press.

Burgess, A. (1964) *Malayan Trilogy*. London: Pan Books.

Burrows, T. (2013) *The Beatles: Day by Day*. London: Chartwell Books.

Buskin, R. (2009) John Lennon 'Whatever Gets You thru the Night'. Sound on Sound, June. www.soundonsound.com/people/john-lennon-whatever-gets-you-thru-night.

Buss, D. M. (2006) Strategies of human mating. *Psychological Topics* 15(2): 239–60.

Butler, W. (2018) John Lennon's self-portrait depicting himself as Hitler sells for $54,000. *NME*, 22 April. www.nme.com/news/music/john-lennon-self-portratit-depicting-himself-as-hitler-sells-for-54000-2299520.

Buzzanco, R. (1996) *Masters of War: Military Dissent and Politics in the Vietnam Era*. Cambridge, UK: Cambridge University Press.

Byrne, R. (2006) *The Secret*. New York, NY: Atria Books.

Calhoun, S. (2012) *Exploring U2: Is This Rock 'n' Roll?* Lanham, MD: Rowman & Littlefield.

Campbell, G. (1975) Bob Dylan and the pastoral apocalypse. *Journal of Popular Culture* 8(4): 697–707.

Capra, F. (1975) *The Tao of Physics: An Exploration of the Parallels between Modern Physics and Eastern Mysticism*. Boulder, CO: Shambhala Publications.

Carlyle, T. (1841) *On Heroes, Hero-Worship, and the Heroic in History*. London: James Fraser.

Carr, G. J. (1945) Health problems in the merchant navy. *British Journal of Industrial Medicine* 2(2): 65–73.

Carrol, L. (1865) *Alice's Adventures in Wonderland*. London: Macmillan.

Carroll, J. (2011) *Reading Human Nature: Literary Darwinism in Theory and Practice*. Albany, NY: State University of New York Press.

Carter, I. (2009) John Lennon, the boy we knew. *The Observer*, 13 December. www.theguardian.com/music/2009/dec/13/john-lennon-childhood-girlfriend-liverpool.

Caute, D. (1961) *At Fever Pitch*. New York, NY: Pantheon Books.

Cavett, D. (2005) *The Dick Cavett Show: John and Yoko Collection* [DVD]. R. S. Bader (Producer). Palisades, NY: Daphne Productions.

Chalmers, D. J. (1995) Facing up to the problem of consciousness. *Journal of Consciousness Studies* 2(3): 200–19.

Chomsky, N. (1965) *Aspects of the Theory of Syntax*. Cambridge, MA: MIT Press.

Chulov, M. (2018) The jihadist 'Beatles': Britons who became the face of Isis cruelty *The Guardian*, 9 February. www.theguardian.com/world/2018/feb/09/jihadist-beatles-britons-face-isis-cruelty.

Citron, S. (1996) *The Wordsmiths: Oscar Hammerstein 2nd and Alan Jay Lerner*. London: Sinclair-Stephenson.

Citron, S. (2001) *Sondheim and Lloyd-Webber: The New Musical*. Oxford: Oxford University Press.

Citron, S. (2005) *Noel and Cole: The Sophisticates*. Milwaukee, WI: Hal Leonard Corporation.

Clark, T. (2020) The 50 best-selling music artists of all time. *Business Insider*, 10 September. www.businessinsider.com/best-selling-music-artists-of-all-time-2016-9?r=US&IR=T.

Clayton, S. (2009) Not from nowhere: identity and aspiration in Bob Dylan's hometown. In C. Shelly and T. Swiss (eds.), *Highway 61 Revisited: Bob Dylan's Road from Minnesota to the World* (pp. 25–38). Minneapolis, MN: University of Minnesota Press.

Cleave, M. (2006) How does a Beatle live? John Lennon lives like this. London Evening Standard, March 4, 1966. In J. S. Sawyers (ed.), *Read the Beatles: Classics and New Writings on the Beatles, Their Legacy, and Why They Still Matter* (pp. 85–91). London: Penguin Books.

Clegg, C. (2015) George Harrison & Bob Dylan – Yesterday (1970). *YouTube: Beatles Bootlegs*. https://youtu.be/oJYYxhjYEMw.

Clydesdale, G. (2006) Creativity and competition: The Beatles. *Creativity Research Journal 18*(2): 129–39.

Cobb, M. C. (2016) 'When I feel a song in me': Exploring emotions through the creative songwriting process. In C. J. Schneider, N. K. Denzin and J. A. Kotarba (eds.), *Symbolic Interactionist Takes on Music* (pp. 61–79). Bingley, UK: Emerald Group Publishing.

Cobussen, M. (2008) *Thresholds: Rethinking Spirituality through Music*. Farnham, UK: Ashgate.

Cole, R. J. (2007) Forty years of chanting: A study of the Hare Krishna Movement from its foundation to the present day. In G. Dwyer and R. J. Cole (eds.), *The Hare Krishna Movement: Forty Years of Chant and Change*. London: I.B. Tauris.

Coleman, E. J. (1998) *Creativity and Spirituality: Bonds between Art and Religion*. Albany, NY: State University of New York Press.

Coleman, E. (2018) Revisit our infamous 1963 profile of Bob Dylan. *Newsweek*, 24 May. www.newsweek.com/bob-dylans-75th-birthday-revisit-our-infamous-1963-profile-462801.

Coleman, R. (1965) Beatles say - Dylan shows the way, *Melody Maker*, 9 January. http://amoralto.tumblr.com/post/60467020158/melody-maker-beatles-say-dyl an-shows-the-way-january.

Coleman, R. (1984) *John Ono Lennon: Volume 2 1967–1980*. London: Sidgwick & Jackson.

Coley, R. (2015) 'I don't believe you . . . you're a liar': The fabulatory function of Bob Dylan. In E. Banauch (ed.), *Refractions of Bob Dylan: Cultural Appropriations of an American Icon* (pp. 83–97). Manchester: Manchester University Press.

Colt, J. (1968) The Rolling Stone interview with John Lennon. *Rolling Stone*, 23 November. www.beatlesinterviews.org/db1968.11jl.beatles.html.

Contosa, D. R. (2008) *Rebel Giants: The Revolutionary Lives of Abraham Lincoln and Charles Darwin*. Amhurst, MA: Prometheus Books.

Cook, G. and Mercer, N. (2000) 'From me to you': Austerity to profligacy in the language of the Beatles. In I. Inglis (ed.), *The Beatles, Popular Music and Society: A Thousand Voices* (pp. 86–104). Basingstoke, UK: Macmillan Press.

Corcoran, N. (2002) Death's honesty. In N. Corcoran (ed.), *Do You Mr Jones? Bob Dylan with the Poets and the Professors* (pp. 143–74). London: Pimlico.

Cormany, K. (2009) John Lennon – you saved my soul. *YouTube: cubfan8290*. https://youtu.be/musbzUWbDpk.

Cortright, D. (2005) *Soldiers in Revolt: G. I. Resistance during the Vietnam War*. Chicago, IL: Haymarket Books.

Cott, J. (2007) *Dylan on Dylan*. London: Hodder.

Cott, J. and Doudna, C. (1982) *The Ballad of John and Yoko*. New York, NY: Doubleday.

Courrier, K. (2009) *Artificial Paradise: The Dark Side of the Beatles' Utopian Dream*. Westport, CT: Praeger Publishers.

Covach, J. (2006) From craft to art: Formal structures in the music of the Beatles. In K. Womack and T. F. Davis (eds.), *Reading the Beatles: Cultural Studies, Literary Criticism, and the Fab Four* (pp. 37–53). Albany, NY: State University of New York Press.

Cowen, A. S., Fang, X., Sauter, D. and Keltner, D. (2020) What music makes us feel: At least 13 dimensions organise subjective experiences associated with music across different cultures. *Proceedings of the National Academy of Sciences* *117*(4): 1924–34.

Cox, K. B. (2017) The road to Rishikesh: The Beatles, India and globalised dialogue in 1967. In K. Womack and K. B. Cox (eds.), *The Beatles, Sgt. Pepper, and the Summer of Love* (pp. 67–88). Lanham, MD: Lexington Books.

Cronkhite, G. F. (1951) The transcendental railroad. *The New England Quarterly*, *24*(3): 306–28.

Crossland, D. (2006) The stars in St Pauli: Hamburg's heady days of rock and roll. *Speigel Online*, 15 February. www.spiegel.de/international/the-stars-in-st-pauli-hamburg-s-heady-days-of-rock-roll-a-400870.html.

Crow, C. (1985) *Biograph* [Sleeve notes]. London: Columbia Records.

Crowley, A. (1909) *Liber AL vel Legis (The Book of the Law)*. Barstow, CA: Thelema Publishing.

Curtis, J. (1987) *Rock Eras: Interpretations of Music and Society 1954–1984*. Bowling Green, OH: Bowling Green State University Popular Press.

d'Aranda, E. (1666) *The History of Algiers and It's Slavery with Many Remarkable Particularities of Africk* London: John Starkey.

Dalton, D. (2012) *Who Is That Man? In Search of the Real Bob Dylan*. Waterville, ME: Thorndike Press.

Davies, H., Lennon, J. and Ono, Y. (2012) *The John Lennon Letters: Edited and with an Introduction by Hunter Davies*. London: Weidenfeld & Nicholson.

de Herrera, N. C. (2016) *All You Need Is Love: An Eyewitness Account of When Spirituality Spread from East to West*. New York, NY: Open Road Media.

de Waal, F., Macedo, S. and Ober, J. (2009) *Primates and Philosophers: How Morality Evolved*, Princeton, NJ: Princeton University Press.

Dederer, C. (2017) 'What do we do with the art of monstrous men?' *The Paris Review*, 20 November. www.theparisreview.org/blog/2017/11/20/art-monstrous -men/.

Denisoff, R. S. (1966) Songs of persuasion: A sociological analysis of urban propaganda songs. *The Journal of American Folklore 79*(314): 581–9.

Denisoff, R. S. (1968) Protest movements: Class consciousness and the propaganda song. *Sociological Quarterly IX*: 228–47.

Denisoff, R. S. (1969a) Folk-rock: folk music, protest, or commercialism. *Journal of Popular Culture 3*(2): 214–30.

Denisoff, R. S. (1969b) Urban folk 'movement' research: Value free? *Western Folklore 28*(3): 183–97.

Denisoff, R. S. (1970) Protest songs: Those on the top forty and those of the streets. *American Quarterly 22*(4): 807–23.

Denisoff, R. S. (1972) The evolution of the American protest song. In R. S. Denisoff (ed.), *The Sounds of Social Change* (pp. 15–25). Chicago, IL: Rand MacNally.

Denisoff, R. S. (1973) *Great Day Coming: Folk Music and the American Left*. Champaign, IL: University of Illinois Press.

Denisoff, R. S. (1983) *Sing a Song of Social Significance*. Bowling Green, KY: Popular Press.

Denlsoff, R. S. and Fandray, D. (1977) 'Hey, hey Woody Guthrie I wrote you a song': The political side of Bob Dylan. *Popular Music and Society 5*(5): 31–42.

Denisoff, R. S. and Levine, M. H. (1971) The popular protest song: The case of 'Eve of Destruction'. *Public Opinion Quarterly 35*(1): 117–22.

Dennett, D. C. (1993) *Consciousness Explained*. London: Penguin Books.

Desjardins, M. (1997) *Peace, Violence and the New Testament*. Sheffield, UK: Sheffield Academic Press.

DiAngelo, R. (2018) *White Fragility: Why It's So Hard for White People to Talk About Racism*. Boston, MA: Beacon Press.

Doggett, P. (2007) *There's a Riot Going on: Revolutionaries, Rock Stars and the Rise and Fall of '60s Counter-Culture*. Edinburgh: Canongate Books.

Doggett, P. (2009) *The Art & Music of John Lennon*. London: Omnibus Press.

Dunlap, J. (2006) Through the eyes of Tom Joad: Patterns of American idealism, Bob Dylan, and the folk protest movement. *Popular Music and Society 29*(5): 549–73.

Dunn, G. D. and McDonald, B. (2009) Six impossible things before breakfast. In W. Irwin and R. B. Davis (eds.), *Alice in Wonderland and Philosophy: Curiouser and Curiouser* (pp. 61–77). Hoboken, NJ: John Wiley & Sons.

Dunson, J. (1963) Birth of a Broadside. *Broadside, 20*: 10–11.

Durkheim, É., Cladis, M. S. and Cosman, C. (2001) *The Elementary Forms of Religious Life*. Oxford: Oxford University Press.

Dutton, D. (2009) *The Art Instinct: Beauty, Pleasure, and Human Evolution*. Oxford: Oxford University Press.

Dylan, B. (1962) 'I Will Not Go Down under the Ground'. *Broadside, 3*: 3.

Dylan, B. (1963) 'With God on Our Side'. *Broadside, 27*: 1.

Dylan, B. (1964) '11 Outlined Epitaphs'. The Times They Are A-Changin' [Sleeve notes]: Columbia Records.

Dylan, B. (1965) Bringing It All Back Home [Sleeve notes]: Columbia Records.

Dylan, B. (1971) *Tarantula*. New York, NY: Scribner.

Dylan, B. (1972) Eat the Document [film]. B. Dylan (Dir.) Los Angeles, CA: Pennebaker Associates.

Dylan, B. (2004a) *Chronicles: Volume 1*. London: Simon & Schuster.

Dylan, B. (2004b) *Lyrics: 1962–2001*. London: Simon & Schuster.

Dylan, B. (2006a) 'Cars'. Theme Time Radio Hour. White Plains, NY: Grey Water Park Productions.

Dylan, B. (2006b) 'Jail'. Theme Time Radio Hour. White Plains, NY: Grey Water Park Productions.

Dylan, B. (2006c) 'Rich Man, Poor Man'. Theme Time Radio Hour. White Plains, NY: Grey Water Park Productions.

Dylan, B. (2006d) 'Weather'. Theme Time Radio Hour. White Plains, NY: Grey Water Park Productions.

Dylan, B. (2009) 'Work'. Theme Time Radio Hour. White Plains, NY: Grey Water Park Productions.

Dylan, B. (2011) To my fans and followers. *News Archive*, 13 May. www.bobdylan.com/us/news/my-fans-and-followers.

Dylan, B. (2013) Bob Dylan songs played live. *BobDylan.com*. www.bobdylan.com/us/songs.

Dylan, B. (2015) Read Bob Dylan's complete, riveting MusiCares speech. *Rolling Stone*, 9 February. www.rollingstone.com/music/news/read-bob-dylans-complete-riveting-musicares-speech-20150209.

Dylan, B. (2017) Nobel Lecture. *NobelPrize.org*. www.nobelprize.org/nobel_prizes/literature/laureates/2016/dylan-lecture.html.

Dylan, B. (2018) In the Garden. *Saved (1980)*. https://bobdylan.com/songs/garden/.#

Dysinger, C. and Gebhardt, S. (Dirs.) (2011) *John Lennon Live in New York City* [VHS, PAL]. London: Picture Music International.

Ehrlich, D. (1997) *Inside the Music: Conversations with Contemporary Musicians about Spirituality, Creativity, and Consciousness*. Boulder, CO: Shambhala Publications.

Elliott, E. (1995) *The Mourning of John Lennon*. Melbourne: Melbourne University Press.

Emerson, R. W. (1837) The American scholar. https://emersoncentral.com/texts/nature-addresses-lectures/addresses/the-american-scholar/.

Emerson, R. W. (1841) *Essays: First Series*. Boston, MA: James Munroe and Company.

Emerson, R. W. (1844) *Essays: Second Series*. Boston, MA: James Monroe and Company.

Engels, F. (1892) *Condition of the Working Class in England in 1844* (trans. F. Kelley). London: George Allen & Unwin.

Epstein, D. M. (2011) *The Ballad of Bob Dylan: A Portrait*. London: Souvenir Press.

Evans, J. S. B. and Stanovich K. E. (2013) Dual-process theories of higher cognition: Advancing the debate. *Perspectives on Psychological Science 8*(3): 223–41.

Evans, M. (2004) *The Beatles Literary Anthology*. London: Plexus.

Everett, W. (1999) *The Beatles as Musicians: Revolver through the Anthology*. Oxford: Oxford University Press.

Eyerman, R. and Barretta, S. (1996) From the 30s to the 60s: The folk music revival in the United States. *Theory and Society 25*(4): 501–43.

Eyerman, R. and Jamison, A. (1998) *Music and Social Movements: Mobilizing Traditions in the Twentieth Century*. Cambridge, UK: Cambridge University Press.

Faithfull, M. and Dalton, D. (1994) *Faithfull: An Autobiography*. New York, NY: Little, Brown and Company.

Fawcett, A. (1976) *John Lennon: One Day at a Time: A Personal Biography of the Seventies*. New York, NY: Grove Press.

Feinstein, R. (2009) *Real Moments: Bob Dylan: The Photographs of Bob Dylan*. London: Omnibus Press.

Filene, B. (2000) *Romancing the Folk: Public Memory and American Roots Music*. Raleigh, NC: University of North Carolina Press.

Fink, L. (2011) *Sweatshops at Sea: Merchant Seamen in the World's First Globalized Industry, from 1812 to the Present*. Raleigh, NC: University of North Carolina Press.

Fish, D. R. (1994) Songs of the Sixties: A Rhetorical Examination of Song as a Protest against the Vietnam War, PhD Thesis, Department of Communication, University of Utah.

Flanagan, B. (2017) Q&A with Bill Flanagan. *Bob Dylan.com*. https://bobdylan.com/news/qa-with-bill-flanagan/.

Flory, M. W. (2012) Postmodern prophecy: Bob Dylan and the practices of self-subversion. In T. R. Clark and D. W. Clanton (eds.), *Understanding Religion and Popular Culture: Theories, Themes, Products and Practices* (pp. 213–22). Abingdon, UK: Routledge.

Ford, M. (2003) 'Trust yourself': Emerson and Dylan. In N. Corcoran (ed.), *Do You Mr Jones? Bob Dylan with the Poets and the Professors* (pp. 127–42). London: Pimlico.

Forland, T. E. (1992) 'Bringing It All Back Home' or 'Another Side of Bob Dylan': Midwestern isolationist. *Journal of American Studies 26*(3): 337–55.

Forster, E. M. (1924) *A Passage to India*. London: Edward Arnold.

Foucault, M. (1965) *Madness and Civilization: A History of Insanity in the Age of Reason*. New York, NY: Pantheon Books.

Freemantle, F. (1975) *The Tibetan Book of the Dead*. Boulder, CO: Shambhala Publications.

Friedman, J. C. (2013) *The Routledge History of Social Protest in Popular Music*. Abingdon, UK: Routledge.

Frith, S. (1978) *The Sociology of Rock*. London: Constable and Company.

Frith, S. (1989) Why do songs have words? *Contemporary Music Review 5*: 77–96.

Frith, S. (1996) *Performing Rites: On the Value of Popular Music*. Oxford: Oxford University Press.

Frontani, M. R. (2009) *The Beatles: Image and the Media*. Jackson, MI: University Press of Mississippi.

Fry, P. (2009) 18. The political unconscious. *YouTube: Yale Courses*. https://youtu .be/GQvp5zoZbvo.

Gadamer, H. G. (1965) *Truth and Method*. New York, NY: Crossroad Publishing Company.

Gallie, W. B. (1956) IX. Essentially contested concepts. *Proceedings of the Aristotelian Society* 56(1): 167–98.

Gascoigne, J. (2006) The expanding historiography of British imperialism. *The Historical Journal* 49(2): 577–92.

Gill, A. (1998) *Don't Think Twice It's All Right: Bob Dylan, the Early Years*. New York, NY: Thunder's Mouth Press.

Gill, A. and Odegard, K. (2004) *A Simple Twist of Fate: Bob Dylan and the Making of Blood on the Tracks*. Cambridge, MA: Da Capo Press.

Gilmour, M. J. (2011) *The Gospel According to Bob Dylan: The Old, Old Story of Modern Times*. Louisville, KY: Presbyterian Publishing Corporation.

Gilroy, P. (2010) *Postcolonial Melancholia*. New York, NY: Columbia University Press.

Giuliano, G. (1989) *Dark Horse*. London: Bloomsbury.

Giuliano, G. (2001) *Lennon in America: 1971–1980, Based in Part on the Lost Lennon Diaries*. Lanham, MD: Cooper Square Press.

Gladden, P. R. and Cleator, A. M. (2018) Sexual assault and intimate partner violence. In T. K. Shackelford and V. A. Weekes-Shackelford (eds.), *Encyclopedia of Evolutionary Psychological Science*. https://doi.org/10.1007/978-3-319-16999-6_1722-1.

Gleed, P. (2012) 'The rest of you, if you'll just rattle your jewelry': The Beatles and questions of mass and high culture. In K. Womack and T. F. Davis (eds.), *Reading the Beatles: Cultural Studies, Literary Criticism, and the Fab Four* (pp. 161–8). Albany, NY: State University of New York Press.

Goldberg, P. (2010) *American Veda: From Emerson and the Beatles to Yoga and Meditation – How Indian Spirituality Changed the West*. Berkeley, CA: Potter/ TenSpeed/Harmony.

Goldman, A. (1988) *The Lives of John Lennon*. New York, NY: William Morrow & Co.

Golson, G. B. (1981) *The Playboy Interview*. Chicago, IL: Playboy Press.

Goodden, J. (2014a) Cover shoot for Sgt Pepper. *The Beatles Bible*. www .beatlesbible.com/1967/03/30/cover-shoot-for-sgt-pepper/.

Goodden, J. (2014b) Days in the life: The Beatles' history. *The Beatles Bible*. www .beatlesbible.com/history/.

Goodden, J. (2014c) Filming: *A Hard Day's Night*. *The Beatles Bible*. www .beatlesbible.com/1964/04/16/filming-a-hard-days-night-33/.

Goodden, J. (2014d) Filming: *Help! The Beatles Bible*. www.beatlesbible.com/196 5/04/05/filming-help-31/.

Goodden, J. (2014e) *Get Back/Let It Be* sessions: Complete song list. *The Beatles Bible.* www.beatlesbible.com/features/get-back-let-it-be-sessions-complete-song-list/.

Goodden, J. (2014f) 'In My Life'. *The Beatles Bible.* www.beatlesbible.com/songs/in-my-life/.

Goodden, J. (2014g) John and Cynthia Lennon, George Harrison and Pattie Boyd fly to Tahiti. *The Beatles Bible.* www.beatlesbible.com/1964/05/04/john-cynthia-lennon-george-harrison-pattie-boyd-holiday-tahiti/.

Goodden, J. (2014h) John Lennon is filmed with Bob Dylan. *The Beatles Bible.* www.beatlesbible.com/1966/05/27/john-lennon-bob-dylan-eat-the-document/.

Goodden, J. (2014i) Press conference: Warwick Hotel, New York, NY: *The Beatles Bible.* www.beatlesbible.com/1966/08/22/press-conference-warwick-hotel-new-york-city/.

Goodden, J. (2014j) Recording, mixing: 'The Ballad of John and Yoko'. *The Beatles Bible.* www.beatlesbible.com/1969/04/14/recording-mixing-the-ballad-of-john-and-yoko/.

Goodden, J. (2014k) 'Serve Yourself'. *The Beatles Bible.* www.beatlesbible.com/people/john-lennon/songs/serve-yourself/.

Goodden, J. (2017) *Riding so High: The Beatles and Drugs.* Cardiff: Pepper & Pearl

Gorra, M. (2008) *After Empire: Scott, Naipaul, Rushdie.* Chicago, IL: University of Chicago Press.

Gould, J. (2007) *Can't Buy Me Love: The Beatles, Britain and America.* London: Portrait.

Gracyk, T. (1996) *Rhythm and Noise: An Aesthetics of Rock.* London: I.B. Tauris.

Gray, M. (2006) *The Bob Dylan Encyclopedia.* London: Bloomsbury Academic.

Gray, M. (2008) *The Bob Dylan Encyclopedia.* Updated and revised edition. London: Continuum.

Graziano, M. S. A. (2013) *Consciousness and the Social Brain.* Oxford: Oxford University Press.

Green, J. (1983) *Dakota Days.* New York, NY: St Martin's Press.

Greene, A. (2012) A history of Rock and Roll Hall of Fame no shows. *Rolling Stone,* 12 April. www.rollingstone.com/music/news/a-history-of-rock-and-roll-hall-of-fame-no-shows-20120412.

Greene, D. (2016) *Rock, Counterculture and the Avant-Garde, 1966–1970: How the Beatles, Frank Zappa and the Velvet Underground Defined an Era.* Jefferson, NC: McFarland & Company.

Grossberg, L. (1984) Another boring day in paradise: Rock and roll and the empowerment of everyday life. *Popular Music* 4: 225–58.

Grossman, M. and Wooding, D. (1999) 'Please pray for Bob Dylan' asks his former pastor. Kenn Gulliksen says Dylan is still 'a believer' and 'God is not through with him yet'. *Expecting Rain: The Bob Dylan Who's Who.* http://expectingrain.com/dok/who/g/gulliksenken.html.

Gura, P. F. and Myerson, J. (1982) *Critical Essays on American Transcendentalism.* Boston, MA: G. K. Hall & Co.

Haidt, J. (2012) *The Righteous Mind: Why Good People Are Divided by Politics and Religion*. New York, NY: Pantheon Books.

Haigha, H. (2017) John Lennon and *Alice in Wonderland*. *Alice is Everywhere*. http://aliceiseverywhere.com/john-lennon-alice-wonderland/.

Hamlin, J. (2015) Top 10 most covered artists. *WhoSampled*. www .whosampled.com/news/2015/02/11/top-10-most-covered-artists/.

Hammill, P. (1975) Long night's journey into day: A conversation with John Lennon. *Rolling Stone*, 5 June. www.beatlesinterviews.org/db1975.0605.beatles .html.

Hampton, W. (1986) *Guerrilla Minstrels: John Lennon, Joe Hill, Woody Guthrie, Bob Dylan*. Knoxville, TN: University of Tennessee Press.

Harker, D. (1980) *One for the Money: Politics and Popular Song*. London: Hutchinson.

Harrell, D. E. (1985) *Oral Roberts: An American Life*. Bloomington, IN: Indiana University Press.

Harris, K. M. (1978) *Carlyle and Emerson: Their Long Debate*. Cambridge, MA: Harvard University Press.

Harrison, G. (2004) *I Me Mine*. London: Phoenix.

Harry, B. (1964) 'The Daily Howl'. *Mersey Beat*, 12 March. www.triumphpc.com /mersey-beat/archives/dailyhowl.shtml.

Harry, B. (2000) *The John Lennon Encyclopedia*. London: Virgin.

Hawksley, R. (2015) Sir Paul McCartney: I'm frustrated Lennon's assassination made him a martyr. *The Telegraph*. 4 July. www.telegraph.co.uk/culture/music/ the-beatles/11718010/Sir-Paul-McCartney-the-fact-that-Lennons-martyred-has -elevated-him.html.

Hay, E. K. (1984) Kipling and Forster: A case for dual biography. *Biography 7*(2): 123–33.

Hegel, G. W. F. (1977) *Phenomenology of Spirit* (trans. A. V. Miller and J. N. Findlay). Oxford: Oxford University Press.

Helm, L. and Davis, S. (2000) *This Wheel's on Fire: Levon Helm and the Story of the Band*. 2nd ed. Chicago, IL: Chicago Review Press.

Henke, J. (2003) *Lennon Legend: An Illustrated Life of John Lennon*. Washington, DC: Becker & Meyer.

Hersch, C. (1998) *Democratic Artworks: Politics and the Arts from Trilling to Dylan*. Albany, NY: State University of New York Press.

Hesmondhalgh, D. (1996) Flexibility, post-Fordism and the music industries. *Media, Culture & Society 18*(3): 469–88.

Heylin, C. (1995) *Bob Dylan: The Recording Sessions 1960–1994*. New York, NY: St. Martin's Press.

Heylin, C. (1996) *Bob Dylan, A Life in Stolen Moments: Day by Day, 1941–1995*. New York, NY: Schirmer Books.

Heylin, C. (2000) *Bob Dylan: Behind the Shades, the Biography – Take Two*. 2nd ed. London: Penguin Books.

Heylin, C. (2010a) *Revolution in the Air: The Songs of Bob Dylan 1957–73*. London: Constable & Robinson.

Heylin, C. (2010b) *Still on the Road: The Songs of Bob Dylan Vol. 2 1974–2008*. London: Constable & Robinson.

Heylin, C. (2011) *Bob Dylan, Behind the Shades: The 20th Anniversary Edition*. London: Faber and Faber.

Heylin, C. (2016) *JUDAS! From Forest Hills to the Free Trade Hall: A Historical View of the Big Boo*. London: Jawbone Press.

Hiatt, B. (2011) George Harrison: The private life of the quiet Beatle. *Rolling Stone*, 2 September. www.rollingstone.com/music/pictures/the-private-life-of-george-harrison-20110902/on-the-courts-with-dylan-0096947.

Higgins, K. M. (2012) The Music between Us: Is Music a Universal Language? Chicago, IL: University of Chicago Press.

Hislope, R. (2018) The Beatles against Machiavelli: Is it better to be loved or feared? In P. O. Jenkins and H. Jenkins (eds.), *Teaching the Beatles* (pp. 37–49). Abingdon, UK: Routledge.

Hobsbawm, E. (1987) *The Age of Empire: 1875–1914*. London: Weidenfeld & Nicholson.

Hollingshaus, W. (2013) *Philosophizing Rock Performance: Dylan, Hendrix, Bowie*. Lanham, MD: Scarecrow Press.

Hopkins, J. (1987) *Yoko Ono: A Biography*. London: Sidwick & Jackson.

Horgan, J. (2012) John Lennon snorting Pepsi in the 1964 classic *A Hard Day's Night. YouTube: Jerry Horgan*. https://youtu.be/i9iysoiB-es.

Hubbard, L. R. (1968) *Dianetics: The Modern Science of Mental Health*. Los Angeles, CA: Hubbard College of Scientology.

Hurston, Z. N. (1937) *Their Eyes Were Watching God*. Philadelphia, PA: J. B. Lippincott & Co.

Inglis, I. (1996a) Presley and the Beatles. *International Review of the Aesthetics and Sociology of Music 27*(1): 53–78.

Inglis, I. (1996b) Synergies and reciprocities: The dynamics of musical and professional interaction between the Beatles and Bob Dylan. *Popular Music and Society 20*(4): 53–79.

Inglis, I. (2000a) *The Beatles, Popular Music and Society: A Thousand Voices*. Basingstoke, UK: Palgrave Macmillan.

Inglis. I. (2000b) 'The Beatles are coming!' Conjecture and conviction in the myth of Kennedy, America, and the Beatles. *Popular Music and Society 24*(2): 93–108.

Inglis, I. (2008) Cover story: Magic, myth and music. In O. Julien (ed.), *Sgt. Pepper and the Beatles: It Was Forty Years Ago Today* (pp. 91–102). Farnham, UK: Ashgate.

Inglis, I. (2012) *The Beatles in Hamburg*. London: Reaktion Books.

Jackson, A. (2006) *The British Empire and the Second World War*. London: Hambleton Continuum.

Jaichandran, R. and Madhav, B. D. (2003) Pentecostal spirituality in a postmodern world. *Asian Journal of Pentecostal Studies 6*(1): 39–61.

James, D. (1989) The Vietnam War and American music. *Social Text 23*: 122–43.

James, J. (1995) *The Music of the Spheres: Music, Science, and the Natural Order of the Universe.* New York, NY: Springer Publishing.

James, W. (1929) *The Varieties of Religious Experience: A Study in Human Nature.* New York, NY: Random House.

Jameson, F. (1981) *The Political Unconscious: Narrative as a Socially Symbolic Act.* London: Methuen & Co.

Jameson, F. (1984) Periodizing the 60s. *Social Text 9*(10): 178–209.

Jameson, F. (1991) *Postmodernism, or, the Cultural Logic of Late Capitalism.* Durham, NC: Duke University Press.

Jardine, C. (2016) *The Best Alan Watts Quotes.* Morrisville, NC: LULU Press.

Jarosinski, A. (2006) *Every Mind Polluting Word: Assorted Bob Dylan Utterances.* 2nd ed. Wrocław, Poland: Don't Ya Tell Henry Publications.

Johanson, D. C. and Wong, K. (2009) *Lucy's Legacy: The Quest for Human Origins.* New York, NY: Harmony Books.

Jones, A. (2012) Bob Dylan –*Tempest. Uncut,* 7 September. www.uncut.co.uk/re views/bob-dylan-tempest-2341/.

Jones, E. (1949) *Hamlet and Oedipus.* New York, NY: W. W. Norton & Company.

Jones, J. (1992) *Let Me Take You Down: Inside the Mind of Mark David Chapman, the Man Who Killed John Lennon.* New York, NY: Villard Books.

Jones, M. (2007) *That Would Be Me: Rock & Roll Survivor to Hollywood Actor.* Bloomington, IN: AuthorHouse.

Julien, D. (2005) Lot #179 John Lennon white suit from *Abbey Road* album cover. *Julien's Auctions: The Auction House to the Stars.* https://web.archive.org/web/ 2018101102351O/

https://www.juliensauctions.com/auctions/2005/autumn-auction/lot179.html.

Kahneman, D. (2011) *Thinking, Fast and Slow.* London: Allen Lane.

Kaiser, D. (2011) *How the Hippies Saved Physics: Science, Counterculture, and the Quantum Revival.* London: W. W. Norton & Company.

Keen, S. (2006) A theory of narrative empathy. *Narrative 14*(3): 207–36.

Keinan, G. (2002) The effects of stress and desire for control on superstitious behavior. *Personality and Social Psychology Bulletin 28*(1): 102–8.

Kelly, A. (2013) Mood swings. In *Bob Dylan Mood Swings Catalogue.* London: Halcyon Gallery.

Kennedy, R. (1967) Far and near: The holes in our roads. *The Daily Mail,* 17 January.

Kenny, F. (2015) *The Making of John Lennon: The Untold Story of the Rise and Fall of the Beatles.* Edinburgh: Luath Press.

Kierkegaard, S. (1843) *Frygt og Bæven* [Fear and Trembling]. Copenhagen: C.A. Reitzel.

King, B. J. (2017) *Evolving God: A Provocative View on the Origins of Religion.* Expanded edition. Chicago, IL: University of Chicago Press.

Kipling, R. (1889) 'The Ballad of East and West'. In T. S. Eliot (ed.) (1941) *A Choice of Kipling's Verse, Made by T. S. Eliot, with an Essay on Rudyard Kipling* (pp. 111–15). London: Faber and Faber.

Kun, J. (2005) *Audiotopia: Music, Race, and America*. Berkley, CA: University of California Press.

Lalvani, K. (2016) *The Making of India: The Untold Story of British Enterprise*. London: Continuum International Publishing Group.

Lander, J. (2010) *Lincoln and Darwin: Shared Visions of Race, Science, and Religion*. Carbondale, IL: Southern Illinois University Press.

Lasky, M. (1998) Defusing the enemy's vocabulary. *Society* **36**(1): 66–71.

Leaf, D. and Scheinfeld, J. (2007) The US vs John Lennon [DVD]. D. Leaf and J. Scheinfeld (Producers). London: Lionsgate Home Entertainment.

Leary, T., Metzner, R. and Alpert, R. (1964) *The Psychedelic Experience: A Manual Based on the Tibetan Book of the Dead*. New Hyde Park, NY: University Books.

Lennon, J. (1961) Being a short diversion on the dubious origins of Beatles (translated from the John Lennon). *Mersey Beat*. www.triumphpc.com/mersey-beat/archives/dubious.shtml.

Lennon, J. (1964) *In His Own Write*. London: Macmillan.

Lennon, J. (1965) *A Spaniard in the Works*. London: Simon & Schuster.

Lennon, J. (1967) What I believe by Beatle John (The Daily Sketch, 9 October). *Beatles Interviews*. www.beatlesinterviews.org/db1967.1009.beatles.html.

Lennon, J. (1986) *Skywriting by Word of Mouth*. New York, NY: Harper & Row.

Lennon, J. and Prabhupāda, A. C. B. S. (1981) *Search for Liberation: Featuring a Conversation between John Lennon and Swami Bhaktivedanta*. Alachua, FL: Bhaktivedanta Book Trust.

Lennon, J., Ono, Y. and Sheff, D. (1981) *The Playboy Interviews with John Lennon and Yoko Ono*. New York, NY: Playboy Press.

Lepidus, H. (2010) Bob Dylan and birthday boy Ringo Starr through the Years. *Examiner.com*. https://web.archive.org/web/20120511221046/http://www.examiner.com/article/bob-dylan-and-birthday-boy-ringo-starr-through-the-years.

Lerner, M. (2007) *The Other Side of the Mirror: Bob Dylan Live at the Newport Folk Festival 1963–1965* [DVD]. M. Lerner, J. Rosen and A. Wall (Producers). London: BBC.

Lester, J. (1968) *Look Out Whitey! Black Power's Goin' Get Your Mama!* New York, NY: The Dial Press.

Lester, R. (1964) *A Hard Day's Night* [DVD]. W. Shenson (Producer). London: United Artists.

Lester, R. (1967) *How I Won the War* [DVD]. R. Lester (Producer). London: United Artists.

Lévi-Strauss, C. (1978) *Myth and Meaning*. Abingdon, UK: Routledge.

Lewis-Giggetts, T. M. (2017) When faith and music intersect: The spiritual evolution of a musical genius. *Journal of African American Studies* **21**(3): 533–9.

Lewisohn, M. (1996) *The Complete Beatles Chronicles*. London: Bounty Books.

Lewisohn, M. (2004) *The Complete Beatles Recording Sessions: The Official Story of the Abbey Road Years 1962–1970*. London: Hamlyn.

Lewisohn, M. (2013) *The Beatles – All These Years: Volume One: Tune In*. London: Little, Brown Book Group.

Lifton, D. (2015) The history of John Lennon's five-year battle with the FBI. *Ultimate Classic Rock*, 21 March. http://ultimateclassicrock.com/john-lennon-fbi-history/.

Lifton, D. (2016) The story of Bob Dylan's infamous 'Judas' concert. *Ultimate Classic Rock*, 17 May. http://ultimateclassicrock.com/bob-dylan-judas-concert/.

Lifton, R. J. (1961) *Thought Reform and the Psychology of Totalism: A Study of 'Brainwashing' in China*. Raleigh, NC: University of North Carolina Press.

Lifton, R. J. (ed.) (1975) *Explorations in Psychohistory: The Wellfleet Papers*. New York, NY: Simon & Schuster.

Lindsey, H. and Carlson, C. C. (1970) *The Late, Great Planet Earth*. Grand Rapids, MI: Zondervan.

Long, T. (2002) *Take What You Need: Musical, Cultural, and Literary Influences on Bob Dylan*. PhD Thesis, Middle Tennessee State University. Murfreesboro, TN.

Lorcin, P. M. E. (2013) Imperial nostalgia; colonial nostalgia. Differences of theory, similarities of practice? *Historical Reflections 39*(3): 97–111.

Lott, E. (1993) *Love and Theft: Blackface Minstrelsy and the American Working Class*. Oxford: Oxford University Press.

MacDonald, I. (1994) *Revolution in the Head: The Beatles' Records and the Sixties*. London: Vintage.

MacDonald, I. (2008) *Revolution in the Head: The Beatles' Records and the Sixties*. Second revised edition. London: Vintage.

MacFarlane, T. (2007) *The Beatles' Abbey Road Medley: Extended Forms in Popular Music*. Lanham, MD: Scarecrow Press.

MacFarlane, T. (2013) *The Beatles and McLuhan: Understanding the Electric Age*. Lanham, MD: Scarecrow Press.

Mäkelä, J. (2004) *John Lennon Imagined: Cultural History of a Rock Star* (Vol. 4). New York, NY: Peter Lang.

Marcus, G. (2009) Hibbing High School and 'the mystery of democracy'. In C. Shelly and T. Swiss (eds.), *Highway 61 Revisited: Bob Dylan's Road from Minnesota to the World* (pp. 3–14). Minneapolis, MN: University of Minnesota Press.

Marques, J. M., Abrams, D., Paez, D. and Taboada, C. (1998) The role of categorization and ingroup norms in judgments of groups and their members. *Journal of Personality and Social Psychology 75*(4): 976–88.

Marqusee, M. (2005) *Wicked Messenger: Bob Dylan and the 1960s*. London: Seven Stories Press.

Marshall, L. (2013) *Bob Dylan: The Never Ending Star*. London: Polity Press.

Martin, G. and Pearson, W. (1994) *Summer of Love: The Making of Sgt. Pepper*. London: Macmillan.

Marvin, C. and Ingle, D. W. (1996) Blood sacrifice and the nation: Revisiting civil religion. *Journal of the American Academy of Religion 64*(4): 767–80.

Marx, K. and Engels, F. (1848) *Manifesto of the Communist Party*. London: J. E. Berghard.

Marx, L. (2000) *The Machine in the Garden: Technology and the Pastoral Ideal in America*. Thirty-fifth anniversary edition. Oxford: Oxford University Press.

Masuda, Y. (1990) *Managing in the Information Society*. Oxford: Blackwell Publishers.

Matthiessen, F. (1941) *American Renaissance: Art and Expression in the Age of Emerson and Whitman*. New York: Oxford University Press.

Maxa, R. (1979) Bob Dylan knocks on heaven's door, accepts Christ, says a West Coast pastor as the music biz and the star's fans await an album to explain it all. *The Washington Post*, 27 May. www.washingtonpost.com/archive/lifestyle/magazine/1979/05/27/bob-dylan-knocks-on-heavens-door-accepts-christ-says-a-west-coast-pastor-as-the-music-biz-and-the-stars-fans-await-an-album-to-explain-it-all/78a25f0a-c879-4539-81db-d4866c3f0508/.

McCarron, A. (2017) *Light Come Shining: The Transformations of Bob Dylan*, Oxford: Oxford University Press.

McCartney, P. and Miles, B. (1997) *Many Years from Now*. London: Martin Secker & Warburg.

McCullough, D. (2017) *The American Spirit: Who We Are and What We Stand For*. New York, NY: Simon & Schuster.

McGeorge, A. (2015) Disturbing footage of John Lennon mocking disabled people leaves fans in shock. *The Daily Mirror*, 20 September. www.mirror.co.uk/3am/celebrity-news/disturbing-footage-john-lennon-mocking-6480508.

McGrath, J. (2010a) Liverpool's black community and the Beatles: Black Liverpudlian angles on the Beatles' history. *Soundscapes Journal on Media Culture* 12(4). www.icce.rug.nl/~soundscapes/VOLUME12/Interview_McGrath.shtml.

McGrath, J. (2010b) *Ideas of Belonging in the Work of John Lennon and Paul McCartney*, PhD Thesis, Leeds Metropolitan University.

McGrath, P. (2007) John & Yoko: Give Peace A Song [DVD]. Pinewood: Fabulous Films.

McIntosh, P. (1988) White privilege: Unpacking the invisible knapsack. Beyond heroes and holidays. Working Paper 189 White Privilege and Male Privilege: A Personal Account of Coming to See Correspondences through Work in Women's Studies. Wellesley, MA: Wellesley College Center for Research on Women. https://codeofgoodpractice.com/wp-content/uploads/2019/05/Mcintosh-White-Privilege-Unpacking-the-Invisible-Knapsack.pdf.

McKay, R. (2019) Bob Dylan's wild night of knife fights and robberies in Glasgow. *GlasgowLive*, 17 December. www.glasgowlive.co.uk/news/history/bob-dylans-wild-night-glasgow-12022386.

McMillian, J. (2013) *Beatles vs. Stones*. London: Simon & Schuster.

Mehr, S. A., Singh, M., Knox, D. et al. (2019) Universality and diversity in human song. *Science* 366(6468): eaax0868. https://doi.org/10.1126/science.aax0868.

Meisel, P. (2010) *The Myth of Popular Culture from Dante to Dylan*. Chichester, UK: Wiley & Sons.

Mellers, W. (1974) *Twilight of the Gods: The Music of the Beatles.* New York: The Viking Press.

Metzinger, P. (2017) *The Mike Douglas Show* S11E122 John Lennon & Yoko Ono, Jerry Rubin, Barbar Loden, Dr Jesse Steinfeld. *YouTube: Paul Metzger.* https://youtu.be/dxh5fY4p72o.

Middleton, R. (1990) *Studying Popular Music.* Milton Keynes, UK: Open University Press.

Miles, B. (2001) *The Beatles Diary Volume 1: The Beatles Years.* London: Omnibus.

Miller, M. E. and Cook-Greuter, S. R. (2000) *Creativity, Spirituality, and Transcendence: Paths to Integrity and Wisdom in the Mature Self.* New York, NY: Ablex Publishing Corporation.

Muir, A. (2019) *Bob Dylan & William Shakespeare: The True Performing of It.* Falmouth, UK: Red Planet Books.

Mulley, C. (2017) *The Women Who Flew for Hitler: The True Story of Hitler's Valkyries.* London: Macmillan.

Nachman, G. (2009) *Right Here on Our Stage Tonight!: Ed Sullivan's America.* Berkeley, CA: University of California Press.

Negus, K. (2007) Living, breathing songs: Singing along with Bob Dylan. *Oral Tradition 22*(1): 71–83.

Negus, K. (2010) Bob Dylan's phonographic imagination. *Popular Music 29*(2): 213–28.

Nickerson, E. (2012) Top 200 most popular names in England and Wales in 1900. *British Baby Names.* www.britishbabynames.com/blog/2012/08/top-200-most-popular-names-in-england-and-wales-1900.html.

Norman, P. (1981) *Shout!: The True Story of the Beatles.* London: Penguin Books.

Norman, P. (2009) *John Lennon: The Life.* London: HarperCollins.

O'Brien, L. (1995) *She Bop: The Definitive History of Women in Rock, Pop and Soul.* London: Penguin.

Ono, Y. (1964) *Grapefruit.* Tokyo: Wunternaum Press.

Ono, Y. (2010) IMAGINE PEACE by Yoko Ono for Peace Day: 21 September 2010. *Imagine Peace.* http://imaginepeace.com/home/faq.

Orwell, G. (1940) Boys' weeklies. In *Inside the Whale and Other Essays* (pp. 89–130). London: Victor Gollancz.

Parker, B. (2010) *Good Vibrations: The Physics of Music.* Baltimore, MD: Johns Hopkins University Press.

Partridge, C. (2017) Emotion, meaning and popular music. In C. Partridge and M. Moberg (eds.), *The Bloomsbury Handbook of Religion and Popular Music* (pp. 23–31). London: Bloomsbury Academic.

Pearson, B. L. and McCulloch, B. (2010) *Robert Johnson: Lost and Found.* Champaign, IL: University of Illinois Press.

Peddie, I. (2006) *The Resisting Muse: Popular Music and Social Protest.* Farnham, UK: Ashgate.

Pennebaker, D. A. (1967) Dont Look Back [DVD]. J. Court and A. Grossman (Producers). Los Angeles, CA: Docurama.

Peters, L. (2000) *Orphan Texts: Victorian Orphans, Culture and Empire.* Manchester: Manchester University Press

Petrie, K. J., Pennebaker, J. W. and Silverstein, B. (2008) 'Things We Said Today': A linguistic analysis of the Beatles. *Psychology of Aesthetics, Creativity, and the Arts 2*(4): 197–202.

Phillips-Silver, J., Aktipis, C. A. and Bryant, G. A. (2010) The ecology of entrainment: Foundations of coordinated rhythmic movement. *Music Perception, 28*(1): 3–14.

Pichaske, D. (2010) *Song of the North Country: A Midwest Framework to the Songs of Bob Dylan.* London: Continuum International Publishing Group.

Pickering, M. (2008) *Research Methods for Cultural Studies.* Edinburgh: Edinburgh University Press.

Pinker, S. (2003) *The Blank Slate: The Modern Denial of Human Nature.* London: Penguin Books.

Polizzotti, M. (2006) *Bob Dylan's Highway 61 Revisited (33 1/3)* London: Continuum Publishing.

Preston, S. D. and de Waal, F. B. M. (2002) Empathy: Its ultimate and proximate bases. *Behavioral and Brain Sciences 25*: 1–72.

Ra, A. (2016) *Foundational Falsehoods of Creationism.* Durham, NC: Pitchstone Publishing.

Raiola, J. (2016) John Lennon's journey to feminism and why it matters in the era of Trump. *The Huffington Post*, 10 October. www.huffpost.com/entry/john-lennons-journey-to-feminism-and-why-it-matters_b_57f9601ee4b090dec0e71412.

Ramachandran, V. S. (2003) *The Emerging Mind: The Reith Lectures 2003.* London: Profile Books.

Ramachandran, V. S. (2005) *A Brief Tour of Human Consciousness: From Imposter Poodles to Purple Numbers.* New York, NY: Pi Press.

Rasmussen, A. K. (2010) *Women, the Recited Qur'an, and Islamic Music in Indonesia.* Berkeley, CA: University of California Press.

Reck, D. R. (1985) Beatles Orientalis: Influences from Asia in a popular song tradition. *Asian Music 16*(1): 83–149.

Reed, T. L. (2003) *The Holy Profane: Religion in Black Popular Music.* Lexington, KY: The University Press of Kentucky.

Rein, L. (2012) Never before published transcript of a conversation between John Lennon, Yoko Ono, Timothy Leary and Rosemary Leary – at the Montreal Bed-In, May 1969. Timothy Leary Archives. www.timothylearyarchives.org/never-before-published-transcript-of-a-conversation-between-john-lennon-yoko-ono-timothy-leary-and-rosemary-leary-%E2%80%93-at-the-montreal-bed-in-may-1969/.

Richards, T. (1993) *The Imperial Archive: Knowledge and the Fantasy of Empire.* London: Verso.

Ricks, C. (2011) *Dylan's Visions of Sin.* Edinburgh: Canongate Books.

Riley, T. (2011) *Lennon: The Man, the Myth, the Music – The Definitive Life.* London: Ebury Publishing.

Risen, J. L. (2016) Believing what we do not believe: Acquiescence to superstitious beliefs and other powerful intuitions. *Psychological Review 123*(2): 182.

Ritter, H. (1986) *Dictionary of Concepts in History.* Westport, CT: Greenwood Press.

Robock, A. (2005) Tonight as I stand inside the rain: Bob Dylan and weather imagery. *Bulletin of the American Meteorological Society 86*(4): 483–7.

Rocheleau, J. (2006) 'Far between sundown's finish and midnight's broken toll': Enlightenment and postmodernism in Dylan's social criticism. In P. Vernezze (ed.), *Bob Dylan and Philosophy* (pp. 66–77). Chicago, IL: Open Court.

Rodnitzky, J. L. (1969) The evolution of the American protest song. *The Journal of Popular Culture 3*(1): 35–45.

Rodnitzky, J. L. (1988) Also born in the USA: Bob Dylan's outlaw heroes and the real Bob Dylan. *Popular Music and Society 12*(2): 37–43.

Rodriguez, R. (2012) *Revolver: How the Beatles Reimagined Rock 'n' Roll.* Milwaukee, WI: Backbeat Books.

Roe, N. (2003) Playing time. In N. Corcoran (ed.), *Do You Mr Jones? Bob Dylan with the Poets and the Professors.* London: Pimlico.

Rogan, J. (2010) *Lennon: The Albums.* London: Omnibus Press.

Rogers, R. A. (2006) From cultural exchange to transculturation: A review and reconceptualization of cultural appropriation. *Communication Theory 16*: 474–503.

Rogovoy, S. (2010) *Bob Dylan: Prophet, Mystic, Poet.* New York, NY: Simon Spotlight Entertainment.

Rojek, C. (2001) *Celebrity.* London: Reaktion Books.

Rosen, R. (2002) *Nowhere Man: The Final Days of John Lennon.* San Francisco, CA: Quick American Archives.

Roskin, M. (1974) From Pearl Harbor to Vietnam: Shifting generational paradigms and foreign policy. *Political Science Quarterly 89*(3): 563–88.

Roylance, B. (2000) *The Beatles Anthology.* London: Weidenfeld & Nicolson.

Sagan, C. (1995) *Cosmos.* New York, NY: Wings Books.

Sahlins, M. D. (1972) *Stone Age Economics.* Piscataway, NJ: Transaction Publishers.

Said, E. W. (1978) *Orientalism.* New York, NY: Pantheon Books.

Said, E. (2005) The pleasures of imperialism. In H. Bloom and P. Loos (eds.), *Edwardian and Georgian Fiction* (pp. 245–78). Philadelphia, PA: Chelsea House Publishers.

Saluszinsky, I. (1992) The genius of Dylan. *The Australian Weekend Review,* 28–9 March. http://expectingrain.com/dok/who/s/saluszinskyimre.html.

Saluszinsky, I. (2001) Tangled up in Bob. In P. Craven (ed.), *The Best Australian Essays 2001* (pp. 529–36). Melbourne: Black.

Sauceda, J. (1983) *The Literary Lennon: A Comedy of Letters: The First Study of All the Major and Minor Writings of John Lennon.* Ypsilanti, MI: Pierian Press.

Sawyers, J. S. (2011) *Bob Dylan: New York.* Albany, CA: Roaring Forties Press.

Scaduto, A. (1996) *Bob Dylan: A Biography.* 2nd ed. London: Helter Skelter Publishing.

Scarza, V. (1985) Live Aid [DVD]. London: Rhino.

Schmidt, C. M. (2003) *David Hume: Reason in History*. University Park, PA: Pennsylvania State University Press.

Schneider, M. (2003) 'What matters is the system!' The Beatles, the 'Passover Plot' and conspiratorial narrativity. *Anthropoetics: The Journal of Generative Anthropology 8*(2). http://anthropoetics.ucla.edu/apo802/beatles2/.

Schneider, M. (2008) *The Long and Winding Road from Blake to the Beatles*. Basingstoke, UK: Palgrave Macmillan.

Schonfield, H. J. (1965) *The Passover Plot*. London: Hutchinson.

Schreiber, D. A. (2012) On the epistemology of postmodern spirituality. *Verbum et Ecclesia 33*(1): 1–8.

Scorsese, M. (1978) The Last Waltz [DVD]. R. Robertson and J. Taplin (Producers). Los Angeles, CA: United Artists Classics.

Scorsese, M. (2005) No Direction Home: Bob Dylan [DVD]. S. Lacy, J. Rosen, M. Scorsese, N. Sinclair and A. Wall (Producers). London: BBC.

Scorsese, M. (2011) George Harrison: Living in the Material World [DVD]. O. Harrison, M. Scorsese and N. Sinclair (Producers). London: BBC.

Scott, P. (1966) *The Jewel in the Crown*. London: Heinemann.

Seaman, F. (1992) *The Last Days of John Lennon: A Personal Memoir*. New York, NY: Random House.

Seybold, E. (1960) Thoreau for everyone. *The Emerson Society Quarterly* **XVIII**: 19–21.

Sharp, K. R. (2011) *Starting Over: The Making of John Lennon and Yoko Ono's Double Fantasy*. London: Simon & Schuster.

Shelton, R. (1986) *No Direction Home: The Life and Music of Bob Dylan*. London: Penguin Books.

Shelton, R. (2011) Tapes reveal Bob Dylan struggled with heroin addiction. *The Times*, 23 May. www.thetimes.co.uk/article/tapes-reveal-bob-dylan-struggled-with-heroin-addiction-zbndg6zg6bk.

Shipper, M. (1978) *Paperback Writer: The Life and Times of the Beatles: The Spurious Chronicle of Their Rise to Stardom*. London: New English Library.

Shotton, P. (1984) *The Beatles, Lennon, and Me*. Lanham, MD: Madison Books.

Shotton, P. and Schaffner, N. (1983) *John Lennon: In My Life*. Briarcliff Manor, NY: Stein and Day.

Shumway, D. R. (2014) *Rock Star: The Making of Musical Icons from Elvis to Springsteen*. Baltimore, MD: John Hopkins University Press.

Sillitoe, A. (1961) *Key to the Door*. London: W. H. Allen & Co.

Silverton, P. (2011) Bob Dylan's back in Britain. Again. Just like he was last year. And the year before that. *Rock's Back Pages*. www.rocksbackpages.com/Library/Article/bob-dylans-back-in-britain-again-just-like-he-was-last-year-and-the-year-before-that.

Simpson, J., Gardham, D. and Haynes, D. (2014) The hunt for British jihadist 'Jailer John'. *The Times*, 21 August. www.thetimes.co.uk/article/the-hunt-for-british-jihadist-jailer-john-w06omkh3sfl.

Small, C. (1998) *Musicking: The Meanings of Performing and Listening*. Middletown, CT: Wesleyan University Press.

Smeaton, B. and Wonfor, G. (1995) The Beatles Anthology [DVD]. N. Aspinall and C. Chipperfield (Producers). London: EMI Records.

Smith, E. L. (1990) *Rape and Revelation: The Descent to the Underworld in Modernism*, Lanham, MD: University Press of America.

Snyder, T. (2008) *The Tomorrow Show with Tom Snyder: John, Paul, Tom & Ringo* [DVD]. P. Burke and T. Blomquist (Producers). Los Angeles, CA: Shout! Factory.

Sounes, H. (2011a) *Down the Highway: The Life of Bob Dylan*. New York, NY: Doubleday.

Sounes, H. (2011b) *Fab: An Intimate Life of Paul McCartney*. Cambridge, MA: Da Capo Press.

Spangler, J. (2019a) Beatles photos & quotes database: 1964. *Beatles Interviews*. www.beatlesinterviews.org/db64.html.

Spangler, J. (2019b) Beatles interview: Memphis, Tennessee, 19 August 1966. *Beatles Interviews*. www.beatlesinterviews.org/db1966.0819.beatles.html.

Spangler, J. (2019c) John Lennon interview: *Red Mole*, 21 January 1971. *Beatles Interviews*. www.beatlesinterviews.org/db1971.0121.beatles.html.

Spangler, J. (2019d) John Lennon Interview: *Newsweek*, 29 September 1980. *Beatles Interviews*. www.beatlesinterviews.org/db1980.0929.beatles.html.

Spitz, B. (2006) *The Beatles: The Biography*. London: Aurum.

St John, G. (2017) Electronic dance music: Trance and techno-shamanism. In C. Partridge and M. Moberg (eds.), *The Bloomsbury Handbook of Religion and Popular Music* (pp. 278–85). London: Bloomsbury Academic.

Stark, S. D. (2005) *Meet the Beatles: A Cultural History of the Band That Shook Youth, Gender, and the World*. London: HarperCollins.

Stewart, C. J., Smith, C. A. and Denton, R. E. (1984) *Persuasion and Social Movements*. Prospect Heights, NY: Waveland Press.

Street, J. (2002) Bob, Bono and Tony B: The popular artist as politician. *Media, Culture & Society* 24(3): 433–41.

Strout, P. (2016) *Core Values & Beliefs*. Stafford, TX: Vineyard USA.

Subirats Miranda, J. L. (2013) Harrison, Dylan, Fogerty, Jesse Ed Davis, Taj Mahal y Amigos 1 de 2. *YouTube: Jose L. Subirats Miranda*. https://youtu.be/r23DKWvFb3k.

Sullivan, H. (1995) *The Beatles with Lacan: Rock 'n' Roll as Requiem for the Modern Age*. New York, NY: Peter Lang.

Sutton, M. (2009) 'Roadmaps for the soul': History and cartography in Bob Dylan's early songs. *Australasian Journal of American Studies* 28(1): 17–33.

Sylvan, R. (2002) *Traces of the Spirit: The Religious Dimensions of Popular Music*. New York, NY: New York University Press.

Tagg, P. (1987) Musicology and the semiotics of popular music. *Semiotoca* 66(1): 279–98.

Taylor, D. (1987) *It Was Twenty Years Ago Today*. London: Bantam.

Taylor, J. and Israelson, C. (2017) *The Political World of Bob Dylan: Freedom and Justice, Power and Sin*. Basingstoke, UK: Palgrave Macmillan.

Taylor, M. (2003) The illusion of independent agency: Do adult fiction writers experience their characters as having minds of their own? *Imagination, Cognition & Personality 22*: 361–80.

Taylor, R. P. (1985) *The Death and Resurrection Show: From Shaman to Superstar*. London: Anthony Blond.

Temple, C. (2016) *Picasso's Brain: The Basis of Creative Genius*. London: Robinson.

Terrarosa, T. (2018) Why GM's claim to use 90% U.S. Steel might not hold water. *The Street*, 2 March. www.thestreet.com/investing/stocks/why-gm-s-claim-to-use-90-u-s-steel-might-not-hold-water-14508408.

Thalbourne, M. A. and Delin, P. S. (1999) Transliminality: Its relation to dream life, religiosity, and mystical experience. *The International Journal for the Psychology of Religion 9*(1): 45–61.

Tharoor, S. (2017) *Inglorious Empire: What the British Did to India*. London: C. Hurst & Co.

Thomson, J. A. (2009a) Who are we? Where did we come from? How religious identity divides and damns us all. *The American Journal of Psychoanalysis 69*(1): 22–42.

Thomson, J. A. (2009b) Why we believe in gods – Andy Thomson – American Atheists 09. *YouTube: Richard Dawkins Foundation for Reason & Science*. http s://youtu.be/1iMmvu9eMrg.

Thomson, J. A. and Aukofer, C. (2011) *Why We Believe in God(s): A Concise Guide to the Science of Faith*. Durham, NC: Pitchstone Publishing.

Thoreau, H. D. (1849) Resistance to civil government. In E. P. Peabody (ed.), *Æsthetic Papers* (pp. 189–213). Boston, MA: The Editor.

Thoreau, H. D. (1854) *Walden; or, Life in the Woods*. Boston, MA: Ticknor and Fields.

Thoreau, H. D. (1860) A plea for Captain John Brown. In J. Redpath (ed.), *Echoes of Harpers Ferry* (pp. 189–213). Boston, MA: Thayer and Eldridge.

Till, R. (2010) *Pop Cult: Religion and Popular Music*. London: Continuum.

Turner, F. J. (1921) *The Frontier in American History*. New York, NY. Henry Holt & Co.

Turner, J. (2005) Performing conscience: Thoreau, political action, and the plea for John Brown. *Political Theory 33*: 448–71.

Turner, J. M. (2003) Pablo Fanque, black circus proprietor. In G. H. Gerzina (ed.), *Black Victorians/Black Victoriana* (pp. 20–38). New Brunswick, NJ: Rutgers University Press.

Turner, S. (2006) *The Gospel According to the Beatles*. Louisville, KY: Westminster John Knox Press.

Ullestad, N. (1992) Diverse rock rebellions subvert mass media hegemony. In R. Garofalo (ed.), *Rockin' the Boat: Mass Music and Mass Movements* (pp. 37–54). Cambridge, MA: South End Press.

Urish, B. (2007) *The Words and Music of John Lennon*. Westport, CT: Greenwood Publishing Group.

Valdez, S. (2017) *Revolver* as a pivotal art work: Structure, harmony and vocal harmonisation. In R. Reising (ed.), *'Every Sound There Is': The Beatles' Revolver and the Transformation of Rock and Roll*. Farnham, UK: Ashgate.

Verplaetse, J., de Schrijver, J., Vanneste, S. and Braeckman, J. (2009) *The Moral Brain: Essays on the Evolutionary and Neuroscientific Aspects of Morality*. Berlin: Springer.

Vinnicombe, C. (2008) Paul McCartney to record with Bob Dylan? *Music Radar*, 18 November. www.musicradar.com/news/guitars/paul-mccartney-to-record-with-bob-dylan-183291.

Walker, D. A. (1979) *Iron Frontier: The Discovery and Early Development of Minnesota's Three Ranges*. St Paul, MN: Minnesota Historical Society Press.

Warren, A. (1986) Citizens of the empire: Baden-Powell, scouts and guides, and an imperial ideal. In J. M. MacKenzie (ed.), *Imperialism and Popular Culture* (pp. 232–56). Manchester: Manchester University Press.

Webb, S. H. (2006) *Dylan Redeemed: From Highway 61 to Saved*. London: Bloomsbury Academic.

Weber, L. (2014) Jewish religious life on the Iron Range. *MNopedia*. www .mnopedia.org/jewish-religious-life-iron-range.

Weinstein, D. (2006) Rock protest songs: So many and so few. In I. Peddie (ed.), *The Resisting Muse: Popular Music and Social Protest* (pp. 3–16). Farnham, UK: Ashgate.

Wenner, J. (2000) *Lennon Remembers*. New York, NY: Verso.

Wenner, J. (2007) Bob Dylan: The 40th anniversary interview. *Rolling Stone*, 3–17 May. www.rollingstone.com/music/news/bob-dylan-hits-the-big-themes-from-religion-to-the-atomic-age-20110511.

Wheeler, S. (2005) *Charlie Lennon: Uncle to a Beatle*. Denver, CO: Outskirts Press.

Whissell, C. (1996) Traditional and emotional stylometric analysis of the songs of Beatles Paul McCartney and John Lennon. *Computers and the Humanities 30*: 257–65.

White, T. (2000) George Harrison: 'All Things' in good time. *Billboard*. 30 December. www.billboard.com/articles/news/80788/george-harrison-all-things-in-good-time.

Whiteley, S. (1997) *Sexing the Groove: Popular Music and Gender*. London: Routledge.

Whiteley, S. (2000) *Women and Popular Music: Sexuality, Identity and Subjectivity*. London: Routledge.

Whiteley, S. (2003) *The Space between the Notes: Rock and the Counter-Culture*. Oxford: Taylor & Francis.

Whiteley, S. (2008) 'Tangerine trees and marmalade skies': Cultural agendas or optimistic escapism? In O. Julien (ed.), *Sgt. Pepper and the Beatles: It Was Forty Years Ago Today* (pp. 11–22). Farnham, UK: Ashgate.

Whitman, W. (1860) *Leaves of Grass* [E-book]. www.gutenberg.org/ebooks/1322.

Whitman, W. (1865) *Drum Taps*. New York, NY: Peter Eckler.

Wiener, J. (1991) *Come Together: John Lennon in His Time*. Chicago, IL: University of Illinois Press.

Wiener, J. (1999) *Gimme Some Truth: The John Lennon F.B.I. Files*. Berkeley, CA: University of California Press.

Wilentz, S. (2011) *Bob Dylan in America*. London: Vintage.

Williams, A. R. (1951) The magazine reading of secondary school children. *British Journal of Educational Psychology* 21: 186–98.

Williams, R. (1977) *Marxism and Literature*. Oxford: Oxford University Press.

Williams, R. (1993) Two worlds collide. *Mojo* 1: 40–60.

Williams, R. (2010) *The Royal Albert Hall: A Masterpiece for the 21st Century*. London: Art Books International.

Williams, W. (2020) *Windrush Lessons Learned Review*. London: Home Office.

Willis, E. (1967) The sound of Bob Dylan. *Commentary,* November. www .commentarymagazine.com/articles/the-guns-of-navarro/.

Wilson, S. (2015) *Stop Making Sense: Music from the Perspective of the Real*. London: Karnac Books.

Winegarten, R. (2008) *Germaine de Staël and Benjamin Constant: A Dual Biography*. New Haven, CT: Yale University Press.

Winkelman, M. (2005) Spirituality and the healing of addictions: A shamanic drumming approach. *Religion and Healing in America* 37(2): 455–70.

Womack, K. (2009) *The Cambridge Companion to the Beatles*. Cambridge, UK: Cambridge University Press.

Womack, K. (2016) *The Beatles Encyclopedia: Everything Fab Four*. Santa Barbara, CA: ABC-CLIO.

Womack, K. and Davis, K. W. T. F. (2006) *Reading The Beatles: Cultural Studies, Literary Criticism, and the Fab Four*. Albany, NY: State University of New York Press.

Woodhead, L. (2017) *War Paint: Elizabeth Arden and Helena Rubinstein: Their Lives, Their Times, Their Rivalry*. London: Weidenfeld & Nicolson.

Wuthnow, R. (2001) *Creative Spirituality: The Way of the Artist*. Berkeley, CA: University of California Press.

Wylde, R. (2020) Bob Dylan & John Lennon chatting in London, 1966 [Restored footage and audio]. *YouTube: Swinging Pig*. https://youtu.be /9g2X_MtVRqk.

Wynne-Jones, J. (2008) Bigger than Jesus? The Beatles were a Christian band. *The Daily Telegraph*, 12 July. www.telegraph.co.uk/news/uknews/2403617/Bigger-than-Jesus-The-Beatles-were-a-Christian-band.html.

Zak III, A. J. (2005) Bob Dylan and Jimi Hendrix: Juxtaposition and transformation 'All Along the Watchtower'. *Journal of American Musicological Society* 57 (3): 599–644.

Zukav, G. (1979) *The Dancing Wu Li Masters: An Overview of the New Physics*. New York, NY: Bantam Books.

Index